VMware ESⅹ Server

Advanced Technical Design Guide

Ron Oglesby
Scott Herold

International Standard Book Number (ISBN:)
0971151067

Printed in the United States of America by United
Graphics, Inc., Mattoon, IL.

Brian Madden Publishing offers discounts of this book
when purchased in bulk. Visit www.brianmadden.com for
details.

First Printing, July 2005

Authors
Ron Oglesby
Scott Herold

Technical Editors
Stephen Beaver
Michael Burke
Ken Cline

Copy Editor
Emily Monaco

Publisher
Brian Madden

Contents at a glance

A note from the authors

This book was written with you, the reader, in mind. As writers, we're always interested in hearing your thoughts about what worked, what didn't, what was good, and what wasn't. We'd love to hear any feedback or comments you might have.

Any mistakes or clarifications found in this book will be posted to www.vmguru.com/books.

For anyone wondering, neither of us work for VMware or EMC. We both work for an independent consulting company in Chicago called RapidApp.

We mention several companies, products, and vendors throughout this book. None of them paid us to be listed. These are simply companies whose products we've used and liked.

Thanks for reading, and we look forward to hearing from you at www.vmguru.com.

Ron Oglesby & Scott Herold, August 2005

6. Managing the Server with the COS and web interface ...265

Acknowledgements from Ron

This book wouldn't have happened without all the great guys out in the VMware Community groups. I would like to thank all those that post day after day and contribute to the overall knowledge of the community. I would like to extend a very special thanks to our technical reviewers that gave of their time to correct our mistakes. As always, any mistakes or omissions are ours and not theirs. (Hopefully the 3.0 update will contain some of the additions you asked for.) I would like to thank the guys at RapidApp that had to listen—yet again—to all the talk about another book being written, and especially to Scott that showed so much enthusiasm and listened as I tried to teach him about writing. He did a superb job for his first run at it. Finally, I would like to say thanks and "I'm sorry," to my wife Dina and daughter Madison. They are the ones that really lose when I begin writing. Sorry, yet again, for the nights and weekends on the laptop. And thanks for not griping about it.

Acknowledgements from Scott

First and foremost, I have to give the most thanks to Ron for offering me this opportunity and being my mentor throughout the entire process. Without him I would not have gotten as far as I did and you would have likely been reading small parts of this on a half kept-up website. I would also like to thank those who post in and run the VMware Community Forums. There are far too many names to mention, but everyone of you has helped keep the technology strong enough to warrant this book. My co-workers at RapidApp have done an unbelievable job supporting (and advertising) the book at various client sites and training classes. Without their enthusiasm for the success of the technology, we would have a lot less to write for. I would like to give a special "Thank You" to our technical reviewers who went above and beyond in making sure we provided accurate content. All of them volunteered their time for the book and their hard work is greatly appreciated. Finally, I would like to thank my mom for always being there and my loving fiancee (and toughest editor) Leah. Their support throughout the entire process has been unbelievable. Sadly, Leah can now say she knows more about VMware ESX than any other elementary teacher in the world.

Foreward

It sure didn't take long for server virtualization with VMware's products to catch on in a big way. Today, nearly every IT organization we work with is looking to use VMware in some capacity. At RapidApp, we have invested heavily in developing our VMware ESX technical skills and have had the opportunity to put those skills to work assisting several Fortune organizations to realize the benefits promised by the technology.

The success stories have been piling up. In the past 18 months we have seen many of our clients make the move from using VMware's GSX product for their application development and testing environments into their first foray using VMware ESX in their production server environment. Most of the same clients have plans for widespread deployment over the next 24 months, and we anticipate that within three years the use of "VMs" will become ubiquitous and a strategic component of an organizations IT infrastructure.

It's likely if you are reading this now you recognize the benefits of the technology. The cost avoidance and TCO benefits are compelling enough on their own to make VMware a sure thing. But don't forget the harder to quantify and sexier benefits associated with recoverability, rapid and dynamic provisioning, and that server virtualization is on the path to the utility computing model the experts are telling us is right around the corner.

This book will help you—the designer, builder, and manager of your organization's IT infrastructur—prepare to provide the benefits of server virtualization. You won't get far in the book before you begin to identify opportunities to use VMware to help tackle some of your key initiatives. Ron and Scott have done an excellent job compressing their extensive research and real world experience into this text. Use it as a field guide to help you ensure that as you begin to tactically deploy VMware, you are building the right foundation for your server virtualization strategy.

Mitch Northcutt, President & CEO, RapidApp

Chapter

VMware Overview

This book is designed to provide you with practical, real-world information about the use and design of VMware ESX Server systems. In order to study the advanced technical details, we need to ensure that you have a good baseline understanding of VMware ESX features, and VMware's other products.

Even if you've already read and understand the VMware ESX admin guide or if you're very familiar with previous versions of ESX or GSX, we still recommend that you at least skim through this chapter so that you can familiarize yourself with the specific terms and phrasing that we'll use throughout this book.

As you read through this book, you should keep in mind that each chapter was written separately and that it's okay for you to read them out-of-order. Of course if you're new to VMware and virtualization technologies, the chapter sequence will guide you through a logical progression of the components. We'll begin in this chapter with an overview of VMware software solutions.

The VMware Solution

In case you don't know why you're reading this book, VMware ESX allows for the "virtualization" of Intel-based servers. This idea will be explored more in this chapter, but the basic concept is that a single piece of physical hardware will be used to host multiple logical or "virtual" servers. The ability to host multiple virtual servers on a single piece of hardware, while simple to understand in theory, can be extremely complex in execution.

When VMware technology is used, a single host allows multiple virtual servers to share the host's physical resources. These resources include processor, memory, network cards, and of course local disk. (We'll refer to these four physical resources as the "core four" throughout this book.) This architecture also gives you the ability to "partition" your host to allow for the server's resources to be fully utilized while you migrate multiple physical servers to a single VMware server running multiple virtual servers. (We'll discuss partitioning and migration strategies in much more depth throughout this book.)

So what does this mean to your environment or your business? It depends on what your business looks like and which product from VMware you're thinking about using. Obviously if you're reading this book then you're at least contemplating an ESX Server implementation. But even with ESX you have a number of alternatives on how to deploy and utilize the system. Also, when investigating VMware technology it is unfair to simply look at ESX and why it is used. You can only decide to use ESX instead of GSX or Workstation after you really understand what each product does and where they truly fit.

So what is "virtualization?"

Simply stated, VMware (the company) provides virtualization technology. All of their products (Workstation, GSX Server, and ESX Server) work in more-or-less the same way. There is a host computer that runs a layer of software that provides or creates virtual machines that Intel operating systems can be installed to. These virtual machines are really just that—complete virtual machines. Within a virtual machine you have hardware like processors, network cards, disks, COM ports, memory, etc. This hardware is presented through a BIOS and is configurable just like physical hardware.

If we were to jump ahead a little and look at a virtual Windows server, you would be able to go into device manager and view the network cards, disks, memory, etc., just like a physical machine. As a matter of fact the whole idea is that the virtualized operating system has no idea that it is on virtual hardware. It just sees hardware as it normally would.

In Chapter 2 we'll go into detail on how virtualization actually takes place with ESX Server, but for now it's just important to understand that from a high level there are a few components that make up any virtualization environment:

1. A host machine/host hardware

2. Virtualization software that provides and manages the virtual environment

3. The virtual machine(s) themselves (or "VM's"—virtual hardware presented to the guest

4. The guest operating system that is installed on the virtual machine

Figure 1.1 The basic virtualization model

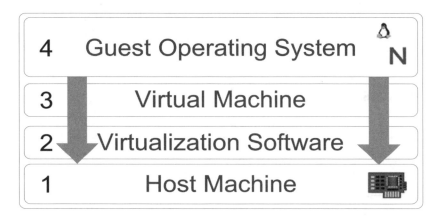

Knowing that each of these four elements must be in place in a virtual environment and understanding that they are distinctly different resources will allow you to understand where different virtualization software is used. Let's examine each of these components a bit before moving into the breakdown of the different virtualization technologies available from VMware.

The Host Machine

The host machine in a virtual environment provides the resources that the virtual machines will eventually have access to. Obviously the more of the resources available the more virtual machines you can host. Or put more directly, "the bigger the host machine, the more virtual machines you can run on it." This really makes sense if you look at Figure 1.1. In Component 1 of the diagram, the host machine has a single processor, some RAM, a single disk, and a single network card. Assuming that the host is going to use some of each of these core four resources for its own operation, you have what's leftover available for the virtual machines you want to run on it.

For example, let's assume that the host is using 10% of the available processor for itself. That leaves 90% of the CPU available for the virtual machines. If you're only running a single virtual machine (VM) then this may be more than enough. However, if you're trying to run 10 VMs on that host then the hosts "extra" 90% CPU availability will probably lead to a bottleneck.

The other challenge is that since all of the VMs are sharing the same resource (the CPU in this case), how do you keep them from stepping on each other? This is actually where Component 2 from Figure 1 comes in—the virtualization software.

The Virtualization Software

The virtualization software layer provides each virtual machine access to the host resources. It's also responsible for scheduling the physical resources among the various VMs. This virtualization software is the cornerstone of the entire virtualization environment. It creates the virtual machines for use, manages the resources provided to the VMs, schedules resource usage when there is contention for a specific resource, and provides a management and configuration interface for the VMs.

Again, we can't stress enough that this software is the backbone of the system. The more robust this virtualization software is the better it is at scheduling and sharing physical resources. This leads to more efficient virtual machines.

VMware provides three versions of this virtualization software. The first two—"VMware Workstation" and "VMware GSX Server"—are virtualization software packages that install onto an existing operating system on a host computer. The third version ("VMware ESX Server") is a full operating system in-and-of itself. We'll explore some of the reasons to help you choose which product you should use later in this chapter. The important idea here is to understand that ESX

Server is both its own operating system and also the virtualization software (Components 1 and 2 in the model we've been referencing), while GSX Server and Workstation are virtualization software packages that are installed on and rely upon other operating systems.

The Virtual Machine

The term "virtual machine" is often incorrectly used to describe both the virtual machine (Component 3) and the guest operating system (Component 4). For clarity in this book we will not mix the two. The virtual machine is actually the virtual hardware (or the combined virtual hardware and the virtual BIOS) presented to the guest operating systems. It's the software-based virtualization of physical hardware. The guest operating systems that we install into these "machines" are unaware that the hardware they see is virtual. All the guest OS knows is that it sees this type of processor, that type of network card, this much memory, etc.

It's important to understand that the virtual machine is not the OS but instead the hardware and configurations that are presented to the guest OS.

The Guest Operating System

In case it's not clear by now, the guest OS is the Intel-based operating system (Windows, Linux, Novell, DOS, whatever) that's running on a VM. Again, understanding that the guest OS (or "guest machine" or simply "guest") is simply the software (Component 4) that's installed onto a VM (Component 3) will make your life easier when it comes to understanding and troubleshooting your environment.

Once all four of these components are in place you'll have a virtual environment. How this virtual environment performs, is managed, and the types of functionality available in your virtual environment are all dependent on the type of software you're using to provide your virtual environment.

Which VMware product which should I use?

Well that's the question isn't it? Since this book is about ESX Server we can probably assume that you've already made your decision. Then again you might be using this book to help make your decision, so we'll go ahead and look at the products and how they fit into the IT world.

Most VMware folks started out using VMware Workstation (simply called "Workstation" by VMware geeks in the know). Workstation allows us to create virtual workstations and servers on our own PC. This lets us create small test environments that we can use to test scripts, new software packages, upgrades, etc. VMware Workstation is perfect for this.

Figure 1.2: Where do the VMware products fit?

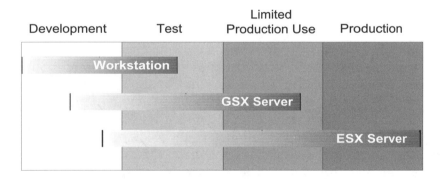

Of course Workstation has its limitations. Probably the biggest one is that VMs can only run while you're logged into your host workstation. Logoff and the VMs shutdown. Also, VMware Workstation is pretty much a local user tool which means that there is really no remote administration capabilities whatsoever. These limitations keep Workstation on the desktops of developers, engineers, and traveling salespeople who have to give multi-server demos off their laptops. No one uses Workstation for production environments.

VMware GSX Server (called "GSX" for short) is a step up from Workstation. GSX is basically a software package that installs onto an existing host operating system (either Linux or Windows). It offers some remote management and remote console access to the VMs, and the various VMs can be configured to run as services without any console interaction required. Its limitation is really that it has to use resources from the host hardware through the host OS. This really limits the scalability and performance of GSX.

The reason for this is that with GSX, VMs do not have direct access to the hardware. Let's look at an example to see how this can cause a problem. We'll look at memory use. Let's assume you configure 384MB of memory for a VM running on GSX Server for Windows. The "catch" here is that since GSX is "just" another Windows application, the VM doesn't get direct access to 384MB of memory. Instead it requests 384MB of memory from Windows.

Sure you'll see the host's memory utilization go up by 384MB when you turn on the VM, but the guest OS has to send all memory requests to Windows. In this case you'll have a host OS managing the "physical" memory for the guest OS. (This is on top of the guest OS managing its own memory within the VM.)

While this is just a simplified example, it points out some of the inherent limits with GSX. Does this mean GSX isn't a good product? Not at all. It just means that it has limitations stemming from the fact the virtualization software runs on top of a host OS. GSX is still used in plenty of production environments—especially those that don't require enterprise class scalability for their VMs, those that have a limited numbers of VMs, and those that do not require maximum performance. GSX is also frequently found in corporate test labs and is used to allow administrators to get the benefits of a "virtual" test environment without the them needing to know all the ins and outs of a full virtual server OS. Finally, a lot of companies use GSX when they don't have the budget to buy ESX-certified hardware when the VMware champions can't win the political "everything has to run on Windows" battle.

What makes ESX different than GSX, Workstation, or even Microsoft's Virtual Server?

VMware ESX Server is its own operating system. Unlike GSX or Microsoft Virtual Server 2005, ESX is not a software package that installs into a host OS—ESX is the host OS. Engineered from the beginning to be nothing more than a VM host, ESX Server is completely designed to give the VMs the best performance possible and to allow you (the admin) to control and shape the way the host resources are shared and utilized.

So what does using ESX instead of GSX or Workstation get you? The answer is simple: performance and reliability.

- Performance. ESX Server provides a level of performance for your VMs that simply cannot be found in GSX or Workstation. It also allows for more advanced resource allocation, fine tuning of performance, a better VM-to-processor ratio, and more advanced resource sharing.

- Reliability. VMware published an ESX Server Hardware Compatibility List (HCL). If the hardware you're using for ESX is on the HCL, then you can be confident that everything will work as expected. ESX also lets you get rid of any problems that exist in the host OS since host OSes don't exist with ESX.

In short if you're looking to implement virtual machines on an enterprise level or if you're looking to host a lot of production servers as VMs, then ESX is the simple choice.

A 60-second Overview of the ESX Server Architecture

An ESX Server is made up of two core components:

- The ESX Server kernel (called "VMkernel")

- The console operating system ("COS", also contains "VMnix")

The term "ESX Server" is usually used to describe all of this stuff together.

Figure 1.3: ESX Server Simplified

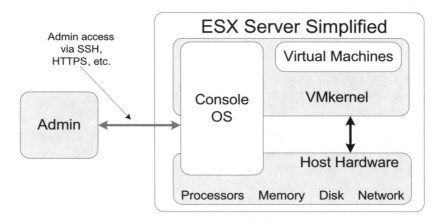

There is quite a bit of confusion in regards to what VMnix and the VMkernel really are. VMnix is a customized linux kernel based on the Redhat 7.2 distribution. Specific kernel options are specified in VMnix that optimize the console operating system for running virtual machines. Various scripts are initialized in the startup process of the console operating system which call and load the VMkernel when the system is booted into runlevel 3. Once the system has completely loaded the VMkernel, resource control and virtual machine management is passed from the COS to the VMkernel.

In Chapter 2 we'll go into great (and sometimes painful) detail about the VMkernel and the console OS. For now we just want you to understand the basic architecture so you see how ESX is different from VMware's other two main products.

Referring to Figure 1.3 you can see that the console operating system is what allows us to interact with this server. This operating systems allows us Secure Shell access, supports a web based management console, allows us to FTP and copy files to and from the host. But, the Console operating system is not ESX by itself, it does not schedule resources or manage hardware access, and basically would be a simple Redhat server if it wasn't for the VMkernel.

The VMkernel manages/schedules access to specific hardware resources on the host. It is the VMkernel that provides the Virtual Machines that guest operating systems can be installed to. This kernel is what makes ESX different from all the other software packages available. The VMkernel allows direct hardware access to the core 4 resources. It manages memory for the VMs, schedules processor time for the VMs, maintains virtual switches for VM network connectivity and schedules access to local and remote storage.

This kernel has been specifically built for this task. Unlike Windows or Linux hosts that have been built to be multi-purpose servers, this kernel's whole purpose is to share and manage access to resources. This makes it extremely light (Less than an 80-MB install package) yet extremely powerful. Overhead in VMware ESX is estimated at 3-8%, while overhead for the host in these other OS's is generally 10-20% and sometimes as high as 30% depending on configurations.

The reduction in overhead basically comes from ESX being a "bare metal" product. Unlike any of the other technologies available, ESX makes the most of your hardware and has been built from the ground up to provide superb VM performance. Contrast this to the GSX, Workstation and Microsoft Virtual Server products that are really add-ons to operating systems that are built to handle numerous tasks and are not focused on providing high end VM performance.

ESX Architectural Overview

Now that you have a basic understanding of the VMware products and a basic knowledge of ESX and how it works, its time to go into detail as to what makes it all possible. As a warning, this chapter is not intended for those with a weak heart or who are prone to falling asleep. If you want to truly understand the magic behind ESX server then this chapter is for you! Also, make sure you have an empty stomach, because there's a lot of information to digest here.

The Console Operating System versus VMkernel

One of the most difficult concepts for new VMware admins to understand is the difference between the Console Operating System (called "COS") and the VMkernel. Both play extremely important roles in your ESX environment and it's important to fully understand what each does and is capable of doing. A common misconception of ESX is that it "runs on Linux." Let's set the record straight once and for all: ESX is not Linux. It's not derived from Linux, and does not run on Linux. Now that that's out of the way, let's get back to the COS and the VMkernel.

The easiest way to distinguish the differences between these two components is to think of the server's console as being the "physical world" and the VMkernel as the "virtual world." The console lets you touch and interact with it directly, and it allows access to modify configurations and manage the environment. The VMkernel manages everything that relates to the "virtual world" and the guests that run within the host.

Console Operating System

The COS is used to boot your system and prepare your hardware for the VMkernel. As the COS loads, it acts as the bootstrap for the VMkernel which means it prepares all the necessary resources for turnover to the VMkernel. Once the COS has loaded ESX, the VMkernel will warm boot the system, assuming the role of primary operating system. The VMkernel will then load the COS and several other "helper worlds" as privileged VMs. The COS is responsible for quite a few things that are vital to the proper operation of ESX, including:

- *User interaction with ESX.* The COS is responsible for presenting the various methods to communicate with the ESX host system. It runs services that allow user interaction with the host using various methods such as:
  - Direct console access
  - Telnet/ssh access to the console
  - Web interface
  - FTP

- *Proc file system.* The proc file system can be utilized by both the COS and the VMkernel to provide real time statistics and to change configuration options on the fly. The proc file system will be discussed in greater detail in Chapter 6.

- *Authentication.* There are several processes that run within the COS that provide authentication. These mechanisms determine what rights a specific user ID has over the COS itself and the various guests running on the host. Chapter 7 is dedicated to these processes and how they interact with each other, the VMkernel, and the COS.

- *Running Support Applications.* There are some applications that may be run within the COS to provide extended support of the host environment. Every major hardware vendor has some form of agent that will run within the COS that can detect hardware issues as they arise (voltage problems, drive failures, fans quitting, etc.) In some scenarios it may also be necessary to install a local backup client to the COS to backup critical system files. The number of applications that are installed and run on the COS should be limited though, as the COS is really designed to support ESX and nothing else.

VMkernel

Once the OS has loaded, the VMkernel is started. At this point the VMkernel will warm boot the system and assume responsibility for all hardware management and resource scheduling is turned over to the VMkernel for management. Even the COS gets reloaded by the VMkernel as a VM and is restricted by the VMkernel and its configurations. (Okay, technically, the COS still manages it's own memory and NIC, but that's it.) The COS must follow the same rules for resource allocations and sharing as every virtual guest running on the host.

The VMkernel performs a number of functions, but one of the main jobs it has is to manage the interaction of virtual machine hardware and the physical hardware of the server. It acts as the "go-between" for scheduling resources for VMs on an as needed and as configured basis. While this may seem like a brief and simplistic description of the VMkernel, the remainder of this chapter focuses heavily on how the VMkernel works its magic and makes ESX what it is.

The ESX Boot Process

By taking a look at the boot process of an ESX host we can see how the COS and the VMkernel interact and at what point the VMkernel takes control of the system resources. There are several steps to the boot process. While we won't cover all of them, we will highlight the ones that perform important system tasks as they relate to ESX.

LILO

LILO (or the "Linux Loader") is a boot loader application (similar to ntloader for Windows) that the system reads when it boots from the hard drive. Based on the information contained in /etc/lilo.conf file, the system begins its boot process. The default boot option for LILO within ESX is to boot and load the VMkernel. The /etc/lilo.conf file also contains information on how the COS should be configured as it is booting. This information contains the amount of memory allocated to it and the devices that are configured for COS use. Many of the LILO configuration items are controlled by the vmkpcidivy command, discussed later in this chapter

Console Operating System

After LILO properly initializes the boot instructions the COS begins to load. The majority of the boot process is contained in the COS.

Most of these steps are used to prepare the VMkernel to take control of the hardware resources.

init

The first process that the COS executes is init. This process reads the /etc/inittab file and determines the system runlevel that should be executed. (A Linux runlevel determines what services are started on the server and the order in which they are started.) Varying runlevels on a Linux system is comparable to the various boot options available on a Windows server such as "Safe Mode" or "Command Prompt Only." The default system runlevel for ESX is 3, which means the system will boot and present a console for system login. Based on this value the COS will run the scripts contained in the /etc/rc.d/rc3.d directory during the boot process.

/etc/rc.d/rc3.d

The /etc/rc.d/rc3.d directory actually contains symbolic links to start scripts in the /etc/init.d directory. By running an "ls" command in the /etc/rc.d/rc3.d directory you will see some scripts that begin with a K and some that begin with an S. Scripts that begin with a K are used to stop (or "kill") a service during the boot process (or ensure it is not running) and scripts beginning with an S are used to start a service. You will also notice a number after the S or the K in the script's file name. These determine the order the script is run, starting at 0 and going up to 99. The S scripts are executed in ascending number order, whereas the K scripts are executed in descending order. The order of the K or S values in the file have no meaning when it comes to what order a script runs in.

S00vmkstart

If you run an "ls –l" command in the scripts directory you'll notice that the S00vmkstart command actually links to a script called vmkhalt. By running this script first, VMware ensures that there are no VMkernel processes running on the system during the boot process.

S10network

The network script (S10network) starts the TCP/IP services on the COS and assigns the IP address and hostname of the system.

S12syslog

The syslog script starts the daemon that processes system logs. Starting this script allows the remainder of the boot process to be logged. After the VMkernel begins to load it also provides a mechanism to capture the log files generated by the VMkernel for review when errors occur.

S56xinetd

The xinetd script starts the services required for the COS to handle incoming requests for access. Each application that can be started by xinetd has a configuration file in /etc/xinetd.d. If the "disable = no" flag is set in the configuration file of a particular application then xinetd starts the application. (Yeah it's a double-negative.) The most important application that is started here is the vmware-authd application which provides a way to connect and authenticate to ESX to perform VMkernel modifications.

S90vmware

This is where the VMkernel finally begins to load. The first thing that the VMkernel does when it starts is load the proper device drivers to interact with the physical hardware of the host. You can view all the drivers that the VMkernel may utilize by looking in the /usr/lib/vmware/vmkmod directory.

Once the VMkernel has successfully loaded the proper hardware drivers it starts to run its various support scripts:

- The vmklogger sends messages to the syslog daemon and generates logs the entire time the VMkernel is running.

- The vmkdump script saves any existing VMkernel dump files from the VMcore dump partition and prepares the partition in the event that the VMkernel generates unrecoverable errors.

Next the VMFS partitions (the partitions used to store all of your VM disk files) are mounted. The VMkernel simply scans the SCSI devices of the system and then automatically mounts any partition that is configured as VMFS. Once the VMFS partitions are mounted the

VMkernel is completely loaded and ready to start managing virtual machines.

S91httpd.vmware

One of the last steps of the boot process for the COS is to start the VMware MUI (the web interface for VMware management). At this point the VMkernel has been loaded and is running. Starting the MUI provides us with an interface used to graphically interact with ESX. Once the MUI is loaded a display plugged into the host's local console will display a message stating everything is properly loaded and you can now access your ESX host from a web browser.

So why do I need to know the boot process?

You need to understand the basic boot process to understand that the VMkernel is a separate entity from the COS. Also if your server fails to boot or certain services or processes fail to start you'll have a good idea of where to start looking for problems. If you're not familiar with Linux then this is all probably very new to you. If you have some experience with Linux then this section just helped you understand how the VMkernel fits into the picture.

Now let's take a look at how the VMkernel does its magic and "virtualizes" the hardware.

Hardware Virtualization

The whole idea behind VMware is to present a standard hardware layer as a virtual machine to the guest operating systems. These virtual hardware resources remain constant regardless of what physical hardware makes up the host.

The VMkernel is responsible for providing the virtual hardware layer to virtual machines. When a guest OS accesses a resource the VMkernel is then responsible for mapping the virtual request through to the physical hardware for processing. Since VMware presents standard hardware to virtual guests, you need to be familiar with this hardware. Some resources such as SCSI and the network have several options, so we need to understand when each option is used and what it changes in the environment with each.

System Devices

When ESX presents a hardware layer to a guest operating system it presents a system based on Intel's 440BX chipset. This is a highly supported chipset and is compatible with every guest operating system that can be run within ESX. You may be wondering how we can run Pentium 4 XEON and AMD Opteron processors in a guest that has a 440BX chipset. While this sounds a little off, we'll describe that in detail a later in this chapter. For now you just need to understand that the 440BX is what is presented to the guest and it allows for a high degree of compatibility across numerous platforms for our guest operating systems.

Processors

Assuming you are utilizing a processor that meets the requirements of ESX server, your guest will see the same type of physical processor that's installed on the host. The VMkernel is capable of accepting processor calls and handing it straight to the physical processors of the host with limited virtualization overhead. By presenting the host processor type to the guest, the VMkernel does not need to perform any conversions to ensure compatibility between the physical and hardware layer. This simply means that the processor is NOT accessed through on emulation layer. And that if your host has an MP or DP type processor then that's what is presented to the guest.

It's important to note that not all registers of the physical CPU are presented by the VMkernel. While VMware is fairly tight-lipped about these registers, one that is known for sure is processor serial numbers. Applications that are licensed to a serial number of a processor or group of processors will not function within VMware.

Network

ESX provides us with two hardware options when presenting virtual network adapters to guest operating systems. Depending on the guest operating system, there may be a requirement for one over the other.

VLANCE

The vlance adapter is a virtualized AMD PCNET driver. This adapter has guaranteed compatibility across every guest operating system that can be run within ESX. Since it's based on legacy hardware it will also have some limitations when utilizing it within a guest. After installing the drivers you'll notice that the connection speed within the guest operating system shows 10Mb/sec. This is a limitation of the driver and in fact doesn't impact the transfer rate of the hardware. The vlance adapter will utilize as much bandwidth as is available to the physical connection. There is native support for this device in every operating system that ESX has been certified for. If you're configuring a DOS boot disk for a network based installation or to use a DOS based tool such as Ghost, this is the only driver that will properly function. Using this driver will require increased virtualization overhead over the other networking option available to us.

VMXNET

VMware has created a virtual network device that was designed from the ground up to interact with the VMkernel. This device is the vmxnet adapter. Because of its tight integration with the VMkernel you will receive enhanced performance when using it in a guest, especially with high speed connections. Since this device is a VMware creation there is no native support for it in any guest operating system. The only way to configure this device is to install the drivers provided by the VMware Tools installation package within the guest. Using this adapter minimizes the amount of virtualization overhead and increases the network performance for a guest OS. It's important to note that not all operating systems will have the capability to use this device. Use of this device is based strictly on the availability of a VMware Tools installation package and vmxnet driver for the target guest.

SCSI

Like the virtual network adapter, VMware provides two different SCSI adapters that may be presented to a guest operating system. The device that's used by your specific guest depends on the operating system that will be installed. The two options available to use are an LSI Logic adapter or a Bus Logic adapter. Each adapter has different levels of support in each of the supported operating systems. To eliminate any error when building a guest, ESX automatically assigns the proper controller during the virtual machine configuration wizard based on operating system choice. While the default controller may be changed in some cases, it typically requires additional drivers to first be installed in the guest. It may also impact the performance of the virtual machine (more on this in Chapter 4). As a general rule of thumb the choices that VMware makes for us guarantee compatibility for our guest servers.

As you can see the virtual hardware presented to the guests create a relatively flexible environment that can be used by almost any mainstream Intel OS. Now that you have a basic understanding of the virtual hardware as presented to the guests, let's look a little more at how hardware is divided between the physical and virtual worlds.

Hardware Allocation

When installing and configuring ESX, you'll see that both the COS and the VMkernel are responsible for controlling certain aspects of the hardware. There are three different settings for your hardware devices: Virtual, Console, or Shared. Devices that are allocated as "virtual" can only be accessed by the VMkernel (the virtual world). "Console" devices are those that are limited to functioning in the console operating system (the physical world). The third option is a mix of the two and allows for a device to be accessed in both the COS and the VMkernel (physical and virtual worlds). There are also several different ways in which the device allocations may be changed to accommodate changing needs of the environment.

Virtual

Virtual devices, as stated above, may only be accessed by the virtual guests running on your host. The first obvious device that would be configured for virtual machines is at least one network adapter. (Later in this book we'll discuss why you would want to strongly consider using multiple adapters). Configuring a network adapter for virtual machine use is the only way that your guests will be able to communicate with the network outside of your host server.

In addition to network connectivity you also need a place to store the data that makes up your guest. In order to do this a SCSI adapter should also be assigned for virtual machine (which means the VMkernel). To simplify things for now, ESX also considers fiber adapters to be SCSI adapters in terms of virtual, console, or shared configuration. Depending on the size of your environment and the type of data you'll be connecting to, you may or may not have a need for fiber HBAs or additional SCSI adapters.

Console

While "virtual" devices are only be seen by your virtual guests, "console" devices, as you may have guessed, are only seen by the COS. Every ESX host has at least one network adapter that is used by the service console. (This adapter is usually, although not always, dedicated to the COS.) When you communicate to the host with the MUI or connect via ssh, you're interacting with this network interface. When you install backup or management agents on the console operating system, this adapter is also used to communicate through the network.

In order for the console operating system to properly boot, it needs a disk controller to be allocated to Console use. Since the COS is a standalone operating system (just like Windows) it needs a hard drive configured so it can create and use the partitions and files required to boot. This can be a physically attached hard drive, or in the case of ESX 2.5 or newer, a remote boot off of a SAN. (More on this in Chapter 4.)

We should note that you don't need a disk controller that's dedicated to the COS only. You just need to have a controller (either "shared" or "console") that's available to the COS so it can boot.

Shared Resources

Shared resources are those that can be accessed by both the VMkernel and the COS at the same time. Consider the situation we just alluded to previously where you have a system with only one SCSI controller and no SAN in your environment. In order to hold large amounts of data you purchase a SCSI drive cage that externally attaches to your ESX host. Since you only have the one SCSI adapter, you need to make sure the console has access to the internal hard drives for the installation of the COS. We also need to make sure that once ESX is installed the VMkernel will have the appropriate access to the external drive cage.

Shared devices are not limited to SCSI controllers, but may also be fiber HBAs or network adapters. In Chapter 4 we'll introduce you to some of the advanced configurations available to you utilizing the shared bus mode.

Modifying These Configurations

During the installation process of ESX we'll show you how to initially allocate your devices in Chapter 3. As your needs change and your virtual environment grows it's essential to know that you can modify which devices are seen in the physical and virtual worlds. Fortunately VMware provides several tools to make this possible.

MUI

Modifying device allocations utilizing the MUI (the web interface) is a relatively simple process. In order to access the configuration screen you need to log into the MUI as the root user. This will enable the "Options" tab on the main page. The top link in the left column of the options tab will be "Startup Profile." This is the area where you can configure HyperThreading options and memory resources for the service console, and device allocations.

Device allocation configuration through the MUI is somewhat limited in that the only devices that can be configured as "Shared" are SCSI and Fiber Storage Adapters. In order to share a device you must choose to allocate it to "Virtual Machines" and then select the "Share with Service Console" checkbox. You'll notice that the network adapters installed in the system do not have this option. Configuring the network devices for shared use is an advanced configuration and not recommended unless certain conditions are met. This limitation should be sufficient for a vast majority of the implementations, but we feel it's important to note that you cannot do everything from the MUI. Details on this can be found in Chapter 4.

Console Operating System

Modifying device allocations through the service console can be done with the vmkpcidivy command. This command can be run in two different ways: interactive and batch mode.

Running vmkpcidivy in interactive mode is the easiest way to configure your devices outside of the MUI. You can run vmkpcidivy in interactive mode by accessing the service console (locally or via ssh) and using the following command:

```
# vmkpcidivy -i
```

After executing the interactive mode command you'll be presented with a list of configurable devices in the system and how they're currently allocated. (This is shown in the Example: 2.1). The devices are presented in a list categorized by their allocations. You'll see "Shared" devices listed twice—once under the Console section and once in the Virtual Machines section.

Example 2.1

```
[root@esx1 root]# vmkpcidivy -i
Checking for existing VMnix Boot Configurations.

The following VMnix kernel images are defined on your
system:
Boot image configuration: esx
Image file: /boot/vmlinuz-2.4.9-vmnix2
```

```
Memory: 192M
Service Console devices:
Ethernet controller: Intel Corporation 82557
[Ethernet Pro 100] (rev 08)
RAID storage controller: Symbios Logic Inc. (formerly
NCR) 53c895 (rev 02) (shared)
VM devices:
Ethernet controller: 3Com Corporation 3c905C-TX [Fast
Etherlink] (rev 78)
RAID storage controller: Symbios Logic Inc. (formerly
NCR) 53c895 (rev 02) (shared)
Type in the name of the boot image configuration you
wish to configure or type "new" to create a new image
[esx]:
```

Following the list of devices is a prompt asking if you would like to modify an existing configuration or create a new one. The default configuration name for ESX 2.1.1 and higher is ESX. Prior to 2.1.1 the default configuration name was VMNIX. You can tell what your default is by either paying attention to the LILO boot menu at start-up or by viewing the /etc/lilo.conf file with the following command:

```
# grep default /etc/lilo.conf
```

By choosing your default configuration you will be presented with each device and its current setting. When presented with a list of devices, the current values will be set as the "default" values. By simply hitting enter the particular device that's listed will keep its current configuration.

There are three possible values to use for allocating your devices: c, v, or s. These represent Console, Virtual Machines, and Shared, respectively. When you get to the particular device(s) you wish to modify, enter the proper value and hit enter. Once you've gone through the entire list of devices you'll be prompted as to whether you want to apply the configuration changes or not. Once you've chosen to apply the changes you will need to reboot the system the changes to take effect. If you're using vmkpcidivy for information gathering you'll either want to break out of the application using CTRL+C or choose not to apply the changes to the configuration.

We strongly recommended that if you're unsure of the change you're attempting to make that you create a new configuration with a proper temporary name such as "esx-test." This will require that you type "new" at the first prompt followed by your temporary configuration name at the second. When you create a new profile, the settings from your original profile are not remembered. You'll have to pay close attention to each option presented to ensure your system comes up in a functional state after its next reboot.

The Core Four Resources

There are four resources that you need to strongly consider when you review and design your virtual environment. (These are what we've starting calling "Core Four.") Properly understanding and configuring these resources are essential to maintaining a stable virtual environment. This section focuses on these "Core Four" resources and how they pertain to VMware ESX Server and its guests.

Processor

As mentioned previously, the virtualization of the processor component that is presented to virtual machines is slightly different than other devices. As we discussed, the motherboard architecture presented to the guest operating system is based on the Intel 440BX chipset which is a Pentium III-based motherboard. So how does this impact the physical processors that are installed in the host server?

This simple answer is, "it doesn't." The best way to describe how VMware virtualizes the processor was described to us by one of the VMware sales engineers that we frequently have the opportunity to work with. Since the system architecture as presented to the guest operating system is 440BX-based, the device manager within Windows shows you all the typical components of that "virtual motherboard." The single exception in this virtual motherboard is that at the hardware level there's a hole cut out of the motherboard where the processor belongs.

The VMkernel, based on processor family, presents the specific capabilities of your host processors to the guest operating system which allows full utilization of the processors installed. While there are some registers that are not virtualized, the guest has the capability to benefit from the key registers of advanced processors such as Pentium 4 XEON and AMD Opteron. Simply put, the processors are not really virtualized the same way as the other "core four" (memory, disk and network) are. The processor utilization is scheduled, but what the guest sees is pretty much what it gets.

Hyper-threading

Hyper-threading is an Intel technology that allows a single processor to execute threads in parallel, which Intel claims can boost performance by up to 30%. If you think about it, what Intel is really doing is presenting two processors to the OS for each physical processor installed. This idea and technology really comes from trying to make up for the poor task scheduling that Microsoft does in its Windows operating systems (but that's another book all together).

VMware ESX 2.1 introduced support for hyper-threaded processors. The additional logical processors are packaged with the physical and are numbered adjacently. For example, processors 0 and 1 would be physical CPU 1 and its logical counterpart (and 2 and 3 would be CPU 2 and its logical counterpart, etc.). This behavior is different than that displayed in a typical x86 operating system in that all physical CPUs are counted first, and then the logical CPU pairs are numbered. It will be important to remember this numbering system if you begin to use the more advanced concepts of "pinning" a Guest VM to a specific processor for performance reasons.

The increase that a system receives from hyper-threading is dependent on how well the applications running on the system utilize the system cache. While a typical operating system requires that hyper-threading be enabled or disabled for the entire system, VMware has provided several mechanisms for configuring hyper-threading sharing on the system that can be configured on a per virtual machine basis:

- *Any*. This is the default setting for virtual machines running on the system. This allows multiple virtual CPUs to share a single processor package at the ESX level. It allows you to get the most out of enabling hyper-threading on your system, but can introduce problems where an inefficient application may impact overall performance of the other virtual machines sharing a package with it.

- *Internal.* This option is only supported by SMP (multiprocessor) machines. It allows both virtual CPUs for a virtual machine to run in a single package and isolates it from any other virtual CPUs in the system. This prevents the configured guest form impacting other guests and protects it from other guests that may have inefficient applications. If overall system utilization allows, a guest configured with internal hyper-threading sharing can still utilize a package per virtual CPU to maximize performance.

- *None.* In cases where an application is known to perform poorly with hyper-threading, sharing can be disabled. This completely isolates each virtual CPU of the system to its own package. This option should only be used when suggested by VMware or an application vendor as it isolates a large amount of system resources.

Modifying the hyper-threading settings of the system may be done one of three ways. Your system must have hyper-threading enabled at the hardware level in order to view and modify these options. Also, the virtual machine must be powered off for these modifications to be possible.

- *MUI.* By using the MUI, the hyper-threading sharing option can be modified two ways. The first is by editing the CPU Resource Settings for the virtual machine. You'll be presented with a checkbox that's labeled "Isolate Virtual Machine from Hyper-Threading." The behavior of this setting depends on whether the system is a single processor system or if it has Virtual-SMP enabled. For a single processor machine this option will set the sharing value to "none." For SMP machines, the value will be changed to "internal. The other option is to use the verbose configuration option for the guest. When presented with a list of configuration options, add (or modify) a value titled "cpu.htsharing." Assign the value of "any, internal, or none" to this option.

- *COS.* You can easily set the hyper-threading sharing value by directly modifying the VMX file for the virtual machine in question. The easiest way to modify the file is to utilize the following command:

```
# echo cpu.htsharing = \"value\" >> /path/to/server-name.vmx
```

Make sure you substitute the proper value inside the escaped quotation marks. The escape character of "\" is required for echo to properly insert the quotation marks into the configuration file. Another thing you MUST be careful of is that you use the double output symbol ">>". If you use a single output symbol the existing text of the file will be overwritten. It's always recommended that you make a backup copy of the VMX file before making any modification. If you're familiar with the vi editor then you may use that to modify the VMX file with the following line:

```
cpu.htsharing = "value"
```

There's one final note about using hyper-threading in your ESX environment. If you're using a system that utilizes a NUMA memory architecture, it's strongly recommended that you only use ESX versions 2.1.2 or higher. There have been specific issues tied to these systems that appear to have been fixed by the 2.1.2 updates. While there is no "official" announcement from VMware on this, internal employees have confirmed that update code was included to enhance this functionality. Non-NUMA systems seem to perform extremely well with hyper-threading enabled regardless of the ESX version.

Symmetrical Multi-Processing (also known as SMP or Virtual-SMP)

SMP is an add-on module for ESX that provides the capability to configure multi-processor guest operating systems. You enable Virtual SMP by plugging in a license key to your ESX host either during the install process or by modifying the licensing options afterwards. (Note that you do NOT need an SMP license to use ESX on a multi-processor host. You only need it to create VMs that use multiple physical host processors.) While SMP can provide enhanced performance to your system, there are several guidelines that should be strictly followed as SMP can just as easily negatively impact an environ-ment.

- Administrators should never start off by configuring a virtual machine as an SMP system
- Once upgraded to SMP, it is extremely difficult (and some-times impossible) to properly downgrade a Windows guest
- Utilizing SMP slightly increases CPU and memory overhead of an ESX host

While performing best practices analysis of environments we've notice there are quite a few people who start off deploying every vir-tual machine as an SMP system. The added virtualization overhead from this configuration can be the source of significant performance problems once the environment becomes fully utilized.

Additionally, "downgrading" the kernel of a Windows system is a sen-sitive process with Windows 2000 and is not possible with Windows 2003. It's recommended that all guests be created as single processor machines and then if performance dictates and the application is capable of fully utilizing SMP technology it's a simple process to upgrade the system to SMP. By only utilizing SMP on guests that are capable of taking advantage of it, the virtualization overhead of an ESX host is kept low allowing the system utilization to be maximized.

One final note, SMP is only supported on ESX Server—not GSX or Workstation.

Memory

Memory utilization within ESX is managed at many levels. To start, the COS is given dedicated memory resources as part of its boot process (based on the configuration choices you made during ESX installation). This memory is used to support the operation of the COS and virtualization overhead for the service console and each running virtual machine. The COS is allocated 24MB of memory from its available bank for its own virtualization. This is performed automatically and cannot be customized. Each virtual machine that's powered on requires memory in the COS space to support virtualization. (This is the "virtualization overhead" that you hear people talking about). We'll further discuss the details on virtualization requirements and console configuration in Chapter 3 when we install ESX server.

The remaining physical memory that's not assigned to the COS is presented to the VMkernel for virtual machine use. The way memory is controlled and accessed is complicated by the fact that the VMkernel intercepts memory pages and presents them to the guests as if it were continuous memory pages. This process is somewhat complex and described about a hundred different ways depending on who you talk to.

Figure 2.1

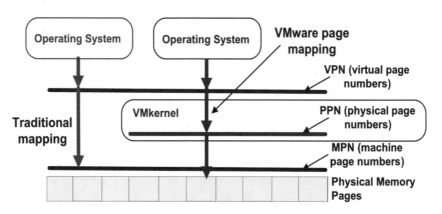

We've found that the process is best described in Carl Waldsurger's "Memory Resource Management in a VMware ESX Server" document. Summarizing this document (and following Figure 2.1):

• VMkernel takes machine page numbers (MPNs) and stores them as physical page numbers (PPNs).

• MPNs are memory pages that are located in the physical memory of the host server.

• PPNs exist only within the VMkernel and are used to map MPNs to virtual page numbers (VPNs) that the VMkernel presents to the guest operating systems. By presenting VPNs to a guest in a contiguous manner, the VMkernel gives the illusion that contiguous memory space is being used within the guest.

- "Shadow page tables" help to eliminate virtual machine overhead by allowing direct correlation of VPNs to MPNs. The VMkernel keeps these mappings up-to-date as the PPN to MPN mappings change.

Later in this chapter we'll describe something called "transparent page sharing." This process (or architecture) allows for a certain amount of secure memory sharing between VMs. The memory resource management used by VMware is what makes transparent page sharing and other memory saving features possible.

NUMA

With the increasing demand for high-end systems, today's hardware vendors needed an affordable and easily scalable architecture. To answer these needs the NUMA (Non-Uniform Memory Access) architecture was developed and adopted by several hardware vendors. NUMA functions by utilizing multiple system buses (nodes) in a single system connected by high speed interconnects. Systems that have NUMA architectures provide certain challenges for today's operating systems. As processor speeds increase, memory access bandwidth becomes increasingly more important. When processors must make a memory call to memory residing on a different bus it must pass through these interconnects—a process which is significantly slower than accessing memory that is located on the same bus as the processor.

NUMA optimizations that were included with version 2.0 of ESX have turned ESX into a fully NUMA-aware operating system. These optimizations are applied using several methods:

- *Home Nodes.* When a virtual machine initially powers on, it's assigned a home node. By default it attempts to access memory and processors that are located on its home node. This provides the highest speed access from processor to memory resources. Due to varying workloads, home nodes alone do not optimize a system's utilization. For this reason it's strongly recommended that NUMA nodes remain balanced in terms of memory configuration. Having unbalanced memory on your nodes will significantly negatively impact your system performance.

- *Dynamic Load Balancing.* At a default rate of every two seconds, ESX checks the workloads across the virtual machines and determines the best way to balance the load across the various NUMA zones in the system. If workloads are sufficiently unbalanced, ESX will migrate a VM from one node to another. The algorithm used to determine which VM to migrate takes into consideration the amount of memory the VM is accessing in its home node and the overall priority of the VM. Any new memory pages requested by the VM are taken from its new node while access to the old pages must traverse the NUMA bus. This minimizes the impact of a guest operating system from a migration across nodes.

- *Page Migration.* While dynamic migration of a virtual machine across nodes limits the impact on the guest, it does not completely eliminate it. Since memory pages now reside on two nodes, memory access speeds are limited by the fact that the processors do not have direct access to them. To counter this, ESX implements a page migration feature that copies data at a rate of 25 pages per second (100 kb/sec) from one node to the other. As it does this the VMkernel updates the PPN to MPN mapping of memory to eliminate virtualization overhead.

Network

Like everything else in the VMware environment, network resources exist in two worlds. The use and configuration of a network resource is quite different depending on whether it's assigned to the COS or to the VMkernel. While the COS configuration is fairly straightforward, virtual adapters have a wide variety of options. In fact, there is enough information around this technology that we've dedicated an entire chapter to it later in this book. Figure 2.2 represents what a typical VMware network configuration would look like on an ESX host.

Figure 2.2

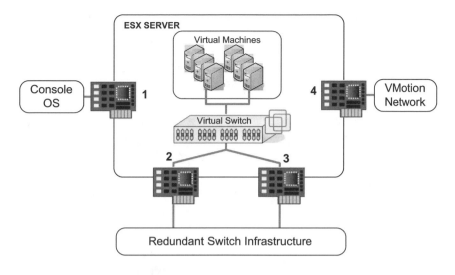

Console NIC Configuration

This adapter is utilized by the COS (remember COS is the "console operating system") for management tasks. ESX management, backups of VMware configuration files, and file copies between ESX hosts are done over this interface.

While this interface is not typically used as much as the interface that the production VMs use, you still want it to be fast if you'll be using it to backup VM disk files. This interface is known to the COS as eth0, and it will commonly be referred to as the "management adapter" throughout this book. By default, the first NIC the COS detects is assigned eth0, and it requires a unique IP address. This does not mean the console NIC will always be an on-board Ethernet interface. Depending on how the system BUS numbering is laid out, it's entirely possible that a PCI slot will act as eth0 for the system.

VMNIC Configuration

ESX assigns adapters configured for virtual machine using sequential names starting with "Outbound Adapter 0" which maps to "Physical Adapter 1." These adapters are labeled as NICs 2 and 3 in Figure 2.2. Like the COS adapter, this numbering is determined by system BUS order. Please refer to Figure 2.3 for Physical Adapter to Outbound Adapter mapping.

Figure 2.3

Outbound Adapter	Physical Adapter
0	1
1	2
2	3
3	4
etc.	etc.

To prevent network bottlenecks on VMware, Gigabit Ethernet connections should be used whenever possible. There are ways to assist in limiting the amount of bandwidth that travels over the wire which will be described later, but for production use, gigabit connections allow you to provide adequate resources to each VM.

Virtual Switch

Virtual switches were introduced in ESX 2.1 as a new way to assign network connectivity to virtual machines. While virtual switches can be created with a single physical NIC (or in some cases, no physical NICs), the failure of that NIC would cause the virtual machines using it to lose their network connectivity. To prevent this downtime, ESX allows us to bond up to 8 gigabit Ethernet adapters (up to 10 10/100 adapters) together to present to virtual machines. A virtual switch is just what its name describes—it emulates a 32-port switch for the guests that are configured to utilize it. Each time a virtual machine references a virtual switch in its configuration it utilizes one port. Virtual switches also load-balance virtual machines across all physical NICs used to create the switch. If one network switch port or VMNIC were to fail, the remaining VMNICs in the bond that makes up the virtual switch would pick up the workload.

Another feature of the virtual switch is that any traffic between VMs on the same virtual switch is typically transferred locally across the system bus as opposed to the across network infrastructure. This helps to lessen the amount of traffic that must travel over the wire for the entire host. An example of where this may be used is a front end web server making database queries to another server configured on the virtual switch. The only traffic that traverses the network infrastructure is the request from the client to the web server.

During the creation process of a virtual switch in VMware you are prompted for a "Network Label." This label serves several purposes, the first being that it's a meaningful way to manage the switch. If you give it a name of "Trusted" or "VLAN17," you have a good idea as to the exact specifications of the switch. The other purpose is for utilizing VMware's VMotion technology. In order to move a virtual guest from one physical host to another, all settings on both hosts must be identical, including virtual switch labels.

Virtual Network (VMnet) Configuration

Feeding off the virtual switch methodology, VMware has also implemented what they call virtual networks, or "VMnets" in ESX. This feature provides the capability to create a private network that is visible only to other hosts configured on the same VMnet on the same physical host. VMnets are simply virtual switches that don't have any outbound adapters assigned to them. Using this feature it's entirely possible to create a multi-network environment on a single host. In the Figure 2.4, traffic coming in through the external virtual switch would have no way to directly communicate to the Virtual Machine 3 and would only be able to interact with Virtual Machine 1 or 2.

Figure 2.4

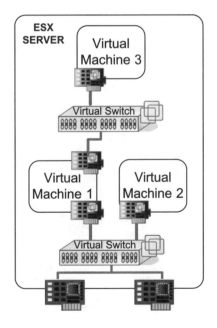

There are several instances in which this configuration may be beneficial:

- Testing in a secure isolated environment. Setting up a VMnet within VMware does not require any physical network connectivity to the box beyond the management NIC. As an example, to see how a group of schema changes impacts an Active Directory, a parallel directory could be created in the virtual environment and tested without ever tying into a production network.

- DMZ Architecture. Since this design creates an isolated environment, it could be created to secure critical systems using network address translation (NAT). This would entail a firewall or reverse proxy being connected to both the virtual switch and the VMnet. Requests from clients would come into this server over the virtual switch. The firewall would then initiate its own connection to the backend web server, which in turn receives data from a database. The information is then returned back to the client without ever having the capability to talk directly to the web or database server.

Storage

Storage for ESX comes in two flavors: local and SAN. With ESX 2.1.2 and lower, every system (at least every supported system) requires local storage for the installation of the COS. In the introduction of ESX 2.5, VMware provided limited support for a "boot from SAN" option which eliminates the need to have local storage connected to the system at all. Before we get into the differences of locally-attached and SAN-attached storage we should understand what it is that will be utilizing these resources.

Virtual Disk Files for VMs

Each VMware virtual disk file represents a physical hard disk that can be allocated to a virtual machine. VMDK files may be up to 9TB in size, which is a limitation that should never really be encountered. Any system that would require that much storage would most likely fall outside of the "VM Candidate" range as described in Chapter 5. ESX does not allow dynamically expanding disks (also known as "sparse" disks) like GSX does. Any VMDK file that is created has all space immediately allocated to it. This is done for a very good reason. It eliminates fragmentation of the hard drive that the VMDK resides on. If you've used VMware's GSX or Workstation products, you may have noticed that heavy fragmentation occurs when a VMDK file must expand itself as it grows. By immediately allocating all space when the vDisk file is defined ESX configures a VMDK file in a relatively contiguous layout on the physical disk.

Allocating the full disk space immediately also ensures that the full amount will be available to the guest OS. There's nothing worse in a datacenter than having a guest crash because it encounters a non-recoverable disk error because it can't write to a section of the disk that it thinks is there.

As a final note, VMDK files may only be presented to virtual machines as SCSI drives. The only device that has IDE support within a guest operating system—at least on ESX Server—is the CD-ROM drive.

VMFS

Any VMDK file that's created for a virtual machine must reside on a VMFS partition. The VMFS file system is optimized for high I/O. It's a flat file system (which means it may not contain subdirectories) that has a 1MB sector size (by default). Unlike the standard way a Windows Server locks a file system, an ESX Server does not lock the entire partition while communicating with it. The lock instead is placed at a file level which allows multiple ESX hosts to utilize the same SAN space and same VMFS partitions (In order to achieve this functionality a SAN is required.)

Standard files should not be stored on VMFS partitions.

There are two different VMFS configuration options you can configure when building a VMFS partition:

- *Public.* This is the default VMFS mode for VMware and fits most needs for configuring and running virtual machines.

When the file system is configured as "public," multiple hosts may access files on the same partition. When a virtual machine is running, a lock is placed on the individual file so no other host can utilize it. If the virtual machine is powered off, power can be restored from any host that has access to the VMDK file.

- *Shared.* This mode is used when configuring clustering across two or more physical hosts as it allows more than one virtual machine to access the same VMDK file at the same time (although only one host can have write access at a time—the other(s) would have read-only access). With Shared mode, ESX allows the guest OS to manage the locking of the file system which is why a "Shared" VMFS volume always seems to be locked or "read only" from the COS. The VMDK files stored in a shared VMFS partition can be clustered with nodes on the same ESX host or nodes that expand across several ESX hosts. For the second option, a SAN LUN must be zoned to all ESX hosts that will host a node of the cluster.

Real World VMFS Mode strategy

At this point some of you may be asking, "why not used shared mode for all my LUNs?" The simple answer is overhead. Managing and monitoring which hosts have VMDKs files opened on a shared mode VMFS partition adds overhead to the system.

In the real world the default mode of public is used as a standard for VMFS partitions. Then, when shared mode is needed, a specific "clustering LUN" is created to host the shared mode VMFS partition and the shared VMDK files.

Local Storage

Local storage for ESX is defined as disk drives directly attached to the system by either a SCSI or IDE interface. (Yes, you can use an IDE interface for storage in an ESX system in a limited configuration.) For example, some blade systems do not have SCSI support for hard drives. In these cases it's possible to install and configure the COS on a local IDE drive. However, it's important to note that IDE cannot be used for a VMFS file system. So although you can install ESX to IDE, you will not be able to run virtual machines unless you have SCSI or fiber-attached storage.

When building an ESX server for a small environment that may only require one or two servers, local storage may fit the bill for VMFS partitions. (This is certainly much cheaper than a SAN infrastructure.) While a SAN does provide significant benefits over locally attached storage, sometimes these benefits do not outweigh the costs.

Nearly all hardware vendors provide external drive cages that can be loaded up with SCSI hard drives at fairly reasonable prices. This allows for very large amounts of storage in a small amount of rack space. There are several advantages and disadvantages to using local storage.

Advantages of Using Local Storage

- Extremely high speed access rates (dependent on the SCSI controller)

- The entire ESX system is contained in one or two rack devices (the server and disk enclosure), making it easy to move

- Easy to manage

Disadvantages of Using Local Storage

- Limited redundancy

- Disk resources are limited to one host at a time (since virtual machines cannot be clustered across physical hosts in this fashion)

- You cannot use VMware's VMotion product to migrate between hosts

Often smaller environments will find that local storage is the only cost-effective solution available. This is not to say that local storage is any better or worse than SAN storage, it just means that it fits them better. Saying outright that SAN Storage is better than local storage for every ESX environment is like saying a Porsche is better than a Ford truck. The truth is that a Porsche is not better than a Ford truck if you are trying to haul a cubic meter of rocks. If one accomplishes your goals at a price you can afford, then that is the right solution.

SAN Storage

ESX Server has a strong dependency on SAN storage when implemented in an enterprise environment. (Just make sure you check VMware's HCL to make sure your SAN is supported!) Since VMware is used to consolidate machines and all space for a VMDK file is allocated upon creation, you'll need quite a bit of storage. As stated previously, VMware configures partitions for VMDK files as VMFS partitions. Strategies on sizing these partitions (or "LUNs" in the SAN world) will be discussed in Chapter 4. While VMware has the capability to expand a VMFS volume by combining several LUNs together, we strongly recommend against this. Combining LUNs within VMware is equivalent to creating a Volume Set in windows 2000/2003. It does not provide a layer of redundancy or striping, and if there are issues with a path or particular LUN, data corruption is more likely to occur than if the VMFS volume were on a single LUN.

In addition to mapping LUNs and configuring them as VMFS partitions, you can map raw SCSI disks through to a virtual operating system. What this means is you can configure a LUN that has an existing file system, such as NTFS, as a disk on the virtual guest. This is useful in a situation where you are setting up clustering in an active/passive configuration with the active node being a physical server and the passive node being a virtual machine. Like using locally attached storage, there are several advantages and disadvantages to using SAN space in your environment:

Advantages of Using SAN Storage

- Multiple hosts may access the same storage space

- Provide large degree of system redundancy

- Ability to cluster virtual machines across physical hosts

- You can use VMware VMotion

Disadvantages of Using SAN Storage

- High level of management. (Many companies have separate departments responsible for managing enterprise storage)

- Expensive to set up storage infrastructure

- Slightly slower than locally attached storage (depending on SAN configuration)

Other Pluggable Devices

In addition to the core four resources, ESX requires special consider-ations for "pluggable" hardware components. These components are those that may be easily added to or removed from the physical hard-ware through either an internal or external connection. While the console operating system may properly detect and utilize many of these devices, a majority of them will not work for the guest operat-ing systems running on the host. This is because special drivers would need to be written and compiled into the VMkernel. Adding addi-tional drivers and support in the VMkernel for a wide variety of available hardware would defeat the purpose of a lightweight kernel with low virtualization overhead.

SCSI

SCSI is one of the resources that's fairly compatible with both the console operating system and the guests running on the host. The VMkernel provides pass-through support for SCSI devices which can include tape backup devices and physical hard drives. The most com-mon use for raw SCSI access is to attach a tape backup unit to a host to either backup the local files on the service console or to have one of the virtual machines directly accessing the backup device acting as a backup server for the other VMs. How ESX accesses any SCSI device is dependent on how the specific SCSI controller that it is con-nected to is configured.

Console Operating System SCSI Device Access
As you saw earlier in this chapter, there are three different ways to configure devices for host and guest access (dedicated to the COS, dedicated to the vmkernel, or shared between the two). By choosing to dedicate the SCSI controller to which a specific physical disk or tape device is connected to the service console, you only will be able to access the device through the console operating system. It's impor-tant to remember that the setting chosen is for the entire SCSI con-

troller and not individual devices attached to it. If the controller is dedicated to the service console only, all devices attached to it will only be accessible by the COS. In the event that a configured device is a physical disk, you could configure additional ext3 partitions for additional storage space for the host.

Virtual Guest SCSI Device Access

In addition to configuring SCSI devices for use by the COS, ESX also gives you the opportunity to pass SCSI devices directly through to a guest operating system. Due to limitations of the SCSI architecture, each SCSI device can only be configured on one guest at a time. In order to configure a guest to access a SCSI resource of the host server, the SCSI adapter that the device is connected to must be configured for either Virtual Machine access or shared access. As you will see when we get to installing ESX in Chapter 3, it's recommended that you configure the primary SCSI controller for shared access.

Configuring a guest to use an attached SCSI device can be performed by using the "Add Hardware" button for the target virtual machine. After choosing to attach a "Generic SCSI Device", a list of compatible devices will be listed. Once you select a device from the presented list, it will become available to the virtual machine after the VM is powered back on. Remember, hardware can only be configured on a virtual machine if the VM is powered off. With the current versions of VMware ESX Server, the only devices that are compatible for pass-through to a guest operating system are hard drives and tape devices. Other device types are not supported on virtual machines as "Generic SCSI Devices".

We feel it is quite important to note that up to ESX 2.1.2 there have been reports of SCSI errors and locking occurring when utilizing a tape drive on the primary SCSI device. It is strongly recommended that if a tape device is required that a second SCSI controller be utilized. This serves two purposes. First, this will enhance the overall throughput of the system. If the second controller is installed on a different system BUS than the original controller there will not be any I/O contention on the system. The second reason for this is that if a SCSI lock does occur it will not impact the system drive. If the controller were to "lock" on the first SCSI controller you would be looking at a purple screen issue and downtime to recover the host and all guests. The I/O compatibility guide should also be consulted prior to making any decisions on adding additional controllers.

iSCSI

One of the most requested features for ESX is the integration of iSCSI for connections to external storage arrays. VMware has been very tight lipped up to this point on anything relating to this functionality. We can verify that this functionality is on VMware's roadmap, but it is still not ready for implementation. ESX 2.5 does not contain any additional code to support this. Our understanding is that in order for ESX to support iSCSI a TCP/IP stack would need to be integrated into the VMkernel. This would more than double the size of the VMkernel in its current state. One of the main selling points to ESX is its lightweight kernel that does not utilize large amounts of CPU cycles.

Chapter 5 has a great description on kernel mode processor calls, we'll summarize the issue here. The amount of TCP/IP calls that would be required for this functionality would also increase the amount of kernel mode calls the VMkernel is required to handle. The VMkernel would have to perform significant amounts of conversion from the guest through to the physical hardware. The performance hit from this does not make iSCSI a viable option at this point in time.

PCI

PCI devices within ESX have extremely limited support. By reviewing the ESX I/O Compatibility Guide, you'll notice that the only devices listed are network, SCSI and Fiber adapters. One of the most commonly sought after PCI cards, Brooktrout Fax cards, is not supported. The main reason for this is driver support. Not only would a Linux level driver be required, but custom VMkernel drivers would also need to be written to properly allow guest access to the resource. This is not to say that other PCI cards will not work. PCI cards that provide additional parallel or serial ports have been reported to work, and work quite well at that. Before choosing a card it is extremely important that VMware support be contacted to verify supportability and functionality of the card in question.

USB/Firewire

While ESX does support USB devices, it only does so at the COS level. Currently, there is no functionality built in to provide USB pass-through to a guest operating system. For this functionality there are several USB network devices that have received excellent reviews in the VMware community and are compatible with guest operating systems. There is no firewire support at the COS or VMkernel level.

Parallel/Serial

Virtual machines running within ESX can be allowed to have direct access to parallel and serial ports of the host operating system. There are several limitations to be aware of before attempting to configure one of these mappings. First, only one guest is allowed to access a single port at any given time. Each guest may have access to one parallel port and two serial ports. Second, there is no way to configure these devices using the MUI. The only way to properly configure them is to manually modify configuration files with the COS. VMware provides this support for external serial modems and external parallel dongles that are required for certain applications.

Configuring Parallel Ports

Parallel ports, as you will see, are more difficult to configure than serial ports. This is because you must first configure the COS to properly see the parallel port as it is not enabled by default. Before attempting to configure parallel pass-through you must ensure that the port is properly configured in the system BIOS. Make sure the parallel port mode in the BIOS is set to either PS/2 or bi-directional. These are typically the default settings within a majority of the systems. Once complete you must add three lines to the end of your /etc/rc.d/rc.local file:

```
/sbin/insmod parport
/sbin/insmod parport_pc
```

```
/sbin/insmod ppdev
```

These lines will properly load the drivers into the COS that are
required to utilize the parallel port. These settings will take effect
on the next reboot. You can force them to take effect immediately
by issuing each of the three commands at the command line.
Once the drivers are properly loaded (you can verify with the
"lsmod" command) you will be able to modify the VMX file of the
guest that needs to access the parallel port. Shut down the guest and
add the following lines to its VMX file:

```
parallel0.present = "true"
parallel0.fileName = "/dev/parport0"
parallel0.bidirectional = "true"
parallel0.startConnected = "true"
```

When the system is powered on, it will have proper access to the system's parallel port.

Configuring Serial Ports

Configuring the virtual machine to use a serial port is very similar to
configuring access to a parallel port. The major difference is the COS
is already properly configured to hand over access. With the proper
virtual machine powered off, add the following lines to its VMX file.

```
serial0.present = "true"
serial0.fileType = "device"
serial0.fileName = "/dev/ttyS0"
serial0.startConnected = "true"
```

When the machine is powered on, the newly mapped serial port will
be presented as COM1 to the guest operating system. In order to configure a second serial port to a guest, use the same lines as above
while swapping out "serial0" with "serial1". The second port will be
recognized as COM2 on the guest operating system.

Resource Sharing

The greatest benefit of using ESX over any other virtualization product is its capability to dynamically share system resources. Since the VMkernel runs on top of and controls the hardware, we're given high levels of flexibility to share system resources across multiple guests. VMware also provides us with several ways to configure sharing of resources giving us an extremely dynamic and flexible platform. Here we'll discuss the various methods that ESX has that allow us to maximize system utilization of the core four resources.

Processor

The VMkernel was designed to provide a high level of interaction with the processors, allowing ESX to dynamically shift resources on the fly (and invisibly) to running virtual machines. If you have three machines that are running in an idle state on the same host as a document processing server, ESX will temporarily shift resources to the highly utilized server to accommodate its immediate needs. If a process is spawned on a low utilization server, the necessary resources are returned to the original VM to effectively run the new application. Generally, a good rule of thumb is to allocate four virtual processors per physical processor, although we've worked in some environments where seeing 5-6 virtual processors per physical was not out of the question based on the processing needs of the virtualized machines. ESX does have a hard coded limit of 80 virtual processors that may be assigned within any single host. With larger systems such as 8 or 16-way hosts, this limit should be considered during the design process. This can be broken down any number of ways mixing single and dual processor virtual machines.

If further granularity is required, ESX provides several mechanisms for manually adjusting processor allocation. This may be useful when one system requires a higher priority than others, such as a database server that is handling transactions for several different applications on the same host.

Processor Share Allocation

One of the easiest ways to modify the default processor allocations of a virtual guest within ESX is to utilize shares. Shares are a mechanism to allocate resources relative to all virtual machines running within a specific host and are used in several instances. Using this method, you can assign priority to specific guests when the host becomes limited on processor cycles. As you add more virtual servers to a host, the total number of shares goes up, and the percentage of total shares to a particular guest goes down. A server that has 1000 shares will receive twice the priority when assigning CPU cycles as a host with 500 shares. The downside to this method is that with each new virtual guest created, the allocation to existing machines decreases, which will slightly decrease their performance when the host system is under a heavy load.

Figure 2.5

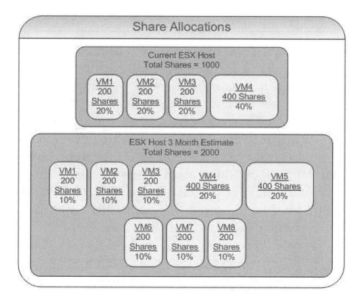

A very important fact to note is that share values do not come into play within ESX until there is sufficient load on the system. Until all available resources are utilized, the VMkernel is happy assigning as many cycles to running guests as they request. Since one of the benefits to ESX server is to maximize hardware, it's unlikely that this will ever be the case, but we've seen hosts that are never utilized to the point that share allocations are required. This does not mean there is no benefit to properly assigning priority, as a runaway guest still has the potential to devour an entire host processor. This could be devastating in a dual or even quad-processor configuration.

Specifying Min/Max Percentages

Within ESX you may assign a minimum and/or maximum percentage value for the processing resources of a virtual machine. By setting the minimum percentage, you're telling VMware to never allow that particular virtual machine to drop below the assigned percent of a single host processor. This is useful if a processor-intensive application requires a bare minimum amount of resources to effectively run. When assigning these values, you need to be extremely careful not to over allocate resources. If you assign eight virtual machines to run with a minimum of 30% in a dual processor server, you will only be allowed to turn on six machines, as three servers per processor will utilize 90% of the resources available on each.

The maximum value is the exact opposite as the minimum. It provides a hard value that a particular virtual machine may not exceed. This would be used in a situation in which an application is known for taking as many resources as the server can throw at it. By setting this value, you tell ESX to allocate a maximum percentage of one CPU to the virtual machine which would provide protection from impacting other virtual machines running on the same host. If you're using the virtual SMP option you can assign a value of up to 200%— the combination of the max percentage per assigned CPU. For example, a value of 140% would mean that each CPU assigned to the virtual machine may be utilized up to 70%.

Assigning a maximum value to an unstable guest operating system would prevent it from consuming an entire host processor. For development guests that are being used to test new code, this configuration could prove to be vital in maintaining a stable environment, especially if multiple developers have guests on the same physical host. Work from one developer will not interfere with work from another.

Setting minimum or maximum processor values are independent of one another. You can choose to set only a minimum value, a maximum value, or both values. Not setting any values allows VMware to have full control over the processor allocation of your virtual machines. While this is sufficient for small deployments with a low number of guest operating systems, it may be crucial to manually change these values as the number of guests increase on a host.

Combination of Min/Max and Share Allocation

When brief periods of contention are expected, one of the best ways to configure the resource allocation of your guests is to use a combination of share values and Min/Max specifications. Before we dive into this theory, we must recommend that very careful planning and utilization analysis be performed before changing any values, as improper settings may impact the integrity of the system. As an example consider Figure 2.6:

Figure 2.6

Guest	Minimum %	Maximum %	CPU Shares
1	15	35	2000
2	40	60	500
3	30	40	1000

Even though Guest 1 has a lower Minimum percentage, he will receive priority of idle shares at a ratio of 4:1 over Guest 2 and 2:1 over Guest 3. This scenario is useful if Guest 1 has a greater benefit than Guest 2 or 3 when additional idle shares are available. With Guest 2 and 3 having a higher minimum CPU percentage, the available cycles will provide enhanced performance on Guest 1 during times of stress.

Until there is processor contention, the systems will run at their maximum allocations. Once resources become limited, ESX will begin to remove cycles from the guests with the lowest share values to best balance them based on the custom share configurations. Based on the chart above, Guest 1 would be the last guest impacted in this scenario due to it having the lowest maximum CPU percentage and highest amount of shares.

We cannot stress enough that modifying these settings should only be done after closely analyzing your system to determine the utilization trends of each virtual machine. While we show an extremely simplistic model with 3 virtual machines, this type of resource management is extremely difficult as the number of guests increase. You should have a solid idea of what impact modifying the settings for a single virtual machine will have on the host and all remaining virtual machines.

Affinity

In addition to setting processing thresholds using one of the previously described methods, you can also specify which physical processor(s) the virtual machine can use. This gives you complete control of the virtual machine processor usage. Not only can you specify that a virtual machine is guaranteed a minimum percentage of processor usage and has a high level of priority in receiving additional allocations, you can also specify the exact processor that provides the resources. Using this methodology one would have complete control over how a production infrastructure reacts on a box, ensuring that every virtual machine has the proper resources and does not step on the toes of other critical applications.

Processor affinity is not limited to specifying a single processor. By specifying a group of processors, you can tell ESX that it is allowed to allocate resources only from the selected processors, leaving the remaining processors inaccessible to the virtual machine. Application servers such as Citrix servers can be pinned to different processors to prevent kernel level calls from interfering with each other. Support servers may then be pinned to the remaining processors and be allowed to share those resources. This allows for a layer of isolation for resource allocations. Typically as shares are granted and removed from the entire pool of processors, every guest on the host is impacted. By utilizing processor affinity, the support servers may dynamically adjust their processing resources while the Citrix servers react as if business is normal.

Memory

Like processing resources, ESX has the capability to dynamically optimize utilization by several techniques: transparent page sharing, ballooning and swapping. These various techniques allow memory of a host to be over allocated, meaning that you can assign more memory to virtual machines than the physical host contains. While we recommend only using sharing and ballooning for production systems, swapping can be utilized to further maximize development hosts and allow more guests. Using the following techniques, it's not uncommon to achieve over allocation of 20-30% in a production environment and up to 100% in development.

Transparent Page Sharing

When a guest operating system is loaded, there are many pages in the memory space that are static and that contain common pages found on all similar operating systems. The same can be said about applications that run on the operating systems. The transparent page tables provide a mechanism to share this space among several virtual operating systems. By mapping identical virtual page numbers back to physical page numbers, guests that are using identical space in the machine page space can share these resources. This lets the system free up memory resources for over allocation without impacting any guests. This is the only memory allocation method that takes place without the host running at maximum memory use.

Idle Memory Tax

When memory share allocation takes effect, VMware provides a mechanism to prevent virtual machines from hoarding memory it may not be utilizing. Just because a particular server has four times the memory share priority than another does not mean it requires it at the time allocation takes place. VMware has a process that applies an idle memory tax. This associates a higher "cost value" to unused allocated shares than it does to memory that is actively used within a virtual machine. This allows the virtual machine to release it for use on other guests that may require it. If the virtual machine in question has a need for the memory, it still has the proper authority to reclaim it as it still has priority over the memory space. A default value of 75% of idle memory may be reclaimed by the tax. This rate may be adjusted by modifying the "MemIdleTax" advanced option. The polling rate of the memory tax may also be adjusted by adjusting the "MemSamplePeriod" advanced option which is set to 30 seconds by default. These values are configured in the advanced options of the ESX host.

Ballooning

VMware has provided functionality to let the guest operating system decide what memory it wants to give back when the system is plagued by high utilization. This is made possible by using a memory reclamation process called "ballooning." Ballooning consists of a vmmemctl driver on the virtual operating system that communicates with the vmkernel. What this driver does is emulate an increase or decrease in memory pressure on the guest operating system and forces it to place memory pages into its local swap file. This driver differs from the VMware swap file method as it forces the operating system to determine what memory it wishes to page. Once the memory is paged locally on the guest operating system, the free physical pages of memory may be reallocated to other guests. As the ESX hosts sees that memory demand has been reduced, it will instruct vmmemctl to "deflate" the balloon and reduce pressure on the guest OS to page memory.

If the vmmemctl driver is not installed or running on the guest, the standard VMware swap file method is utilized. The vmmemctl driver is the preferred method of memory collection as the guest operating system gets to call its own shots. The amount of memory reclaimed from a guest may be configured by modifying the "sched.mem.maxmemctl" advanced option.

Paging

ESX has its own application swap file. This file is independent of both the console operating system and page files setup within the virtual guest operating systems. VMware recommends that this swap file capacity be set to the total amount of memory that will be allocated to all virtual machines. This allows up to a 100% over allocation of memory resources using paging. This is not recommended though, as paging large amounts of data requires additional CPU resources and tends to have a negative impact on the host. When an ESX system becomes over allocated, it takes guest memory that is infrequently used and stores it in the swap file. If VMware requires the resources, it retrieves the memory from the swap space and brings it back into local memory. It may be useful in the development environment, where paging will have less of an impact on the solution, but should be avoided at all costs on a production host.

Network

Each virtual machine configured in an ESX environment shares the combined bandwidth of a virtual switch. In its default configuration, ESX provides limited load-balancing across each physical connection of a virtual switch. If there is only one physical adapter that makes up a virtual switch then you won't gain any benefit from load balancing. The reason we called VMware's default load balancing mechanism "limited" is because of the way it actually functions. We'll go into more detail in Chapter 4, but will briefly summarize here: Each virtual NIC that's assigned to a virtual machine is assigned a virtual MAC address. When a virtual NIC is activated on the guest, the VMkernel ARPs the virtual MAC address for that adapter down one of the physical paths of the virtual switch. The algorithm used for this does not take network load into consideration so it is possible that one path of a virtual switch may become heavily loaded. This behavior limits the sharing benefit gained from load balancing.

ESX provides a single method for throttling network bandwidth. While this may seem limited, the tool used is actually quite powerful. VMware provides the nfshaper module, which allows the VMkernel to control the outgoing bandwidth on a per guest basis. This module only limits outgoing traffic since there is no way (at the host level) to configure how much bandwidth is received by the system. This module is not enabled on a global basis, so must be configured for each virtual machine that you wish to throttle. It's extremely useful if there are a limited number of physical adapters in a system configured with low bandwidth uplinks. A server that's network intensive that will utilize all resources given to it can be limited to allow multiple guests to have access to the networking resources they need.

The nfshaper module can be configured by utilizing the MUI. After logging into the MUI and opening the properties for the target guest, navigate to the "Network" tab. The machine may be in any power state to perform this action. In the right column, the "Edit" button will be active. Clicking on it will present several options.

- *Enable Traffic Shaping.* This one is pretty much a no-brainer. This enables and disables the nfshaper module.

- *Average Bandwidth.* This setting is the sustained throughput that you would like the nfshaper module to maintain for the guest. Remember, this is only for outbound bandwidth. There are no controls to limit how much information a guest receives.

- *Peak Bandwidth.* This is the maximum amount of throughput allowed by the nfshaper module. A guest may hit its peak bandwidth to assist in properly processing all data that needs to be sent. Peak bandwidth is often configured to double the value of average bandwidth. This allows the system to properly send all packets when the system comes under load.

- *Burst Size.* The amount of data that the system may send while hitting its peak bandwidth. If the burst amount is hit, the nfshaper driver will drop below the peak bandwidth until the next burst cycle is available. The burst size should be configured as a byte value of 15% of the average bandwidth. This should be more than enough data to properly fill the peak bandwidth rate.

If the application or guest operating system being filtered starts to display errors such as dropped connections or failed ICMP requests, you should consider increasing these values accordingly.

Disk

Like processor and memory resources, the VMkernel applies a share-based allocation policy to disk access. (Note that we're talking about disk access here, not disk space usage.) The way ESX determines disk access resources is by tracking what VMware calls "consumption units." Each SCSI command issued to a disk resource uses one consumption unit. Depending on the amount of data transferred in the request, additional consumption units are allocated to the guest. When disk resources become stressed on the host system, the share values will determine how many consumption units a guest can utilizes at a given time. After share allocation kicks in, it acts no differently that it does for CPU or memory resources, so we don't need to discuss it again. When choosing the default settings provided by VMware, the following values are used: Low = 500, Normal = 1000, and High = 2000. There are several options available that we'll discuss in Chapter 4 that maximize the utilization of disk resources and yield the best performance available.

Summary

If you managed to get this far then you have more than enough information to build and configure your own ESX server. By understanding the various components of ESX and how they operate, you're well on your way to managing an ESX host. In the next chapter we'll take this information and apply it to the configuration of your first ESX server. By knowing the information presented in this chapter you'll have a good understanding of the various options presented to you during the installation process and why we make the recommendations that we do. Whether you're planning an environment of 2 hosts or 50, the information in this chapter will act as a reference baseline for the rest of this book.

## Chapter 3

VMware ESX Implementation

Now that you have a solid understanding of how ESX works, we need to move on to making decisions about your new environment. This chapter focuses on hardware selection, hardware design, and ESX installation in your environment.

In this chapter, we'll look at the various elements affecting the performance of ESX servers. Then we'll examine various real-world server sizing strategies so that you can create your own strategy. Lastly, we'll go through a basic installation of ESX and describe the configuration options available to you.

ESX Server Hardware

Server sizing in ESX environments is quite a bit different than server sizing in traditional server environments. Since the ESX host will have multiple guests simultaneously accessing the ESX server resources, the hardware tends to be much more robust than that of standard servers.

In order to be able to adequately create your server sizing strategy, it's worth inspecting how server sizing works in ESX environments. To do this, we'll focus on each of the major server hardware components and how they affect the virtual environment.

Before addressing hardware, however, there are a few things that you should keep in mind.

First of all, when you design your ESX servers, you need to make sure that you have "real" server hardware. Desktop computers turned on their side do not constitute "real" hardware. VMware ESX Server has a very strict hardware compatibility list. Unlike some operating systems, you will *not* be able to run ESX successfully on hardware components that are not on the HCL. At this point I usually will hear the argument that since ESX is really Redhat, "We can get it to work". With ESX this simply isn't true. Even if you can get the hardware to work in the Console OS, it does not mean that the VMkernel will recognize the hardware you are "forcing" into the system. Save yourself hundreds of hours and maybe your job, and get a server or components from the VMware HCL.

Now, let's get started with our exploration of server hardware in ESX environments. We'll begin with memory utilization.

ESX Server Memory Usage

When estimating the amount of memory you will need to account for in an ESX build, it is important to not only allow for Console memory, but to also take into account memory sharing, over allocation of memory, and the amount of memory used by the VMs themselves. Every VM on your ESX server (that is powered on) will use some memory. The amount of "real" physical memory in use will depend on a number of factors, but you will have to design your environment factoring in a number of variables.

If ESX Server had a completely flat model, where no memory was shared between VMs, calculations would be simple. You would need to purchase enough physical memory for your host to supply each VM with the amount of memory you wish to assign to it, and enough memory for console operation. Some engineers actually do this so that they ensure that little, if any, swapping occurs. However since ESX's memory model is not flat, and memory is shared and reclaimed in the environment, it is important that you take this into consideration.

In addition to the memory sharing, you should also look at the types of VMs you will be hosting. You should create a list of the types of OS's, the applications they will host, their environment (Prod, dev etc), and the general amount of memory you wish to assign to the VMs. In Chapter 5 we discuss creating a VM standard for Memory and other configurations, but here we will describe some real world recommendations and discuss the other design attributes that go into sizing the memory on your server.

The amount of memory put into a server is closely tied to the number of processors in your system. This is simply because you will create most of your estimates for number of virtual machines per host based on the number of processors in that host. This number (the number of VMs per host) will determine the amount of RAM you will need to design into that host. If you are going to use dual processor servers, and are expecting 8 to 10 VMs per dual processor server, then you need to have enough memory in the server to support those 8 to 10. This is much different than using an 8-way server and expecting 32-40 VMs on the host.

So how much memory is enough to support those 8 to 10 or 32 to 40 servers? Well the answer can be found in the following items:

• Workloads placed on the VMs

• Performance requirements for VMs (Performance SLAs)

• OS's being hosted

• Memory standards for VMs

Workload of the VMs

So what is a workload? Simply put, the workload is the applications or types of applications running on the VMs. Different applications (workloads) require different amounts of physical resources, including memory. But workload is much more than just the application. Imagine a development Exchange server that you use to test upgrades. This server will require less memory than a production VM hosting Exchange mailboxes for 100 users, thus there will be different loads placed on the system by these two machines.

Mixing Test and Dev with production VMs

The other question about workloads is how you are going to spread them out in your environment. Some companies choose to separate the production VMs from dev and test VMs. In doing so they create specific farms or specific hosts for production and specific hosts for dev and test environments. The big advantage in this configuration is that it guarantees that test VMs will not impact the performance of production VMs. The obvious drawback of this model is that you could be creating an environment where all of your "eggs" are in one basket, and a single ESX server failure will increase the number of production VMs affected.

On the other side of this equation are environments that mix test and production VMs all on the same hosts. In this configuration, administrators generally allocate a higher number of resource shares to production VMs to help ensure that test VMs do not negatively impact production VMs. The big advantage of this model is that test and dev servers are often idle. This idle time can allow for better performance of the production VMs since fewer of the server's resources are in use all the time. Of course depending on the security model in your environment, this configuration (test and dev mixed with production) may not meet your security requirements.

Advantages of Mixing Dev, Test, and Production Environments

- Dev and test servers are idle a majority of the time, offering best performance for Prod VMs

- During a host failure, a smaller number of Prod VMs are affected

- Dev servers often require less memory resources, allowing you to allocate more to Prod VMs

Disadvantages of Mixing Dev, Test, and Production Environments

- A runaway process on a test box creates the possibility that performance can be impacted on a production VM

- May require more network ports if the prod and test networks are kept separate

- May not meet your company's security standard

The mixing of workloads and resulting improvement in overall production VM performance is a large factor in some decisions. Your VM configuration, the amount of memory you allot for each VM, and your hardware may keep you from having to install memory expansion boards in your servers, resulting in a reduction in your server costs.

Real World Recommendation: Mix workloads when possible, and when security policies allow. Mix High memory VMs with VMs that require little physical memory. In addition, assign less memory, memory shares and processor shares to test and dev VMs than you do to your production VMs.

Performance Requirements for VMs

Performance SLAs will have a large impact on the memory design in your ESX server. As stated in the previous chapter, ESX allows you to control (to some extent) how memory is shared and distributed among VMs. Memory design for your host should take into account performance SLAs for your VMs. If your VMs are required to act identically to a physical server, or as close to a physical server as possible, you may not be able to over allocate memory in your environment.

Some of this configuration may also depend on your previous decisions about mixing (or not mixing) dev and test workloads with production VMs. The idea is that you may be able to over allocate more memory if you have dev and test VMs on the host. If the host server only has Production VMs on it and your performance requirements dictate a high SLA, you may not be able to over allocate memory.

Real World Recommendation: Mix Guests that have stringent SLAs and loose SLAs. This will allow you to give more shares and or allocate more memory overall to the guests that need it, without having to purchase huge amounts of memory.

Operating Systems Being Hosted

Obviously the types of operating systems being hosted will have a major impact on the memory design for the ESX Server. The memory required to host 10 Windows 2003 Server guests is much higher than the requirement for hosting 10 Windows NT Servers. Take this comparison a step farther and compare a Windows 2003 Server guest with a guest running Linux to test a simple firewall. The difference can be huge.

In addition, the more VMs you have that have the same types of OS's, the more you will be taking advantage of ESX's memory sharing abilities. We have found that when running all like OS's you will generally see about 20-25percent memory savings due to sharing. The long and short of it is that you have to create a list of servers that will be hosted, or project what will be implemented in the environment, to gauge the amount of memory you will need.

Advantage of Mixing guest OS's

• Mixing guest OS's often gives you a mixed workload and therefore better performance

Disadvantage of Mixing guest OS's

• Savings from memory sharing will be reduced

Memory Standards for VMs

In Chapter 5 we will discuss creating a VM standard, but here we need to at least understand the theory. Much like physical hardware standards, you need to create a VM hardware standard. For memory this will mean a standard memory configuration per type of VM being built. Much like physical hardware, people tend to over allocate memory to VMs. Often we will visit a site where the admin in charge of VMs has basically enabled every option and given every VM as many resources as possible. He may have a test Windows 2000 VM with 2GB of RAM assigned and Virtual SMP for a server that is only used to test ADSI scripts.

The problem with this type of over allocation is that it is not a linear move in cost. With a physical server 2GB of memory can be attainted very cheaply if using 512MB DIMMs. Of course to be able to support a large number 2GB VMs you will need a large amount of memory in the ESX host. This often requires that you purchase all 2 or 4GB DIMMs and possibly a memory expansion board. As you can see, the cost will not be the same MB for MB.

It is important to understand and have memory standards for your environment. Once you have these standards you can use them, the workloads of the guests, OS types and environments to determine the amount of memory needed.

Real World Recommendation: Create a standard that is realistic. 2GB of memory for every VM regardless of actual requirements is not good engineering. Instead create a standard that allows you to provide good performance for all VMs and allows you to change memory configurations as needed. Often we will recommend that 384-768 MB of memory per Windows 2003 VM is a good starting place. This can also be adjusted up or down depending on development or production environments (this is detailed in Chapter 5). If the server requires more memory (say 1-1.5GB), we will then increase the memory for that VM. This increase is often offset by all the VMs that are running at 512MB and will keep the average at or a little less than 1GB per VM.

Console OS Memory Requirements

When installing ESX you are asked how much memory you wish to assign to the Console Operating System. VMware allows you to select a number of VMs that the host will support and based on that number selects the appropriate amount of memory. The table below shows the current VMware Console OS recommendations:

Console Memory	Number of VMs
192M	Up to 8 Virtual Machines
272M	Up to 16 Virtual Machines
384M	Up to 32 Virtual Machines
512M	More than 32 Virtual Machines

As you can see, as the number of VMs increase, the amount of memory required by the ESX host increases. We have found these memory settings to be quite appropriate for the Console. If you think about it, this memory is used to support the web server for admin access, secure shell access, basic operating system functions, and virtualization overhead, etc., and it is really important that these be configured properly.

In the real world we have found that if you are getting close to the active number of VMs you have configured, and the console is beginning to seem a little sluggish, a boost in Console OS memory could bring performance back to where it should be. So when you get to 15 or 16 VMs and are thinking of more, you might as well use the next maintenance period to go ahead and up the console memory to the next level.

As for the final recommendation (512 for 32 or more virtual machines), we think this is fine. Some will say that as you get into the 45-50 range and higher, you may want to select (other) from within the Web Interface and set this up to about 768 (max available is 800mb). Some ESX admins swear that boosting this above VMware recommended settings helps increase performance in their environment. We personally feel that assigning more processor shares to the console has shown more performance increases, but this is definitely something to try if you are experiencing console sluggishness.

So Much Memory Per Processor

On servers hosting nothing but production VMs, we like to recommend 3-4 GBs per processor in the host ESX Server. This falls nicely in line with the average of 4-5 VMs per processor. Additionally, when factoring in the memory allocated to the Console OS, memory saved through sharing, and any lost to virtualization overhead, you still will be able to allocate an average of 768MB – 1GB per VM.

If you plan on running development or test VMs only, then you have the ability to run a much higher ratio of VMs to processors. In addition, you can more easily over allocate memory to VMs in test and dev environments since these servers are often idle and performance is not as important as it is in production environments. We have found that in a number of test environments the average ratio is about 5 to 7 VMs per processor

The long and short is that we like the 3-4GB range per processor for most environments. It allows you enough memory to host production VMs and still allows you the flexibility to over allocate for test and dev Environments.

ESX Server Processor Usage

When it comes to sizing ESX Server processors, don't take the time to calculate how many megahertz or gigahertz you need to support your VMs. Processor speeds are dictated by Intel, AMD and the hardware vendors, and you're pretty much forced to take what they offer. While processor and system bus architectures play a role, the real decision when sizing processors is the number of processors overall and number per host. In most cases, you need to figure out whether your server will be a dual proc blade, a standard dual, a quad-processor, Eight-way, or maybe even a 16 processor box.

In deciding how many processors you want in your servers, keep in mind that you will have to find a balance between number of processors in a server, the amount of VMs hosted per server, and the number of ESX servers you are willing to manage. Also consider the amount of risk associated with a hardware failure on your ESX host. There is a big difference between a 16 processor host failing with 80 VMs on it and a 4 processor host going down with only 16-20 VMs on it.

Each VM will have to share processor time with each other VM. Even if a VM is doing nothing at all, servicing no requests, hosting no files, etc., some processor will be used. In this design, if one VM does not need much processor time, then more processing power is available for other VMs. Due to the way ESX server shares the processor and the fact that each VM's processor requests can (by default) be executed on any processor on the server, it is fairly easy to scale ESX up to 16 processors. But one thing to remember is that the more processors you have, the greater your risk of running into a bottleneck in another part of the server.

In a perfect world, your processor utilization would constantly be in the 80-85percent range. This would indicate that you didn't waste money buying too many processors, but also that no VMs are waiting for processing bottlenecks.

Real-World Processor Recommendation
Processors are very fast and very cheap. When sizing servers, many people buy dual processor servers that are quad processor capable. This allows them to test and start with a dual processor configuration and then add more processors if the testing is successful. Later in this chapter we will discuss Duals vs. Quads vs. 8-ways vs. 16-ways. If you need to make that decision now you may want to skip ahead.

Xeon processors in the MP architecture will yield better performance in ESX than the standard DP architecture. The reason for this is simple. Often the MP processors have larger cache sizes, which is better geared toward the large amount of processing that will happen within ESX Virtual environments. The trick will be to determine whether they are worth the added cost for your environment. (See the sizing techniques in Chapter 9.)

ESX Server Hard Drive Usage

In most environments your ESX server hard drive configuration will depend on your company's storage strategy (if they have one). The hard drive configuration for your ESX host will look extremely different if you plan on using a SAN for storing VMDK files instead of local storage. In the next chapter we discuss infrastructure design (Basically network and Storage strategies). If you plan on designing your SAN solution for ESX based on this book, you may want to jump ahead after reading this. This section will purely focus on the local drives and partitions for the ESX host.

In the 2.5 version of ESX, VMware introduced its boot from SAN feature. This feature was pretty much made for the Blade servers now being implemented in some organizations. Personally, I feel that boot from SAN is really not needed outside the Blade world. Storage on the SAN is generally so much more expensive than local storage that using the SAN for the OS on an ESX server (including swap space and all) is pretty much useless.

Because of the way that hard drives are typically used in ESX environments, you don't need very much storage space on individual servers. Typically VMDK files are stored on a SAN solution and the only things that are stored locally are the console operating system and VM configuration files. Most people buy two or three drives for this and configure them in a simple RAID 1 or 5. The size of the drives often depends on the amount of memory you have in the system and whether or not you wish to store VMDK files locally.

One of the first steps in the ESX setup process is configuring the installation of the console operating system. Based on a combination of VMware best practices and our personal experiences with VMware, we recommend a partitioning scheme that will create a very flexible environment regardless of how you move forward with ESX.

/boot: 50MB

The first partition that should be created as a primary partition on the disk is the /boot partition. This partition contains the kernel of the Console OS, which tells the system how to boot and what drivers to load to properly initialize the system.

This does not have to be a large partition as VMware has an optimized kernel for its Console OS that is a set size. The recommendation here is to set the /boot partition to 50MB. It is highly recommended that this partition be the first created on any disk as some systems may have an issue detecting the /boot partition if it is created beyond the first 1024 cylinders.

Swap: 768MB

The second partition created should be the swap partition and should also be created as primary. This should be set to two times the amount of memory assigned to the service console during the install process. We often configure the service console with 384MB of memory, which allows for up to 32 virtual machines to run at one time. Based on the best practices, we create at least a 768 MB swap partition. If your Console OS memory is set at other than 384, set this partition to 2x your configured memory.

/ (or root): 2.5GB

The third partition and final primary partition created should be the / partition, which is commonly referred to as the root partition. This is where all files of the Console OS will be installed. All partitions that begin with a /, including /var and /boot, will be mounted in a directory under the root file system. This allows partitions to be created that fall under the directory structure of the console operating system. A value of 2.5GB is recommended for this partition, as that should be more than sufficient to hold the entire ESX console operating system.

/var: 1GB

The next partition that we recommend be created is the /var operating system. This mounts underneath the root file system and is the default directory for all log files. In addition, this directory is used for temp files when creating unattended install scripts via the VMware Web Interface. Creating a separate partition for log files prevents a troublesome system from filling up the entire root partition with error logs, which would prevent the system from booting. If the /var partition fills, the system will still be bootable, and the directory may be cleaned up or the logs may be reviewed to determine the cause of the errors. Generally 250MB should be sufficient for log files, as VMware regularly rotates log files to prevent the /var directory from filling, but the additional 750 MB is allocated in case you decide to use the unattended script creation process (see Chapter 9 for more details).

/vmimages: 10 GB

The final partition that is created during the initial VMware install process will contain CDROM ISO images for OS installation files and can be used as temporary storage space for exporting disks or installing third party applications. The name of this directory depends on the direction you wish to go with an enterprise management solution. The size should be configured at 10GB and allow for numerous images and files to be stored.

/home: 300MB

VMware's VirtualCenter application, in its current state, uses this directory to store VM configuration files. 300 MB should be enough since the configuration files for the VMs are nothing more than small text files.

Figure 3.1 Partition and Directory overview

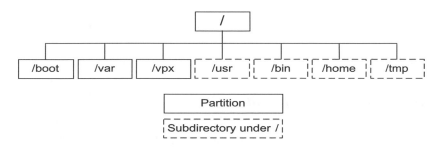

Local VMware Partitions

ESX requires additional partitions on local storage in addition to the console operating system partitions. The first of these partitions is a 100MB Core Dump partition. In an instance where the VMkernel crashes, it will dump down a core dump and log file to this partition, which can be extracted and sent to support for troubleshooting.

The second partition created for VMware's exclusive use is a VMFS partition for the VMware Swap File and possibly local VMDK file storage. VMware utilizes this VMware Swap file for advanced dynamic memory management across VMs. This partition must be large enough to hold a VMware swap file that is capable of supporting more memory than is being allocated to all virtual machines. In our environments we often create this swap file as large as the physical amount of memory in the server. If your server has 16GB of memory we would recommend a 16 GB Swap file on the VMFS.

Assuming 16 GB of physical memory in the server, 50 MB for /boot, 800 MB for SWAP, 2.5 GB for root, 1GB for /VAR, and 10 GB for /vmimages, we have a total of about 30 GB of writable storage. Assuming you are using a SAN solution for storing VMDK files, you could host this on a single set of 36GB mirrored drives. If you plan on storing VMDK files locally you will need to estimate the number of VMs, the size of the VMDK files, and calculate the amount of storage required for these VMs in addition to the original 30GB we have just allocated.

Obviously some of the estimates given here were for larger ESX servers (like quads and eight-ways). If you plan to use blade technology or smaller duals, this will reduce the number of VMs and obviously change the memory assigned to the console, and thus change the swap space for the Console OS. In addition, the amount of physical memory in the server will be lower and you will most likely need to reduce the size of the VMware swap file accordingly.

Hard Drives and Controllers

Obviously the hardware on the ESX host should be utilized to its fullest extent. One of the most under-designed aspects of the server is often the drives and controllers in the host. New VMware admins tend to load up on memory and processors at the expense of really hot disk controllers and fast drives. Depending on the load placed on your ESX server (the bigger the server, the more VMs; the more VMs, the more load on the host) you may want to investigate implementing separate controllers for the Console OS and the Local VMFS partitions. If you plan on storing VMDK files locally, this is probably a good idea and will separate traffic bound for the VM VMDKs and increase your overall performance.

On the controller side of things it is probably a good idea to use a hot SCSI controller with at least 128MB of cache. Most of the off the shelf RAID controllers from HP and IBM now come with 64 or 128 MB of cache. It is also important to ensure that the write cache is enabled. I have seen certain instances where these settings have come from the manufacturer disabled, and I hate paying for things that I don't get to use.

If you are using local storage for your VMDK files and would like to separate them to a separate controller, but still save some money, your best bet is to use the integrated RAID controller for the Console OS and the additional RAID controller for the VMFS partition that will host VMDK files. If separate controllers are not possible, then shoot for a different SCSI BUS on a local controller.

As a final thought on this, we should probably talk about drive speed. There is often an argument between buying 10K or 15K drives. My opinion is up in the air. If the local drives are only used for the Console OS and swap files, I would say it is ok to use 10K drives. If you are going to use local disk to host the VMDK files it wouldn't hurt to move up to 15K drives for everything. This will help to ensure optimal performance for your guest VMs and doesn't add that much cost to the overall system.

ESX Server Network Connectivity

Each ESX Server will at a minimum have at least 2 network cards. One network card (generally the first NIC in the system) is assigned to the console operating system and another is dedicated to Virtual Machine use. While this configuration will function, it obviously provides no redundancy for the VMs and does not allow for other network based functions (like VMotion) that you may want to use. For a minimal configuration with redundancy and VMotion functionality, you may want to design at least a 4 NIC configuration as seen in Figure 3.2.

Figure 3.2 Typical ESX Server Network Configuration

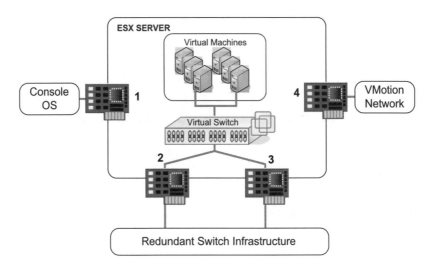

Console NIC Configuration

Referring to Figure 3.2, NIC number 1 is utilized by the console operating system for management tasks. ESX management, backups of VMware configuration files, and file copies between ESX hosts are done over this interface. With the amount of network traffic traveling through this device, a 100mb Full-Duplex connection will be more than sufficient.

This interface is known to the console operating system as eth0, and will commonly be referred to as the management adapter or console NIC throughout this book. By default, the first NIC the Console OS detects is assigned eth0, and requires a unique IP address. It may be a good idea to put the Console NIC on your management network if you have one. This network could be shared with the network connections used by HP RILO boards, etc.

Virtual NIC (VMNIC) Configuration

In this example, Network Cards 2 and 3 are combined into an ESX VMnic bond. In this configuration the NICs are both associated with a single virtual switch on the ESX server. This configuration of NICs 2 and 3 not only supply additional bandwidth to the VMware guests, but also provide fault tolerance. It is important to size these NICs appropriately. In this configuration we often use Gigabit network cards for NICs 2 and 3. Using 100 MB as a baseline for each VM, this configuration supplies enough bandwidth for 16 - 20 VMs. For sizing purposes it is good to assume at least 1 Gig NIC per 5-10 VMs. If fault tolerance is required, you will have to make a decision about bandwidth availability during a NIC failure. Is it acceptable for say 16 VMs to run from a single GB NIC if one NIC fails?

The final network card (Number 4) is dedicated to VMotion. In environments that utilize VMotion technology we have found it beneficial to dedicate a NIC to this traffic and even to isolate that traffic onto its own non-routable network. This network can be a simple VLAN that handles nothing but this traffic and is isolated from the rest of the network.

Virtual Switch

While it is possible to assign standalone vmnics to virtual machines for network connectivity, there is no redundancy involved. If the NIC or connection were to fail, the virtual operating system would not be able to talk to the network. To prevent this downtime, ESX allows you to create virtual switches. These virtual switches allow you to bond two 2-8 gigabit Ethernet adapters together to present to virtual machines. In Chapter 2 we discussed how virtual switches worked. For more detailed information on VM networking please jump to Chapter 4. For now, you just need to understand that you will need at least 1 virtual switch in your environment.

Real-World Network Connectivity

We definitely recommend a three NIC configuration for most production systems. If you plan on implementing VMotion, then a fourth NIC should be used to isolate that traffic away from the NICs used by the VMs. If you are planning to implement servers that are larger than 4-ways, you may want to look into adding another two network ports to accommodate the amount of bandwidth that will be required by the VMs. A good rule of thumb is 8 to 12 VMs per

Gigabit network card dedicated to VMs. If you are looking at an eight-way server and possibly 30 or 40 VMs, you should really be looking at three or four NICs dedicated to VMs.

As an alternative, you can break this down into bandwidth requirements if you wish to get very granular. This requires that you estimate the amount of bandwidth required by each VM, then add that total up to determine the number of NICs you need. Obviously we have done this assuming 100MB or a little less per VM in using the 8-10 VMs per NIC.

Real-World Sizing Strategies

Now that you know how server hardware components work in ESX environments, you need to think about your strategy for sizing your servers.

The objective is simple: you want to build your servers to be big enough to support your VMs and keep the number of OS's you need to manage down, while still making them small enough so that you don't spend too much money on them.

At first, this statement may seem extremely obvious. Nevertheless, there's plenty to think about when you get ready to size your servers.

Why Should You Care About Server Sizing?

Server sizing is not about buying the fastest processors and the most memory. When it comes to server sizing, the maximum number of VMs a server can support is less important than the cost for each VM on that ESX server. If you build a 16 processor server that can handle 64 VMs, but two 8-ways would have cost you 25 percent less and would have handled just as many VMs, you may find yourself out of a job. In addition, server sizing is finding a balance between hosting as many VMs as possible, while still maintaining a manageable number of hosts and keeping the cost per VM at a reasonable level.

A proper server sizing strategy involves creating a balance between too many small servers and too few large servers. For example, it's possible to build a sixteen processor server with 48 gigabytes of memory. But just because you can build one gigantic server for all of your VMs, should you? There are plenty of servers out there that have 48-64 VMs on them, however the cost per VM in these solutions begins to rival the normal cost of adding a blade into a blade chassis.

Server Sizing Options

By building several smaller ESX servers, you're able to increase the redundancy of your ESX environment. If you build one gigantic $60,000 server and something happens to it, all of your VMs are down. However, if you build three $20,000 servers and you lose one, only one-third of your VMs are affected.

Your server environment will ideally balance between the two extreme options:

- Build a few gigantic servers

- Build many small servers

- Take the middle road

Option 1. Build a Few Gigantic Servers

Drive space, processors, and memory are so incredibly inexpensive these days that many people are transfixed by the idea of creating a few massive servers that can each support tons of VMs. They like the concept of only having a few servers to manage and the fact that they can spend money on large chassis, redundant drives, processors, tons of memory, NICs, power supplies, etc.

The general issue here is that the price / performance ratio of big servers might not be there. When looking at building large servers (read 8 and 16 processor servers), the cost per processor when compared to a similarly configured 4-way may be 25 percent more. This translates to a cost of 25 percent more per VM. Of course a benefit of having large ESX servers is that you have fewer ESX servers to manage. This will reduce time spent for monitoring the host, patching, upgrading and managing the host, and of course reduce the "number" of servers in the datacenter, but maybe not the footprint/rack space.

Advantages of Building a Few Gigantic Servers

*   Fewer hosts to manage and monitor

*   Less time spent upgrading and patching hosts

*   Amount of resources (as a percentage) used by the Console OS is extremely low

Disadvantages of Building a Few Gigantic Servers

*   Single point (or fewer points) of failure

*   Possibly an increase in cost per VM

Option 2. Build Many Small Servers

Instead of building a few gigantic servers, you might choose to build several smaller servers. This option lessens the risk that one system's failure could take out a significant number of your VMs.

When thinking about building multiple smaller servers, two advantages become apparent: redundancy and scalability. Because you have multiple servers, you could lose one without a large part of your environment being down. (This means that you might not get paged if this happens, allowing for a full night's sleep.) Also, you can schedule servers to be taken down for maintenance or to be rebooted without affecting large portions of your environment.

Furthermore, you might be able to support more VMs with the same amount of money. (Or, you could look at this as being able to save money.) Many ESX administrators also like the fact that building multiple smaller servers gives them more flexibility to dynamically deploy and re-deploy VMs as requirements and resource needs change.

Another benefit in favor of multiple, smaller servers, is the ease with which servers are managed and provisioned today. Many companies are leveraging blade servers to build large farms of redundant servers. (Think of it as "RAIS"—Redundant Array of Inexpensive Servers.)

Advantages of Building Many Small Servers

- Redundancy

- Often a lower cost per processor

- Flexibility. Redeploy applications and move them around as needs shift

Disadvantages of Building Many Small Servers

- Some utilization might be wasted

- Additional ESX hosts to manage

- Amount of resources used by the Console OS is larger (as a percentage) than when using large servers

Option 3. Build Servers in the Middle Ground

Finally, you have the option to move into the middle ground. Instead of going to either extreme you can find a middle ground like a quad processor server. In a number of engagements we have found that the quad processor is the "sweet spot" when comparing price, performance, and manageability.

With all else being equal, quad processor servers often fall right into an environment's sweet spot. Quad processor servers are more of a commodity than the 8- and 16- processors servers, which lowers their prices when compared to the larger servers. In addition, they often have the flexibility in their design to allow you to configure Network cards, HBAs, and other components for your environment. This is often a huge advantage over blades and 1U's.

Generally, the disadvantage seen in quads is either from a political front where someone is set on one technology over another, or the fact that your ESX environment will still be too small for quads, and would be better off with just a couple of dual processors.

Advantages of Building Mid size servers

• Often sweet spot for price per VM

• A good balance between number of VMs and number of hosts

• As flexible as small servers if your environment is large enough

Disadvantages of Building Mid size servers

• Might not provide enough redundancy in smaller environments

• Additional ESX hosts to manage when compared to large servers

Installing ESX Server

Now that you have figured out (or at least have an idea about) the type of server you will use for your ESX environment, it is time to get to understand the installation process. This section will not show you a series of screen shots of the install, but instead give you a break down of the options you are given during the installation and what they really affect. We will also provide you with a few best practices and some post-installation steps that you may want to follow to ensure your environment is tight.

If you happen to be using some hardware that is, shall we say, "not of the classic configuration" (meaning a blade or boot from SAN technology), make sure to look at the final sections of this chapter since we have outlined some special steps you need to take and documents you may want to review.

Installation Options

During a manual install of ESX server (Scripted installs are discussed in Chapter 9) you have the ability to use either a GUI based installation or a simple Linux text based installation. In either version of the installation you have the ability to configure a number of options.

This section describes those options and how the choices you make during the install effects your ESX environment.

The setup we go through below is process oriented and assumes a "classic" server configuration and not a blade or SAN based installation. When installing to a blade or SAN, the majority of the options are the same. The big differences are either the way the initial boot for the install is handled, or the destination for the console operating system's files.

Pre-installation Steps:

If you currently have an ESX media kit it is important to check VMware.com and make sure a later version of ESX installation is not available. There have been a number of admins that built their first or second ESX server only to find out a day later that there was a new incremental update that they could have downloaded a new installation CD for. Instead they wind up downloading the upgrade and having to put in some extra effort to upgrade the server they just built.

1. Disconnect SAN connections: If you are not using boot from SAN, VMware recommends that you disconnect the connections from the host to the SAN. Leaving these connected exposes the SAN disk to the install and has caused more than one admin to install part of their OS to the SAN instead of the local disks

2. Verify you have all the information for your host. This should include the fully qualified host name, the IP address and config info for the Console OS, and one or more DNS name server IP addresses. The most important piece of information is the FQDN for the server. If you wind up needing to change this after the installation, you will have to go through a process to reconfigure the server certificate on the ESX server.

3. Estimate the number of VMs you will have on the server and how you will create your partition structure. Please refer to the previous section of this chapter for some good rules of thumb for partition sizes.

4. Ensure you have network connectivity: Make sure that, at the very least, the Console OS's NIC is plugged into the network (the first NIC found in the system BUS scan). It is generally a good idea to have all the NICs plugged in during install but the Console OS is the most important.

5. Finally, verify that you have functioning hardware. VMware says the most important pieces of hardware to test are the memory modules. These tend to have the most failures once VMware is up and running. Use your vendor's diagnostic tools for a complete memory test, or download an application like memtest86 (www.memtest86.com). This may take a couple of days to run if you have a large server, but if it finds a memory error before you move this server into production, the 2 days are worth it.

   Obviously you will have to check all your hardware, not just memory, and make sure all of your hardware is solid and that you have run any diagnostics available before installing ESX.

6. Ensure you have a solid SSH client available for connecting to the console. I would recommend a simple client called PuTTY. Any quick google search of PuTTY will link you to the download sites for this great – and free – tool.

Installation Steps

Boot your Server and Select an Installation Mode

During the first boot of the ESX media you will be asked to select an installation mode. Depending on the version of ESX Server you are installing, these options may very. In the table below we have listed all the options available in ESX 2.1 and 2.5. ESX Server 2.5 introduced a number of new options and carried over the original options from 2.1.

ESX 2.1 Options	ESX 2.5 Options	Function
Noapic	Noapic	Disables IO-APIC
Text	Text	Text version used for servers that have unsupported Video chipsets or mice that do not work with the GUI based installation
	driverdisk	Used to install ESX using a VMware supplied driver disk that contains updated drivers for newer hardware
	bootfromsan	Used when you wish this server to install its boot files to a SAN
	bootfromsan-text	A text version of the boot from SAN option
press enter (GUI Install)	press enter (GUI Install)	Recommended standard installation (GUI based)

As you can see, the biggest change in the install in 2.5 was the addition of the boot from SAN option. Prior to 2.5, several VMware customers were "making this work" but it was not officially supported. If you are planning a boot from SAN system, this is the install you want to select.

It is important to note that you should not sit there reading the install options. If you wait too long the default (press enter – for a standard installation) will dump you to a GUI based install. If you want this option anyway, it's not a big deal. But if you were planning to use a text based install or boot from SAN, you pretty much have to restart the server.

The text options allow you to not use a GUI and mouse based installation. This is generally used when your video card chipset or mouse are not compatible with the ESX install. The text version will give you all the options that the GUI install has and some people actually prefer it.

Finally, we will discuss the "noapic" option. Linux users will recognize this immediately. As it is often said with most options "you will know when you need this". With certain servers (very few tier 1 type servers) the linux install will crash or have problems with the apic enabled mother board of the host. For most users you will never need this option but if you do have install problems – such as kernel panics, installs freezing, etc. – you may want to give this install option a shot and get VMware support involved.

Once you have selected your installation type/option the install will begin. You will be prompted to verify or configure the items listed below. You may note that some of these are out of order. The sequence of these may depend on the version of ESX you are installing, but in all current versions the options are pretty much the same.

Setup keyboard and mouse

This option is really the only difference between a "custom" and standard install once you are in the GUI. In most cases this is a "no brainer". And even if it isn't, it may not be much of a problem. The installation defaults to a standard English keybord configuration and a two button mouse. If you don't have a real need to change these settings, then don't. Very little work will be done through the console keyboard and a mouse is rarely required beyond the initial install in GUI mode.

Accepting license agreement

Again, another "no brainer", just like Microsoft or any other vendor, you must accept the license agreement.

Entering ESX Server and VSMP licensing

During the install you have the option of entering your server license and a license for Virtual SMP, if you would like to. Most admins will do this for their first couple of servers then realize that they don't have to. Often carrying around a piece of paper or e-mail with a license number in it is not nearly as convenient as just cutting and pasting the numbers from your own desk once the Web Interface is up. So you can choose not to enter a license number during the install and can instead add the licenses after the install from the comfort of your own desk.

Configure Console Memory

This option allows you to make an estimate of the amount of memory you will allocate to the Console OS. It is important to have an estimate of the number of VMs you are going to host before configuring this. Another important note is the fact that the amount of memory selected here will have a direct impact on the size of the swap partition for the console

The default is 192MB for up to 8 VMs. There are also selections for up to 16, 32, and above 32 VMs. We often suggest that if you are going to be close to the upper number (IE 8, 16 or 32) that you go ahead and configure the console memory for the next highest increment, as it will save you a reconfiguration later if you are interested in adding additional VMs.

Ethernet Devices and SCSI controllers

During the install you will be asked to verify the configuration of the console's network card (eth0) and the SCSI device that will be used to store the Console OS. The default configuration assigns the first Ethernet adapter in the server to eth0 and thus to the console. In addition, the SCSI controller presented to the console is also set to "share with virtual machines". While you won't need to reconfigure the NIC at this point, the SCSI config should be noted.

Verify that the SCSI device shown is the correct one to install the OS to and determine whether you will share that controller with Virtual Machines or not. If you are using a separate SCSI or SAN connection for storing VMs, you can configure the local device for console access only. If the local device is a large RAID array that you will partition for both the Console OS and a VMFS partition for VMDK and swap file use, then you need to ensure that the device is shared with the VMs. It should be noted that even when using a SAN, it is a best practice to store the VMFS swap locally and therefore the controller will be shared whether you are storing VMDKs locally or not.

Partition Creation

This is one of the most confusing sections for some Windows engineers. In the Microsoft world it has been a long time since they have been required to create numerous partitions manually for an installation. That, and the fact that most Windows installations do not span multiple partitions, often confuses the newbies to ESX.

With this in mind, you should use some of our rules of thumb from earlier in this chapter and remember the following rules:

1. Make the partitions / or root, /boot and the swap all primary.

2. Create an extended partition that will be used for /var, /home, /vmimages, and VMFS.

3. Use common sense on sizes of these partitions. Good rules when you aren't sure are listed below:

```
/boot: 50MB
/ or root: 2.5 GB
swap: 2x memory allocated to the console
/var: 250MB
/vmimages: 10GB (or enough to handle ISO images and
configurations)
/home: 300MB
```

IP Address for the Console
Once you have configured the partitions, you will be asked to configure the IP information for the Console Operating System. You can use DHCP if you wish, though it is not advisable, and some versions of ESX calculate the MAC address from VMs based on the Console's IP. If the IP changes, you have a chance of changing MACs on the VMs. Also, it's just a best practice to keep server IPs static.

Location and Time Zone
Since this is an "advanced" design guide, we think you might be able to figure out where you and your servers are in the world.

Root password and account configuration
During the install you will need to set a root password (root for you Windows guys is like the Administrator account). Anyway, the password must be at least 6 characters and of course we recommend you make it a secure password and not your first name or something like that.

At this point you can also create accounts for use on the ESX server. If you are using a management tool like VirtualCenter or plan on using PAM for authentication against another directory, you may not need to create any accounts here. If you plan on running a stand alone ESX server, we highly recommend you create some accounts (and an account strategy) so that users are not all using "root" to access and manage VMs.

Installation

At this point you are ready to install the server. The partitions will be created by the install process and the ESX server packages will be installed. At the end of the installation you will be prompted to reboot and the remaining configuration will take place after the first boot via the Web Interface.

Final Web Interface Configuration (post install)

Once the server reboots, you are installed and almost ready to rock and roll. The final steps of the server's configuration will take place via the Web Interface and include the following items:

- Configuration of a VMFS partition, ESX swap file, and a Core Dump location (if not done during the install process)

- Configuration of additional mass storage devices (if needed)

- Configuration of Virtual Switches

- Installation of licenses if they were not entered during the install

Finally, once the server has been rebooted, you will need to sign into the Web Interface of your server. You can access your server by using a web browser by going to http://servername or http://serverip. When accessing this page you will be prompted by a browser security warning. This is because the certificate used by your server was not issued by a trusted CA. You can click past this warning or install the CA into your browser so you aren't bothered by the message again.

During this login you should use the root account. This login will kick off the ESX Server Configuration screen.

This screen will walk you through the following:

- License agreement and license serial numbers (again)
- Configuration of the Startup Profile
- Storage Configuration
- Swap Configuration
- Network Connections
- Security Settings

License Agreement and Serial Numbers
Again you will have a chance to enter and or verify your license serial numbers and agree to the license agreement. This is not a big deal; just enter your serials numbers if you have not already done so and move on to the next screen.

Startup Profile
The startup profile screen shows you the amount of console memory you configured during the installation, the console Ethernet adapters, and the SCSI controllers in the system.

In this page you should configure which of your controllers are used for the console, shared, or dedicated to VMs. Be very careful when doing so as many VM administrators have dedicated a SCSI controller to virtual machines and found that the host has experienced a Kernel Panic and the service console no longer functioned. If a controller has multiple disks or multiple arrays in use, that both VMs and the console will use, ensure that the controller is shared and not dedicated to either VMs or the Console.

In addition to the SCSI controllers, you should now configure which NICs will be used by the VMs. Dedicate as many as possible to ensure optimal VM performance from a network perspective. Take care not to change the console's adapter unless you specifically need to. This may cause you to loose your Console's IP configuration and create connectivity problems after your reboot.

Storage Configuration

In this screen you will be able to review your existing partitions created during the install and if needed, create any additional VMFS partitions from unused disk space.

Swap Configuration

Don't confuse this with the Console OS's SWAP space. This is a swap file that will be stored on VMFS and used by the VMkernel to over allocate memory within the system for VMs. This defaults to a size equal to the amount of physical memory you have in the system (allowing for almost 100% over allocation). If you are planning on over allocating more than that, you may want to increase this number.

Network Configuration

This screen will ask you to create a virtual switch configuration. These switches can later be reconfigured but it is often good to go ahead and get these set now. Each Virtual switch can be configured as an "internal switch", meaning it has no outbound adapters associated with it and traffic will be local to VMs on this host. In addition, you can create switches associated with single network cards. (For more information on network bonds please refer to Chapter 4.)

Security Settings

The final settings configure the security level of the host. By default the ESX server will configure itself at "high". You have four options to choose from:

- *High:* Enables only secure access to the console and Web Interface. In addition, it disables services like FTP, NFS file sharing, and telnet.

- *Medium:* Maintains the requirement for encrypted access to the console but enables NFS, FTP, and telnet.

- *Low:* Opens up the server wide. Un-encrypted access to the console and Web Interface with all services enabled.

- *Custom:* This setting allows you to configure each of the mentioned services and connections individually, including:

- Encrypted connections to the Web Interface
- Encrypted connections to console sessions
- Secure remote login
- FTP service
- Telnet Service
- NFS File Sharing

If you aren't familiar with Linux or UNIX security, you may want to check with your UNIX team (if you have one) to ensure your ESX matches current security policies. Often security teams will ask you to disable things like remote root login, change the SSH port, etc. If you don't have a UNIX team or UNIX background, go ahead and leave the security settings at High, as this is the simplest way to ensure your server is pretty secure with very little knowledge.

Chapter

Storage and Network Strategies

In the last chapter we went through the different local partitions and storage requirements to setup ESX server. In this chapter we dive into the real meat of ESX storage: VMFS partitions for VM disk storage. VMFS 2.11 is the current version of the VM File System created by VMware. VMFS was created to provide storage for the extremely large files that make up VMs. In turn, the requirements for large amounts of storage put a special emphasis on local and SAN based storage for your VMs.

This chapter delves into the uses of storage in an ESX environment along with the real network requirements for ESX in an enterprise environment.

Local Storage versus Remote (SAN) Storage

So, I know I want to implement ESX, but have not decided on the storage solution yet. Which should we use in our environment: Local SCSI disks or remote SAN LUNs? Well the answer may well be both. While it is possible to run ESX without a local VFMS partition, that doesn't mean it's the best solution. Also, while it is possible to use all local VMFS partitions for VM storage, it may not offer the flexibility you need in your environment.

Local Storage

At a bare minimum (excluding boot from SAN configurations) it is best to have a local VMFS partition to support your VMswapfile. This swap file is used when the memory assigned to your VMs is over allocated – meaning more than you have physically in the server – and the least used portions of memory need to be swapped out to disk. In addition to the VM swap file, you can also store VM disk files on the local storage. In many small environments this is how ESX is first implemented. Then as disk needs or the environment grows, SAN connectivity is implemented and the VMs are moved to the SAN.

The primary reason for using local storage for your VMs is cost. When comparing local SCSI disk costs to that of SAN storage, local disk is much cheaper. In addition, if you are a small environment that does not have a SAN right now, the initial implementation of a SAN can be a substantial investment.

The major drawback to not using centralized SAN storage is that you loose the ability to move VMs quickly and easily from host to host. Touted VMware features like VMotion require that you have a SAN infrastructure in place to use them. In addition, if a host fails and you are using local storage, you must recover the VM disk files from either a backup solution or some other form of network storage used for disk file backups. Where, if you had a SAN, you could simply restart the VMs using the existing disk files on a new host.

Advantages of using local VMFS Storage

*   Cost. Local SCSI storage will always be cheaper than a SAN solution

*   Simple to implement; requires no special SAN experience of any additional configuration within ESX

Disadvantages of using local VMFS storage

*   Makes recovering VMs from a failed host more complex and time consuming

*   Eliminates your ability to use features like VMotion and cross host VM clustering

*   Reduces the overall scalability of your implementation

*   Limits the ESX environment's scalability

Remote/SAN Storage

The exact opposite advantages and disadvantages of local storage applies to Remote or SAN based storage for ESX. While a SAN solution requires additional expense and configurations, the benefits are enormous.

SAN based VMFS partitions allow you a number of benefits over local storage. The simple use of VMotion is a huge benefit to any environment. But add on top of the ability to have a fast, central repository for VM templates, the ability to recover VMs on another host if you have a host failure, the ability to allocate large amounts of storage (we're talking terabytes here) to your ESX servers, and the list goes on and on.

The real idea here is that a SAN implementation offers you a truly scalable and recoverable ESX solution. The options and features available to SAN users are enormous, while the limitations found in local SCSI storage are like an anchor around an ESX admin's neck.

In this section we will discuss SAN and LUN configuration for VMFS partitions at some length, but we would be negligent if we didn't touch on other technologies like iSCSI, NAS, and even RAW disk access for VMs. For now let's just look at the advantages and disadvantages of using SAN storage for your VMFS volumes.

Advantages of using SAN based VMFS Storage

- Allows for VMotion functionality

- Allows for a centrally maintained template location that is extremely fast

- Allows for fast recovery of VMs in the event of a host failure

- Provides a more scalable storage solution for your environment

- Allows for VMs to be clustered across hosts

- Allows for physical to Virtual Clustering

- Provides the ability for your VMs to use RAW Fiber Channel disk, just like a physical machine

Disadvantages of using SAN based VMFS Storage

- More complex to manage and implement

- More expensive than local storage

What this all comes down to is money. For a scalable environment that offers you all of the features of ESX, you should really look at a SAN based implementation. If you are using ESX for a small test environment or are just proving it out, then local storage may fit the bill. But if you plan on expanding and running a real scalable system, some type of SAN will be required.

SAN Implementation Options

These days almost every network has some type of SAN or NAS device in use. The trick is to figure out how ESX Server can fit into your organization's existing storage strategy, or, if you don't have a strategy, how to ensure that your storage will support your ESX implementation properly.

In a majority of environments the 'non-local' storage for ESX is SAN based and using Fiber Channel accessible SAN LUNs. The reason for this is two fold. The first is that ESX, in its current form (version 2.5), only supports remote SAN connectivity for VMFS volumes when accessed via fiber cards. While this 'limitation' of the current system dictates which HBAs and SAN configurations can be used for VMFS storage, it doesn't rule out all Raw disk and LUN access completely. In some environments the system/business requirements dictate a more 'creative' use of the storage.

It is not uncommon to find ESX used in an environment that supports both fiber accessible LUNs and iSCSI targets. This is not to say that iSCSI is used for VMFS volume access, but instead administrators have figured out that just like physical machines, iSCSI drivers can be loaded into VMs and connectivity to iSCSI storage for a VM becomes a reality. In addition to this VMware also offers the ability to use raw fiber disk with VMs while still maintaining some of the benefits of a VM disk file. In this section we will review some of the options available to you when designing your storage strategy and take a look at their benefits to try and give you some configuration tips for each.

VMFS Based

The first thing we need to look at is why you would use VMFS based storage instead of all RAW LUN/disk access for all your VMs. The first compelling reason for using VMFS is all of the benefits you get with VM disk files: VM snaps, the four available VM disk modes, portability of the VMs, etc. In addition to that, using VMFS allows you to configure a single LUN for a large number of virtual machines. If you were required to configure a LUN for each VM that ran within VMware, you would probably create a management nightmare for your storage team.

Using VMFS does not necessarily remove your ability to use RAW disk access when it is appropriate. In reality, when using VMFS you have all the benefits of VM encapsulation, while still leaving you the ability to use RAW LUNs when appropriate. VMFS will be explained in detail later in this chapter.

RAW Disk Access

For the purposes of VMware documentation, RAW disk access is basically the ability to map a specific SCSI disk to a single VM. In the real world you have a few more options than just the RAW mappings VMware provides. In addition to the direct disk access through the vmkernel, you can also use iSCSI access and Network Attached Storage, in most cases, just as you would with a physical server.

VMware Disk Mapping

With ESX 2.5, VMware introduced the new feature of disk mapping files. When using disk mapping files, you are basically using a vmdk type file stored on a VMFS volume that acts as proxy disk access for the VM to a raw LUN.

The mapping file manages the metadata for the LUN that the VM uses as its disk. The metadata is basically the locking information for the LUN and the location of the LUN. Notice here that we say LUN and not partition. Disk mapping files only support mapping directly to an entire LUN and not a partition on a LUN.

A major advantage of using the new mapping file scheme instead of physical device numbers is that a change in a physical device would change the vmhba number of the connection used to access LUN. Assume that an HBA being used to access the raw LUN fails or is removed from the machine. Since the vmhba numbering system contains the device ID being used, then the number would change. This would require a manual change to the vm's configuration to rectify the situation.

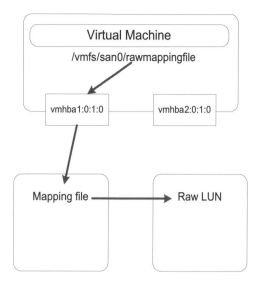

When using a mapping file the VM configuration references a disk file using the VMFS volume name and not the vmhba numbering. This is what makes it possible to VMotion VMs using these types of disks and allows your VM to continue operation without issue even after a hardware failure or reconfiguration.

The most common uses for these mapping files is as the quorum and data disks for clustered VM nodes, and physical to virtual clusters. In addition, these types of mappings are sometimes used when an administrator knows that a VM's disk needs will expand dramatically but does not want to (or can't) allocate all of the disk space they feel the VM will need.

Disk Modes
Raw disks that are mapped through these files have two compatibility modes: physical and virtual. In virtual mode, the disk will act just like a normal VM disk file. You will have the ability to change its modes, add redo logs, and import and export the contents of the disk just like a normal VM disk file.

In physical mode, the virtualization of the SCSI device is limited. As a matter of fact, all SCSI commands from the VM are sent to the physical device other than the Report LUNs command. By keeping this command from being sent to the device, the system is keeping the VM from seeing all the physical characteristics of the hardware that it is accessing. This mode is often used when you are required to run SAN agents that are required within the VM for management, or if you are configuring physical to Virtual Clusters.

Creating Disk Mapping Files

Without regurgitating a number of VMware 'How To's', we want to at least give you the basic requirements for creating a disk mapping file. Like many of the VMware based filesystem operations, you will be using vmkfstools to create and configure disk mapping files.

Before creating the mapping, ensure that each of the following statements are true:

• The LUN must be on a SAN and it cannot contain any VMFS or core dump partitions

• The LUN is not on a SCSI controller that is being shared with the ESX Server service console

• The LUN must provide a unique ID. Some RAID and block devices do not provide a unique ID

Basically you are looking for a completely raw, unused LUN, that is not accessed by any shared controllers. So let's assume you are using a boot from SAN configuration and want to use a mapping file. If you only have a single HBA in your system, and it is shared with both the Console and the vmkernel, this is not an option. Additionally, if you are trying to map to only a single partition on a LUN, and not the entire LUN, that will not work, either.

Creating your mapping file can be done a couple of ways. Here we explain the basic steps for creating the mapping file when deploying a VM using VirtualCenter. If you plan on using command tools, please jump ahead to the next set of steps.

Creating a Mapping file using VirtualCenter

1. During the creation of the VM, you should select System LUN instead of existing Virtual Disk or New Virtual Disk.

2. Select the LUN that you wish to use and select a LUN to store the mapping file on.

   Note: The mapping files should be stored on a single VMFS volume that is accessible by all the ESX servers in the farm. This will help ensure that VMs using mapping files can be easily VMotioned and will help to keep you from creating duplicate mapping files to the same LUNs

3. Once the LUN has been selected, you need to select a compatibility mode.

It should be noted that the process we just described is only a small deviation from the normal VM creation process you use when creating a VM using a virtual disk. The one major difference is that if you are using this mapping file as the primary (boot) disk for the VM, you cannot deploy the VM from a template. The template deployment in VirtualCenter is based on copying an existing disk file. If you need to use a raw LUN for a boot disk, you should create the mapping in the console using vmkfstools and then import the disk contents from another VM (also using vmkfstools).

Creating a Mapping file using the Web Interface

If you are creating a mapping file using the ESX Server Web Interface, the process is pretty much the same, but the difference is in the terminology. In the ESX Web Interface, the file is referenced as 'Disk Metadata'. When you select the option to use a Raw/System LUN, you will have an option to 'Use MetaData'. This option is the mapping file option. When selected, you will be asked to select a VMFS volume to store the mapping file and you will need to select a compatibility mode just like in VirtualCenter.

Finally, once you have clicked OK to add the disk, select 'Use Text Editor' and verify/add the following lines to VM's configuration file (note this can also be done via the console with a text editor):

```
scsi1.present = "TRUE"
scsi1.virtualDev = "vmxbuslogic"
```

```
# This disk is mapped directly to a physical disk.
scsi1:1.present = "TRUE"
scsi1:1.name = "vmhba2:0:1:0"
scsi1:1.mode = "persistent"
```

Here, scsi1:1.name = vmhba2:0:1:0 means that the virtual disk is actually the entire physical disk at LUN 1, target 0 on adapter vmhba2. Note that even though we can't map this to a partition on the LUN, you need to specify 0 in the final position. This 0 tells ESX to use the entire LUN.

Creating Mapping files using vmkfstools

You can also create the mapping file using vmkfstools. The –r switch will allow you to specify the target LUN and the mapping file name. The syntax is as follows: vmkfstools –r <Raw disk> <disk mapping file>. As an example, the command we use below will map LUN 3 on Target 0 of vmhba1.

```
vmkfstools -r vmhba1:0:3 /vmfs/san0/mappingfile.vmdk
```

NAS Storage

To bring everyone up to speed we need to 'define' NAS, here. Unlike a SAN, a NAS device attaches to an existing network and provides a stand-alone storage solution that can be used for data backup or additional storage capabilities for network clients. The primary difference between the NAS and SAN is at the communication level. NAS communicates over the network using a network share, while SAN primarily uses the Fiber Channel protocol.

NAS devices transfer data from storage device to server in the form of files. NAS units use file systems, which are managed independently. These devices manage file systems and user authentication. While SANs are typically connected over networks using a Fiber Channel backbone and deliver data in device blocks, NAS devices are similar to servers using embedded external RAID arrays.

The basic idea here is that the NAS device itself is managing the storage, file system, and access, and not the host. This leaves ESX sitting high and dry. Without the ability to manage the raw file system, its locking and access, ESX server (as far as VMFS storage is concerned) can't use this type of storage. This is not to say that the guests can't use the storage just as a normal network client would, but storing VMFS on a NAS is not possible at this time.

What about my iSCSI?

One of the most frequent storage questions we get is 'does ESX Server support iSCSI?' The 'official' answer to this is no. ESX server, and more specifically the VMkernel, does not support using iSCSI to connect to for VMFS volumes or raw disk access. Generally this leads to a couple of follow-up questions: 1) Why? 2) Even if it's not supported, can I get it to work? Generally these questions come from individuals whose company just dumped a boat load of money on an iSCSI based solution. To go back and tell the organization that their brand new, bleeding edge technology isn't supported by their new virtualization platform may be a huge poke in the eye. On top of that, there may be a pretty good size cost associated with implementing a fiber channel based SAN.

So the first question is 'why doesn't it work/is it not supported'? Not being the head of development and engineering at VMware, I can only pass on our assumptions and some of the information we have been told. The first issue is that the VMkernel does not contain an IP stack. The kernel is kept as small as possible to reduce the amount of overhead in the virtualization layer. Each driver and 'application' added to the kernel adds more overhead. We have been told that adding an IP stack to the kernel is a pretty daunting task. Not to mention adding the drivers for the iSCSI cards that you would want to support.

Generally the criticism of iSCSI in the industry focuses on the TCP-based architecture it uses. This architecture creates a huge processing overhead on the host system's CPU. To 'fix' this issue most vendors create iSCSI adapters that have a separate TCP/IP stack to offload some of the processing needed when using iSCSI. In addition, there has been some lack of standardization in the iSCSI field. Numerous vendors have really negotiated out what their devices will do and how their communications will work between devices. When this happens you wind up needing to support a large number of different drivers to be able to effectively implement the solution in a number of environments and configurations. And unlike Windows, you can't just install a new or different driver into the VMkernel based on your need of the day.

So, that is the short version of the problem. The answer is that VMware is working on supporting iSCSI for VMkernel use in the future, but right now it's not supported.

So, if you want to use your iSCSI solution with ESX you have two options with the current versions:

- Use an iSCSI Gateway that connects fiber channel to iSCSI accessible disk

- Install iSCSI drivers into your VMs to access the iSCSI disk

Using an iSCSI Gateway
To be honest this alternative is not used very often. Adding an iSCSI Gateway from a vendor like Nishan Systems is not an inexpensive option. Their iSCSI gateway, the IPS 3300, is one of the few that allows for you to connect fiber HBAs to iSCSI disk. Most gateways are built to expose fiber based disk as iSCSI targets. Also, when you do this, you may be moving into uncharted territory with components that VMware hasn't certified.

The benefit of this solution is that you have the ability to use your existing disk with very little additional infrastructure. Also, the addition of an iSCSI Gateway keeps you from having to install iSCSI drivers into your VMs and adding the additional overhead directly to your ESX server.

Using iSCSI Directly
Using iSCSI drivers within your VM to access iSCSI disk is another alternative you have. While this does allow you to access and leverage an existing iSCSI solution, there are still a number of things you have to be aware of.

First, the reason for making an iSCSI adapter with its own processor and TCP stack is to keep from having that processor load on the server itself. When you install iSCSI drivers into your VM guests, they will be using the network cards that the kernel supports. This leaves you in a position of significantly increasing the utilization on your ESX servers just to access disk resources.

The next major drawback is that you still need a location to store at least the OS partition of the VM. The VM needs to have a VMFS partition somewhere, whether it is local or SAN based. If it is local then you are back to having all the limitations of local disk storage; if you use a SAN then you need to use a supported HBA anyway. In essence, you either loose all of the benefits of SAN storage for ESX or you wind up implementing both solutions anyway.

Local Storage Configuration

Since local ESX storage is fairly simple to configure, you will notice that this section is pretty small when compared to the SAN storage section. To be honest, there isn't a whole lot you need to know as far as local storage is concerned. You need to understand how to create the VMFS partition (which is explained later in this chapter and done during the install) and you need to understand how to assign SCSI controllers to either the Console OS or to the VMkernel, but beyond that the local storage is fairly straight forward.

Configuring Controllers

The first thing you need to be aware of is that the VMkernel only supports a specific set of controllers. The kernel itself is not the Console OS, therefore drivers cannot simply be added to support a non supported controller. As explained earlier in the book, VMware supports a specific list of hardware for ESX implementations. The current list can easily be found on VMware's support site and should be referenced before configuring hardware for ESX.

The next thing you will have to decide on is how to configure your controller and the options available to you. If you have a controller capable of creating multiple arrays, you have a lot of flexibility. If you have multiple controllers in your box, you are really set.

Like database servers, it is best from a performance perspective to split up the OS and the application. In this case (though it is a crude analogy) it is best to split up the Console OS from the VMkernel. Having two controllers will allow you to store your VM disks (VMDKs) on one controller and set of disks and your Console OS files on another. If you only have one controller with the ability to create multiple arrays, then that is the next best thing. Split the Console OS onto the first array and the VMs onto the second. Spread the VMFS partition for the VMs across as many spindles as possible. A RAID 5 would be my recommendation for the VMs while a simple mirrored set RAID 1 would suffice for the Console.

If you don't plan on storing VM disk files on your local storage, then a single RAID controller – even if it only supports a single array – will suffice. But this section is really focusing on the configuration for the local storage of VMs.

Assigning the controller

During the base install, you most likely configured the VMkernel to be shared between the Console OS and the Virtual Machines. You can review this configuration in the Web Interface by selecting the Options tab and then 'Startup Profile'. Here you will see the installed and supported SCSI controllers. If you have only one controller in your server, then it is most likely configured for use by the Virtual Machines and has the check box checked for 'Shared with the Service Console'.

This configuration indicates that both the Console OS and the VMkernel can access and use the controller. If you have multiple controllers in your server you will see a second controller in the startup screen. This controller can be dedicated completely to the Virtual Machines. This will allow for the best performance for both the Console OS and the vmkernel.

In addition to assigning the controller as either a Console OS, Virtual Machine, or shared resource, you will also need to create your VMFS partition. For information on how to do this, you can jump to the 'VMFS Partitions' section of the chapter.

At this point you may be thinking that if you use SAN storage for your VMs, you should assign your local controller only to the Console OS. It's a best practice to stay away from that idea. The local controller still provides access to the local disk for the VMkernel to use both the VM core dump location and to use the local VMFS swap file. If you do not allow the controller to be used by the VMkernel (read virtual machines), then you have to allocate space on the SAN for your VMswap, and this is really a waste of good SAN space if you ask me.

SAN Storage Configuration for VMFS

When using a SAN for your VM storage, you have a huge number of decisions to make. Unlike local storage, using a SAN adds a layer of complexity to the environment that you wouldn't believe. Also the very nature of ESX and its VMFS file system tends to throw most Windows admins for a loop.

Without getting too deep into VMFS at this point, there is one thing that you need to understand about it that is different from normal Windows type file systems. When building Windows servers and SAN connecting them, you generally dedicate a LUN for each Windows server. When the server boots, it locks the entire file system on that LUN. When using ESX to connect to a SAN based VMFS partition, this volume level locking does not occur. Instead, the ESX host only locks the disk files that it is using. This allows numerous ESX servers to all see and use the same LUNs. This is what allows VMotion to work. Anyway, understanding that ESX only locks specific files on a LUN and not the entire file system will help you understand the following sections.

SAN/LUN Sizing

Determining the number and size of LUNs required in your environment is one of the most important things that you will do when dealing with your SAN configuration for ESX. The first thing you have to do when determining the number and size of LUNs you need is to estimate how much writable disk space you will present to the ESX servers in total (i.e., how much space are your VM disk files going to take up plus room for growth). And the second thing is how you are going to break these up into usable LUNs.

VMware has a number of guidelines out there that are sometimes hard to convert into something usable. Let's go over their guidelines quickly then do some math as an example:

- Recommended limit of 16 ESX servers per VMFS volume, based on limitations of a VirtualCenter-managed ESX setup

- Recommended maximum of 32 IO-intensive VMs sharing a VMFS volume

- Up to 100 non-IO-intensive VMs can share a single VMFS volume with acceptable performance

- No more than 255 files per VMFS partition

- Up to 2TB limit per physical extent of a VMFS volume

Using these guidelines, let's set up three quick equations; one using a dual processor server, one using quads, and one using quads with twice the number of VMs. To do this in your own environment you need to gather the following information:

- Number of expected VMs the overall environment is supposed to host

- Average size of the VM Disk files (VMDKs)

- Number of processors in your ESX servers

- Estimated number of VMs you will host per processor

With this information in hand you can begin to work with the configurations and calculations in Table 1.

Table 1. Dual processor ESX Servers

Server specifications
Number of processors per server: 2
Number of Guests per processor: 4
Total VMs per ESX Host: 8
Average VMDK size (GB): 14
Total Storage per host (GB): 112

Total number of VMs: 200
Total Storage Required (GB): 2800
Number of ESX Servers: 25
Number of farms needed: 2
Number of servers per farm: 13 (rounded up)

Farm Configuration
Total VMs per farm: 100
Total Storage needed for farm: 1400

High I/O LUN Sizing
Total LUNs for disk-intensive VMs (VMs / 32): 3.13
Size per LUN (w/ 10% growth): 492.8
Avg VMs per host per LUN: 2.56

Let's take a look at table 1 very quickly. In this case we have made the following assumptions:

Number of projected VMs: 200

Average VMDK file size: 14 GB

Number of guests per processor: 4

Using these assumptions we first calculate that we will require 2.8 TB of storage for these VMs (14Gb * number of VMs). We can also tell that we will need 25 ESX servers (number of VMs / total VMs per host). Now that we know we need 25 ESX servers, we then divide that number by 16 (the maximum number of ESX servers sharing a VMFS volume). This tells us how many farms we will have, as illustrated in the example above, we need 2 farms with 13 servers each (or 12 in one 13 in the other).

With all of that done we can do the final calculations on LUN sizes. In this case, the 200 VMs have now been split between two farms, leaving us with 100 VMs per farm. We will need 1.4TB of storage for those VMs (number of VMs in farm * estimated VMDK usage). We then assume all 100 VMs are high IO to be on the safe side and divide the number of VMs by the maximum number of high IO VMs per partition that VMware recommends (32). The result is 3.13 LUNs for each farm. By taking the safe route and assuming that all VMs were disk intensive, we can now round down that 3.13 number to give us an even 3 LUNs per farm. Finally, knowing we need 1.4TB of storage per farm, and knowing we need 3 LUNs, we divide 1.4TB/3 and add in 10 percent for growth to come up with a LUN size of 492GB.

Final results:

2 ESX Server farms

13 ESX servers in each farm

3 LUNs per farm

Each LUN is at least 492 GBs

Now let's take a look at the same example, but we will use a quad processor configuration instead of a dual:

Table 2. Quad processor ESX Servers

Server specifications
Number of processors per server: 4
Number of Guests per processor: 4
Total VMs per ESX Host: 16
Average VMDK size (GB): 14
Total Storage per host (GB): 224

Total number of VMs: 200
Total Storage Required (GB): 2800
Number of ESX Servers: 13 (rounded up)
Number of farms needed: 1
Number of servers per farm: 13

Farm Configuration
Total VMs per farm: 200
Total Storage needed for farm: 2800

High I/O LUN Sizing
Total LUNs for disk-intensive VMs (VMs / 32): 6.25
Size per LUN (w/ 10% growth): 492.8
Avg VMs per host per LUN: 2.56

Much like the first table, we arrive at the exact same LUN size. LUN sizing at this level is more a combination of the number of VMs and their estimated disk storage needs than anything else. Notice the table also shows that this time we have a single farm configuration. Since we were able to go to a quad processor configuration, we cut the required number of ESX servers in half. So while the LUN size and overall number of LUNs stay the same, we have reduced the overall management and SAN zoning issues by simply going to a larger server for ESX.

Now let's take a look at a quad processor configuration with two times the amount of storage per VM AND two times the number of VMs:

Table 3. Quad processor ESX Servers with 2x disk and VMs

Server specifications
Number of processors per server: 4
Number of Guests per processor: 4
Total VMs per ESX Host: 16
Average VMDK size (GB): 28
Total Storage per host (GB): 448

Total number of VMs: 400
Total Storage Required (GB): 11200
Number of ESX Servers: 25
Number of farms needed: 2
Number of servers per farm: 13 (rounded up)

Farm Configuration
Total VMs per farm: 200
Total Storage needed for farm: 5600

High I/O LUN Sizing
Total LUNs for disk-intensive VMs (VMs / 32): 6.25
Size per LUN (w/ 10% growth): 985.6
Avg VMs per host per LUN: 2.56

Notice once again that the number of LUNs have remained the same per farm. The two changes we see here are the size of the LUNs – due to the increase in storage – and the number of farms is back up to two because of the increase in the number of VMs.

In either case the number of LUNs and their size are really determined by the number of VMs and the average VMDK file usage and not by the number of hosts. The only limitation hosts offer is that you should never have more than 16 sharing any one LUN and this limitation is what dictates the farms sizes.

One thing to note here is that we have designed the system assuming all VMs are high IO. By assuming this, we limit ourselves to 32 VMs per LUN and stay well below the VMware recommended maximum per VMFS volume. If you are building a purely development environment, it is possible to change that calculation and increase the number of VMs per LUN, but by designing it this way, you stay well within the 'safe' performance envelope.

Finding and Configuring Your LUNs

Now that you know the size and number of your LUNs, it's time to configure ESX to see and use these LUNs. Over the next few sections we will be discussing numerous types of configurations and discussing each one's benefits and drawbacks. While we may have a bias to one configuration or another, it is important to find the options that best fit your environment.

vmhba numbering

You may have already been poking around ESX and noticed the number for your RAID controller or Fiber cards; it looks something like this:

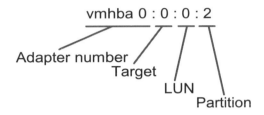

Before we get to deep into this you need to understand first how VMware identifies the HBAs in your system. This numbering scheme can be seen from either the Web Interface of your server, or from within the Console OS. Generally when dealing with SAN LUNs or other disks presented to the server, you will see the first three sections of this identifier as ESX sees it: a simple disk attached to the system via a Virtual Machine host bus adapter (vmhba).

The first section shows the adapter number, the section shows the SCSI target ID, and the final section shows the LUN number. When this numbering scheme has four sections, the fourth section is used for partitions on specific LUNs—not by the adapter itself.

You can use the Web Interface to see the available SCSI adapters and HBAs or you can use the service console. Via the Web Interface, you can go to Options – Storage Management – and view each available disk with an entry like: Disk vmhba1:0:1: (0% of 546.93 G Available). You can also go to the adapter bindings tab within storage management and view the world wide name for your adapters. This is shown like this:

```
vmhba1: QLogic Corp QLA231x/2340 (rev 02)
(21:00:00:E0:8B:1A:9C:6B)
```

At the end of that string you will notice the world wide name for the adapter. This is similar to a MAC address but for fiber controllers.

Scanning Devices for new LUNs

When ESX is booted, it scans fiber and SCSI devices for new and existing LUNs. You can manually initiate a scan through the VMware Management Interface or by using the cos-rescan.sh command. VMware recommends using cos-rescan.sh because it is easier to use with certain Fibre Channel adapters than with vmkfstools. Personally, I have used the rescan feature from within the Web Interface – Options-Storage Management-Rescan SAN – without issue, but it is something to be aware of.

If you need to use cos-rescan.sh, simply login to your ESX Console or via a remote shell and enter the command at a shell prompt. You should rescan devices or LUNs whenever you add a new disk array to the SAN or create new LUNs on a disk array.

Once the LUNs are available to the ESX Server you can use the Web Interface or Console to configure the LUN with a new VMFS partition. If the partition was previously created on another ESX server, you should be able to view the VMFS volume and its contents.

Detecting High Number and 'missing' LUNs

ESX Server, by default, only scans for LUN 0 to LUN 7 for every target. If you are using LUN numbers larger than 7, you will need to change the setting for the DiskMaxLUN field from the default of 8 to the value that you need. Before proceeding with this change we should mention that you should not make this change unless you are using high number LUNs. Making this change without high numbered LUNs in place could cause extremely slow boot times and other issues.

In its current versions, ESX Server can see a maximum of 128 LUNs over all disk arrays on a SAN. Let's assume you need to see LUNs 0 through 12 on a specific target. You would need to change the DiskMaxLUN setting to 13. Now assuming you have 12 LUNs on 12 different targets, you would be well above the limit of 128 and a number of LUNs would be unavailable. While this example is extreme and rarely seen, it is something to be noted.

But what if you have a number of LUNs that are numbered above 7, but they are not all in sequential order? Let's assume you are using 0 through 6 then numbers 8, 10, and 12. What then? Well by default, ESX server will support sparse LUNs. Sparse LUNs is when some LUN numbers in the range you are scanning (our example 0-12) are not present, but LUN number 12 is present. This issue with sparse LUN support is that it slows the scan of the LUNs. If you are only using sequentially ordered LUNs without any missing, you can disable this support by changing the Advanced Configuration setting DiskSupportSparseLUN to 0. This change will reduce the time needed to scan for LUNs.

Masking LUNs
Masking of SAN LUNs is often used for administrative or security purposes. LUN masking allows you to prevent the server from seeing LUNs that it doesn't need to access. Often this is done at the SAN configuration level by Zoning or port ACLs on the SAN switches. If this is not being done on the SAN level, or if you have a requirement to 'hide' certain LUNs from your ESX servers, then you can use LUN masking to accomplish this.

The DiskMaskLUNs configuration option allows the masking of specific LUNs on specific HBAs. These masked LUNs are not scanned or even accessible by the VMkernel. To configure this option, you need to go into Options-Advanced Configuration. The value of the DiskMaskLUN is comprised of the adapter name, target, and a comma separated LUN list.

As an example, let's assume you want to mask LUNs 3, 5, and 12-15 on vmhba2 target 5. The value of the DiskMaskLun would be set to 'vmhba2:5:3,5,12-15'. Let's now assume you want to add a few more

LUNs on vmhba3 to be masked. These will be on target 2 LUNs 3 through 6. To do this you would put a semi-colon';' in between the first entry and the next vmhba entry in the DiskMaskLUN, like so: 'vmhba2:5:3,5,12-15;vmhba3:2:3-6"

When using LUN masking you should be aware that VMware documentation states that 'the DiskMaskLUNs option subsumes the DiskMaxLUN option'. The gist of this is that if you configure an adapter to use LUN masking with the server's DiskMaxLUN, settings will not take effect and all LUNs not masked will be scanned down those HBA paths. For this reason is it a good practice to put in the high range LUN numbers you don't want scanned. So using our previous example of 'vmhba2:5:3,5,12-15', if there are no available LUNs above number 12, you should configure the final range of LUNs to include all possible LUN numbers up to 255: 'vmhba2:5:3,5,12-255'

HBA Configurations

The first thing to know about HBA use with ESX is that, like everything else, there is a very specific list of supported HBAs. The HBAs in this are the ones that have been tested and have the drivers available to the VMkernel. In its current form, ESX supports a number of both Emulex and Qlogic drivers. It should be noted that a number of hardware vendors OEM these cards and that these OEM'd cards are often in the supported list. A prime example of this is the 'HP' Fiber HBAs that are really QLogic 23xx's. If you are not sure about the cards you are planning to use, it is best to check the VMware support site for its current list of supported HBAs.

With that said, let's hit some quick configurations that are required by ESX and then get into multi-pathing options.

Configuring the Fiber Channel Queue Depth

In high IO environments, VMware recommends increasing the maximum queue depth for the Fiber Channel adapters. This change is done by editing the hwconfig file in /etc/vmware directory. A typical /etc/vmware/hwconfig file contains lines similar to the following:

```
device.0.0.0.class = "060000"
device.0.0.0.devID = "0009"
device.0.0.0.name = "ServerWorks CNB20LE Host Bridge
(rev 05)"
device.0.0.0.subsys_devID = "0000"
device.0.0.0.subsys_vendor = "0000"
device.0.0.0.vendor = "1166"
device.0.0.1.class = "060000"
device.0.0.1.devID = "0009"
device.0.0.1.name = "ServerWorks CNB20LE Host Bridge
(rev 05)"
device.0.0.1.subsys_devID = "0000"
device.0.0.1.subsys_vendor = "0000"
device.0.0.1.vendor = "1166"
```

In this file look for the appropriate fiber device you are using. If you are using QLogic, look for the "QLogic Corp QLA2312/2340 (rev 02)". If you are using an Emulex card, look for a device listing with something like "Emulex Corporation LP9802 2Gb Fibre Channel Host Adapter (rev 01)". Once you have found the device line, note the device number that is in a format of 'device.2.5.0 – device[PCI bus].[slot].[function]'.

With that number located, add the following line with the appropriate device number for each QLogic adapter/port you have:

```
device.esx.3.12.0.options = "ql2xmaxqdepth=64"
```

If you are using Emulex cards, your additions will look like the following:

```
device.esx.3.12.0.options="lpfc_lun_queue_depth=64"
```

It should be noted that users have seen some issues with Emulex cards when deploying multiple VMs via VirtualCenter. The workaround requires that you set the queue depth back to 16 to get around the problem. Personally I would just get the QLogic HBAs and avoid the rush.

Increasing the number of outstanding requests per VM

In addition to the queue depth changes, VMware also recommends increasing the Disk.SchedNumReqOutstanding parameter in the Web Interface. The idea here is that you are sharing disk (a LUN) between a number of virtual machines. And since we have just increased the queue depth on the HBA to allow for more requests to stack up, we should increase the number of requests each VM can have against a single LUN at any given time. A good rule of thumb is to adjust this number from its default of 16, to 64.

Multipathing Features

During a rescan of the LUNs, ESX scans all HBAs, all devices on the HBAs, and all LUNs on all devices. During a scan, each LUN reveals its SCSI ID. If a LUN responds with the same SCSI ID as a previous LUN, then this indicates that there are two paths to the same LUN. This is also why it is extremely important that your storage administrator published LUNs down both paths using the same ID. If two different LUNs are exposed to ESX with the same SCSI ID, ESX will assume they are the same LUN shown down different paths.

To this high availability connectivity, ESX supports two different multipathing configurations. The two available multipathing options are Fixed/Preferred Path and Most Recently Used (MRU).

The MRU option is the default configuration that is used with Active/Passive storage devices, such as small arrays that have dual controllers in an active passive configuration. These are devices that maintain a single active path to the exposed disk and failover in the event of a component failure. The Fixed/Preferred Path option is the default for Storage that is configured for Active/Active accessibility. Generally higher-end SANs will support an active/active configuration.

In an MRU configuration, the HBA being used to access a specific LUN will be used until it is unavailable. In the event of a failure, either in the card, the connection, or the storage processor level, ESX will automatically failover to the other HBA and begin using it for connectivity to the LUN. If the first card/path comes back online, the path currently being used will not change. As the name states, ESX will continue to use the path that it has failed over to since it is the 'Most Recently Used'.

Advantages of using MRU

• Automatically configured to the available path

• Very little configuration required

Disadvantages of using MRU

• Possibility that all VMs will run over a single HBA

• Since the first HBA in the system is scanned first, this path is likely to be found and used first by the system

Contrast this to the Fixed/Preferred Path multipathing. In this configuration, the Preferred Path is used whenever it is available. So if a connection is lost, and the ESX Server fails over to another HBA/Path, it will only use that path until the preferred path becomes available again.

Advantages of using Fixed Multipathing

• Allows you to 'manually' balance your LUNs between HBAs

• System will automatically return to your original configuration when the path is returned to an operational state

Disadvantages of using Fixed Multipathing

• Requires a little manual setup initially to ensure LUNs are split evenly between HBAs

So what happens during a failure?

When an active path to a SAN disk is lost, the I/O from the VMs to their VMDK files will freeze for approximately 30-60 seconds. This is the approximate amount of time it will take for the SAN driver to determine that the link is down and initiate failover. During this time, the VMs using the SAN may seem to freeze, and any operations on the /vmfs directory may appear to hang. Once the failover occurs, I/O requests that have queued up will then be processed and the VMs will begin to function normally.

If all connections to the storage device are not working (assume a disastrous loss or a single path configuration), then the VM's will begin to encounter I/O errors on their virtual disks.

HBA Settings for Failover of QLogic Adapters

For QLogic cards, VMware suggests that you adjust the PortDownRetryCount value in the QLogic BIOS. This value determines how quickly a failover occurs when a link goes down.

If the PortDownRetryCount value is <n>, then a failover typically takes a little longer than <n> multiplied by 2 seconds. A typical recommended value for <n> is 15, so in this case, failover takes a little longer than 30 seconds.

Note on Windows Guests

When using Windows Server OS's in your VMs, you may want to adjust the standard disk time out for disk access. During the failover of an HBA, the default timeout in a Windows guest may cause issues within the guest OS that is used to having extremely responsive disks. For the Windows 2000 and Windows Server 2003 guest operating systems, you should increase the disk timeout value in the registry so that Windows will not be extensively disrupted during failover. The registry value can be found at the following location:

```
HKEY_LOCAL_MACHINE\System\CurrentControlSet\Services\D
isk
```

The entry you wish to change is the TimeOutValue. Set the data to x03c hex or 60 decimal. This will configure the Windows Operating system to wait at least 60 seconds for disk operations to finish before reporting errors.

Configuring your Preferred Path

The preferred path settings that can be configured in the Web Interface under storage management are referenced here:

```
http://www.vmware.com/support/esx25/doc/esx25admin_mod
_storage_server.html
```

These settings basically allow you to set a preferred HBA for connecting to a specific LUN. If you have two SAN HBAs in your server, it's easy to do an odd/even configuration against the LUNs. This allows half of your traffic to flow over one HBA and the other half over the other. In the event of a failure, the remaining active HBA will assume the increased load, but during normal operations, your traffic will be somewhat split between the devices.

Figure 4.2

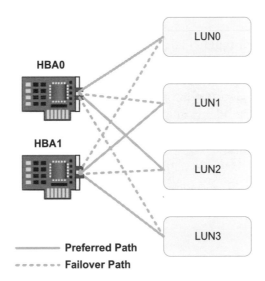

──────── **Preferred Path**
- - - - - - **Failover Path**

The vmkmultipath command
Besides using the Web Interface, you can also use the command vmk-multipath in the service console to view and change multipath settings. To view the current multipathing configuration, use the '-q' switch with the command. This will return a report showing the state of all paths used by the ESX server.

```
Disk and multipath information follows:

Disk vmhba0:0:0 (34,679 MB) has only 1 path.
```

```
Disk vmhba1:0:1 (289,562 MB) has 2 paths. Policy is
fixed.
vmhba1:0:1 on (active, preferred)
vmhba2:0:1 on

Disk vmhba2:0:2 (300,714 MB) has 2 paths. Policy is
fixed.
vmhba2:0:2 on (active, preferred)
vmhba1:0:2 on
```

By looking at this report I can see my first 'disk' available to ESX has only one path to it. This happens to be my local SCSI controller. The following two entries show two different LUNs, both of which use a Preferred Path/Fixed Policy. Also note that each LUN has a different HBA marked as its Active/Preferred path.

Setting the Preferred Path with vmkmultipath
Using the -r switch will allow you to specify the preferred path to a disk. Using the information from the –q report in the previous section, let's assume you want to change the preferred path to disk vmhba1:0:1 to use the vmhba2 controller. The syntax for the command is as follows:

```
vmkmultipath —s <disk> —r <NewPath>


# vmkmultipath —s vmhba1:0:1 —r vmhba2:0:1
```

It should be noted that even if you set the preferred path, it will be ignored if your multipath policy is set to use MRU. Ensure that your policy is set to 'fixed' by setting the path policy using the –p switch with the command.

```
vmkmultipath —s <disk> —p <policy>
```

The valid values for <policy> are fixed or MRU. So if you are setting a preferred path, set the policy for the disk to 'fixed'.

```
vmkmultipath -s vmhba1:0:1 -p fixed
```

Multipath settings should be saved when shutting down ESX Server normally. However, VMware suggests that you run the vmkmultipath command with the –S switch, as root, to ensure that they are saved.

```
# /usr/sbin/vmkmultipath -S
```

VMFS Volumes

The primary storage for VM information is the VMFS volume. VMFS is a unique file system created by VMware as a low overhead, high performance file system. The primary concern when they created this file system was to be able to create a file system that could handle extremely large files, and provide near raw disk access speeds for VM usage.

VMFS is a flat system. This means that you cannot create a directory structure on it. The very idea of a directory structure is to add a layer of manageability and organization to be able to store thousands of files. VMFS on the other hand, is meant to store a small number of files with limited management needs.

So what is stored on VMFS? A number of different items can be/are stored on VMFS volumes. The first (and most obvious) is the virtual machine disk files. In addition to these files, ESX also stores the redo logs for VMs that have their disks in a disk mode other than persistent. On top of the redo logs and disk files, WMware's vmkernel swap space is also stored on VMFS. One reason for storing it on VMFS instead of a standard swap partition is the sheer size potential for the swap file. In some environments this swap file can be as large as 32 or 64 GB.

The current version of VMFS is VMFS 2.11. Some of its more important features/characteristics are listed below:

- Ability to span multiple VMFS-2.11 partitions on the same or different SCSI disks

- Ability for multiple ESX Servers to access files on the same VMFS-2 volume

- Up to 128 VMFS volumes per ESX system

- Up to 32 physical extents per VMFS volume

- 2 TB per physical extent

- Approximate maximum size of 27TB per VMFS volume

So what does this all mean to you? Let's review each of these features quickly and see what they mean.

Ability to span multiple SCSI disks/LUNs

So what this really means is that you can create a single VMFS volume that spans multiple LUNs or multiple disks. Obviously a VMFS partition will span multiple disks like any file system when placed on a RAID array, but what we are talking about here is making a volume span a number of different presented devices (like different LUNs). The benefit here is obvious: you can create enormous volumes. The problem here is the same problem that befalls RAID 0 configurations. You get to span multiple disks, but if you loose one of the disks, you loose the volume. In this case you would need to loose a LUN, and all the LUNs sharing that volume would have issues.

Ability for multiple ESX Servers to access files on the same volume

This is really the functionality that enables VMotion and fast recovery in the event of a host failure. The idea here is that your ESX hosts can all see the same LUN. Because of this, the host almost becomes irrelevant when it comes to storing disk files. Since multiple servers can use the same LUN, you can simply stop a VM on one host and start it on another. Or if the host fails, you can simply create a new VM using the existing disk file.

Up to 128 VMFS volumes per ESX System

This one is pretty obvious. 128 VMFS volumes is a lot of space. Generally we see ESX systems with no more than 10 or 15 VMFS volumes exposed to them. So having the ability to go to 128 allows you more scalability than you may need.

2 TB Per physical extent and 32 extents per volume

These two are pretty much interwoven. The first means you can have up to 2 TB per LUN exposed to ESX that you are going to create a VMFS volume on. And if you have a need to create a single large VMFS volume, you can have up to 32 different physical extents (read LUNs) that comprise a single VMFS volume.

Approximately 27TB per VMFS volume

This is pretty straight forward: you can create VMFS volumes up to 27TB in size. The word 'approximately' comes from VMware and not from the authors so we can't give you an exact size limitation since we don't have 27+ TB of storage to try it out on.

File size and VMkernel "Gotcha"

While it is possible to use almost all of your native linux tools with files and directories mounted under /vmfs, you may run into certain limitations. Standard file commands such as ls and cp generally work without issue. The problem generally becomes apparent when trying to manipulate or work with the large VM disk files. Some tools available in the service console (such as nfs) may not support files greater than 2GB. Also, when using commands like df, you will not see the /vfms directory. Instead, you need to use vdf, which reports all of the normal df information plus information about the VMFS volumes. Generally ftp, scp, and cp do not seem to be a problem. But it is something to be aware of as you manipulate files in VMFS.

Now you understand the basics of VMFS. It's a high performance, flat file system, made to handle a small number of large files. Now it's time to get down into the how's and why's of VMFS. Let's take a look at creating VMFS volumes, their disk access modes, and the basics of creating and working with VMFS.

Creating a VMFS File System

Creating a VMFS volume can be done from the command line or from within the Web Interface. The method of using the Web Interface is pretty self evident. Within the Options tab under Storage

Management you can create new VMFS volumes on disks that your ESX server has access too. Below we describe creating VMFS volumes via the command line and go into some of the options available during volume creation.

When creating a VMFS volume using the command line, you will use a VMware tool named 'vmkfstools'. This utility was built by VMware specifically to work with VMFS volumes and the data stored on them. Vmkfstools' syntax is pretty simple. You run the command followed by its options and then specify the device or volume name and file name you are dealing with.

As you have seen by now, all VMFS volumes exposed to an ESX server are mounted under /vmfs. When you look in the /vmfs directory you will also note that the vmfs volumes are listed by both their volume label and their vmkernel device name. Below we show a sample of the return from an ls -l in one of our /vmfs directories.

```
login as: root
root@esx1.ronoglesby.com's password:
Last login: Sat Feb 19 16:49:01 2005 from ramf1.rapi-
dapp.net
[root@esx1 root]# cd /vmfs
[root@esx1 vmfs]# ls -l
total 0
lrwxrwxrwx    1 root       root      64 Feb 18 14:46
local0 ->vmhba0:0:0:5
lrwxrwxrwx    1 root       root      64 Feb 18 14:48
san0 -> vmhba1:0:1:1
drwxrwxrwt    1 root       root     512 Jan 29 13:08
vmhba0:0:0:5
drwxrwxrwt    1 root       root     512 Feb 17 12:39
vmhba1:0:1:1
[root@esx1 vmfs]#
```

Notice that both local0 and san0 are nothing more than logical links to vmhba0:0:0:5 and vmhba1:0:1:1. When dealing with VMFS volumes, almost every vmkfstools command can use either the volume name or the device name. This makes typing in the commands and remembering the volume you are dealing with much easier.

With that said, how do you create a VMFS volume on a raw LUN? Let's use the previous sample as an example. Assuming that there was not a VMFS volume on vmhba1:0:1:1, we could create a VMFS volume with the default settings using the following command:

```
vmkfstools -C vmfs2 vmhba1:1:0:1
```

The syntax is very simple: vmkfstools <option> <file system type> <Device>. In this case we use the '-C' option to create a new file system. Please note that it is an uppercase C, the lower case c creates files and not files systems. Then we specify the file system type as VMFS, and finally the device we are creating the VMFS volume on.

In addition to the basic syntax, you have the ability to specify a couple of other options such as:

```
-b --blocksize #[gGmMkK]
-n --numfiles #
```

The –b switch allows you to change the block size for the VMFS volume. The default block size is 1MB and used in almost all cases, but you do have the option of changing it. Using the –b switch, you can specify a block size number that is a power of 2, and at least equal to 1MB. Once you have added the numeric value, you then append a suffix to it that specifies whether the value is in kilobytes (k), megabytes (m), or gigabytes (g).

The –n switch specifies the maximum number of files that can be hosted on the file's system. The default (and maximum) number of files is 256. You can set this to any number greater than 1 or less than 256.

An example of both of these used to create a VMFS volume on the same device we used before is illustrated below:

```
vmkfstools -C vmfs2 -b 2m -n 64 vmhba1:1:0:1
```

Labeling VMFS Volumes

If you create a VMFS volume on a SCSI disk or partition, you can give a label to that volume and use that label when specifying VMFS files on that volume. In addition to making it easier to type in command lines, these volume names can also be specified in VM configuration files when pathing the VM to its disk file.

This is extremely important when it comes to environments with numerous servers and LUNs. Using the volume labels as paths, instead of the vmkernel device name, helps to prevent problems when vmotioning a VM from one host to another. Using these labels also allows you to change HBAs and have disk and target numbers change, while not affecting the VM's ability to find the proper disk.

```
vmkfstools -S <Volume_Name> <Device>
```

Notice that the option used here is a uppercase 'S.' Using a lowercase s instead of an uppercase 'S' will not result in a volume label but instead a re-scan of your LUNs. So assuming you want to label the volume you just created in the previous step, your command would like the following:

```
vmkfstools -S san_0 vmhba1:1:0:1
```

VMFS Volume Naming Conventions

While we highly recommend that you label all of your VMFS volumes, we follow that up with a recommendation to come up with a standard naming convention for your VMFS volumes. Since the name assigned to the volume will be seen by all ESX servers in your farm, it is important to have a system to identify the volumes and their uses very easily. Another important piece of the system should allow you to differentiate between local and SAN based VMFS partitions.

Through numerous deployments we have come up with a rather simple system for VMFS volume labeling. It may seam very simplistic to some, but it seems to have worked every time so far. The volume names we use are simple 2 or 3 part names. The first part of the name denotes whether the volume is local or stored on a SAN. The second part of the label is a unique incremental number that increases each time we create a new VMFS volume. And the third piece is a small suffix to denote whether or not this is a special LUN.

When put together, the name of a volume often results in simple names like san_0, san_1, and local_0. If you happen to have a 'special' volume out there such as a deployment LUN that contains all of your VM templates, that may be labeled with a suffix such as the following 'san_5_t'. The 't' in this case is a template LUN. Or if you happen to have a 'shared' mode VMFS volume used by a VM cluster, you can denote it with an 's' like this: 'san_6_s'. By naming the volumes this way, you make it extremely easy for your organization to identify the LUNs within tools like VirtualCenter or the Web Interface. Some organizations have taken this a step further and placed another piece into the name that identifies the farm that the LUNs should be zoned to. Personally I think this is a bit much but it is another option you have.

VMFS Accessibility Modes

VMFS accessibility modes define how ESX servers are able to access the volume and files on the VMFS partition. It's important that you understand each of these modes, because if you simply go by their names (Public and Shared), you will wind up utterly confused.

Early versions of ESX used a 'Public' VMFS mode that only allowed a single ESX server to use a VMFS volume. With the introduction of VMFS 2, the public accessibility mode changed the locking mechanism used by ESX. Instead of locking the entire disk/file system, ESX instead only locked the files it was actively using. This change created the ability to have multiple hosts accessing VM disk files on a shared piece of storage.

Because of this locking design, multiple ESX servers can now run, access, and change files on the shared storage. New files can be created on the storage and the only real limitation is that only one ESX server can have any specific file locked at any given time. Public is now the default (and recommended) access mode for SAN based VMFS volumes.

A second accessibility mode used with ESX is 'Shared'. I know it's confusing already. Shared mode VMFS is used for failover based clustering between virtual machines. The idea here is that a 'shared' mode VMFS is used for the quorum and data disks that are shared between VMs. One major drawback of using shared mode is that once the volume is in use, you cannot make any changes to the disk. Basically you can create the new disk files and configure them for use by your cluster nodes, but no new files can be created on the disk.

This limitation has led VMware to recommend using Disk Mapping files to raw LUNs instead of using shared VMFS for clusters. If you are interested in setting up a VM to VM cluster, please check out the disk mapping files section earlier in this chapter.

Now that you are armed with enough information to build a solid storage infrastructure and begin laying out guest strategies we want to switch gears slightly and introduce the second half of this chapter: ESX and the Network.

ESX and the Network

When designing your ESX network, you need to consider several things such as the amount of traffic generated and components that communicate directly to a server that may be able to utilize a private virtual switch or benefit from being on the same physical host.

Creating an effective network design for a virtual infrastructure requires a solid understanding of all of the components involved. ESX introduces a new way to look at networking design, and before we jump into the new methodologies, we feel that an in-depth description of the various networking components involved is critical. For the various components involved, we will be referencing the Figure 4.3 which is a simplified diagram of the virtual network infrastructure.

Figure 4.3

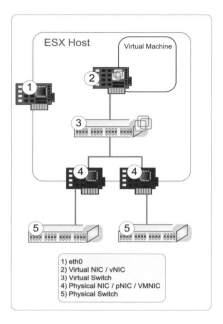

eth0

In Chapter 2 we introduced eth0, which can also be referred to as the Management or Console NIC. If you connect to your ESX server to manage it through the MUI or ssh, eth0 is utilized. Outgoing communication from the console operating system also traverses eth0, making it possible to use backup and monitoring agents on the ESX COS.

Speed and Duplex

One of the first configurations that is typically required with eth0 is the speed and duplex setting. Several factors need to be considered when performing this configuration. By default, ESX sets up eth0 to auto-negotiate its speed and duplex settings. Anyone who has attempted this configuration in the past knows that if Gigabit Ethernet is not being utilized, there is a good chance the NIC will not properly negotiate. Before we jump into how to configure the speed and duplex settings, we should assist in making a decision in whether Gigabit networking should be used over 100Mb.

To make a determination on eth0 speed, we need to analyze the type of traffic that will be generated by the console operating system. In a typical ESX configuration, the following services are running and generating traffic over eth0:

- ESX MUI

- ssh sessions to COS

- Remote Console connections to guest operating systems

- VirtualCenter communication to vmware-ccagent on host

- Monitoring agents running on the COS

- Backups that occur on the COS

With the potential exception of the final bullet point, a 100Mb connection should be more than sufficient for eth0. ESX backup traffic needs extra consideration if a decision between gigabit and 100Mb networking is necessary. If the COS is utilized to backup only the virtual machine configuration files, connections faster than 100Mb will not be required. If utilizing the COS to backup VMDK files, this may be justification enough to upgrade eth0 to a gigabit network adapter.

Another determining factor in making a decision between gigabit and 100Mb connections will be switch port availability within the data center. More often than not, we have seen that the number of gigabit ports available drive us to utilizing 100Mb ports for eth0, and in some cases for the VMNICs, as well. When utilizing ESX for server consolidation, networking ports are often freed up, but again, we typically see the number of 100Mb connections increasing far more than gigabit. It may be that the decision to use 100Mb switch ports is as simple as not having a gigabit network infrastructure or having no high speed port availability in the existing infrastructure.

Advantages of using 100Mb networking for eth0

- Highly available in most cases

- Inexpensive to implement if availability is limited

- Can handle the utilization needs of most ESX implementations

Disadvantages of using 100Mb networking for eth0

- Typically requires additional configuration of the network switch equipment and ESX host

- Speed may not be sufficient for performing network intensive tasks such as VMDK backups

Advantages of using gigabit networking for eth0

- Easy to configure on network switch and ESX host

- High speed suitable for performing VMDK backups from the COS

Disadvantages of using gigabit networking for eth0

- Not always available in the data center

- Expensive to introduce to data center if infrastructure does not exist

- May be underutilized if throughput does not meet gigabit capabilities

Configuring Speed and Duplex

There is an easy way to determine the current configuration of your eth0 interface when utilizing the service console. There is a statistics file in the /proc file system that will show the various settings of the eth0 interface. It is not possible to view the configuration of eth0 utilizing the MUI. The path to the statistics file, which contains the speed and duplex configuration for the adapter, varies depending on NIC manufacturer. Typically, the statistics file is stored in a subdirectory under /proc/net. The following are the locations for the two most common network adapters utilized for ESX – Intel and Broadcom:

For Intel Adapters:

```
/proc/net/PRO_LAN_Adapters/eth0.info
```

For Broadcom Adapters:

```
/proc/net/nicinfo/eth0.info
```

The eth0.info file actually contains a significant amount of data in regards to your eth0 adapter. Information such as MAC address, amount of data transferred, and, most importantly, link state and speed and duplex settings. You can use "less" to view the information contained within this file. The values we are interested in are Link, Speed, and Duplex.

```
# less /proc/net/{Vendor Specific
Directory}/eth0.info
```

When the eth0.info file shows undesired connectivity settings such as 100Mb/Half Duplex or a link status of "Down", additional configuration of eth0 is required. The /etc/modules.conf file allows for the manual configuration of the speed and duplex settings for eth0. Before we dig too far into the /etc/modules.conf file, we feel that it is important to mention that adapters that will be running at gigabit speeds should be configured to auto-detect their speed and duplex settings. We have seen that setting the switch port and eth0 to both auto-detect gigabit connections works nearly every time without additional configuration.

Each supported vendor has a unique configuration in the /etc/modules.conf file for their adapters. When configuring the proper settings in modules.conf, the network port should also be configured with the same settings. If the settings of the NIC and switch port conflict, there is a chance that no link will be established between the two. In order to properly configure eth0 of an ESX host to 100Mb/FD, the following modifications must be made to the /etc/modules.conf file depending on the vendor of the network adapter.

There are two sections to the modules.conf file that need to be considered when statically setting the speed and duplex setting. The first section, which ESX configures properly during installation, is the alias section. The alias defines a mapping between a COS device and the driver that it utilizes within the COS. Depending on the vendor and chipset of the network adapter, you should see a line similar to one of the following:

```
alias eth0 e100
alias eth0 e1000
alias eth0 bcm5700
alias eth0 3c59x
```

The options section of the /etc/modules.conf file defines the options that are utilized by the driver to properly configure the hardware device. Each network vendor utilizes different options to properly configure the speed and duplex of their network adapters. Below, we show the proper lines that need to be added to the /etc/modules.conf file to change the most popular adapters to 100Mb Full Duplex. For a complete list of configuration options, please refer to VMware's KB Answer ID 813.

Intel e100
```
options e100 e100_speed_duplex=4
```

Intel e1000
```
options e1000 Speed=100 Duplex=2
```

Broadcom 5700
```
options bcm5700 line_speed=100 full_duplex=1
```

3Com 3c59x
```
options 3c59x full_duplex=1 options=4
```

When utilizing 100Mb networking, there is an additional utility that can be utilized to temporarily change the speed and duplex settings. The mii-tool command is a command line utility that can be utilized to modify speed and duplex settings of 100Mb connections in real time. It is useful for testing a configuration change before permanently modifying the /etc/modules.conf file. It is important to note that mii-tool can be utilized to configure gigabit adapters at 100Mb, but not at gigabit speeds. If you notice slow speeds or disconnected sessions to your ESX console, the following command may be run to determine your current speed and duplex configuration:

```
# mii-tool
eth0: 100 Mbit, half duplex, link ok
```

As you can see from our example, eth0 is stating that it is connected at 100Mb/Half Duplex. This has been known to cause significant performance issues on the COS. A temporary way to change the console NIC to 100Mb/Full Duplex is by utilizing a switch with the mii-tool command. By typing the following command, we instantly modify the negotiation settings of eth0. There will be no output from this command.

```
# mii-tool -F 100BaseTx-FD
```

Once the speed and duplex settings have been modified with the mii-tool command, we can again check the currently negotiated settings with mii-tool.

```
# mii-tool
eth0: 100 Mbit, full duplex, link ok
```

Assuming the network switch is configured statically for 100Mb/Full Duplex, we should see that eth0 is now properly negotiating at the preferred configuration. If all network connectivity to the ESX host is lost, it typically means the network switch port is configured for auto negotiation. To quickly recover from the outage generated from an invalid setting, we can force eth0 to renegotiate its settings automatically with the following command. If network connectivity has been lost to the COS, this command will need to be run directly from the console.

```
# mii-tool -r
restarting autonegotiation...
```

Assuming forcing eth0 to 100Mb/Full duplex was successful, we know we can modify the /etc/modules.conf file utilizing the steps described earlier.

Configuring Network Settings

Although ESX configures the network settings during the installation process, there may be a requirement to modify the IP configuration settings. There are several files that are involved with the configuration of the IP information for the COS. Refer to the table below to determine which file is required to modify a specific setting.

/etc/sysconfig/network-scripts/eth0/ifcfg-eth0
IP Address
Subnet Mask

/etc/resolv.conf
Search Suffix
DNS Servers

/etc/sysconfig/network
Hostname
Default Gateway

We feel it is important to know the files behind the configuration of the networking of eth0, but it is not absolutely necessary. For those that are impatient, there is a very simple way to modify the IP Address, Subnet Mask, Default Gateway, and Primary DNS server. By running "setup" from the command line, a menu will appear that will allow for the configuration of several COS components, including network configuration. This provides an easy mechanism to modify the network information of eth0.

While it is possible to change the hostname of an ESX server it is strongly discouraged. The SSL certificate that is generated during the ESX installation process is tied to this hostname. If the hostname of the server changes, the SLL certificate is not updated. An error message will be generated stating that the SSL certificate does not match the name of the site.

Regardless of how the configuration for eth0 is modified, the new settings do not take effect by default. The networking components of the COS must be restarted in order for the configuration changes to become permanent. A simple command run at the console will perform the necessary tasks.

```
# /etc/init.d/network restart
```

When the services restart, the new IP configurations will take effect. It is typically best practice to perform these actions directly at the console. This will provide a mechanism to troubleshoot any issues that may occur from an invalid configuration.

Statistics

In the event that statistical information for eth0 is required, there are several mechanisms that make this possible. We have already touched on one of the methods a little earlier in this chapter when covering speed and duplex settings.

The /proc/net/{Vendor Specific Directory}/eth0.info contains the most information about the physical adapter. This file contains information in regards to the actual hardware and does not dive into details such as IP Address or other information that is assigned by the COS.

The best way to find the most useful information quickly is by utilizing the /sbin/ifconfig command. By utilizing this command, it is easy to retrieve the MAC address, IP configurations, any errors or collisions that are occurring, and the amount of data transferred since the last restart of the networking service. The following command will provide the stated information for eth0:

```
# /sbin/ifconfig eth0

eth0 Link encap:Ethernet  HWaddr 00:50:8B:CF:ED:3D
inet addr:192.168.0.9  Bcast:192.168.0.255
Mask:255.255.255.0
UP BROADCAST RUNNING MULTICAST  MTU:1500  Metric:1
RX packets:92076 errors:0 dropped:0 overruns:0
frame:0
TX packets:103019 errors:0 dropped:0 overruns:0 car-
rier:0
collisions:0 txqueuelen:100
RX bytes:9982118 (9.5 Mb)  TX bytes:31299052 (29.8
Mb)
Interrupt:17 Base address:0x2400 Memory:f4fff000-
f4fff038
```

The final method we are going to discuss involves utilizing 3rd party monitoring agents in the COS. There are too many monitoring tools to discuss here, but the majority of them have Linux agents that have the following similarities:

•   Statistical analysis of network performance

- Real-time throughput analysis

- Alerting or notification on high utilization events or "offline" status

Virtual NICs / vNICs

Using the methods and tools discussed up to this point, we have armed you with enough information to properly plan for and configure the networking for the console operating system. When it comes to ESX, we have not even scratched the surface of its capabilities and have yet to describe some of the advanced techniques surrounding connecting our virtual machines to the network infrastructure. We want to hold off just a little bit longer on connecting to the physical network so we can talk about the network configuration of the virtual machines in the virtual infrastructure.

A Virtual NIC is a network adapter that is configured within ESX for a virtual machine. Each virtual machine may have up to 4 network adapters configured, providing significant amounts of flexibility when connecting a virtual server to multiple subnets. Each vNIC that is assigned to a virtual machine receives its own unique MAC address, just as a physical adapter in a physical server would. When we discuss VMNICs and Virtual Switches, and how the virtual machines integrate with the physical network, we will see that this unique MAC address makes its way to the physical switch infrastructure.

As was discussed in Chapter 2, VMware provides two different hardware emulation options when configuring virtual network adapters for virtual machines. Chapter 2 goes into the differences between the two drivers, so in this chapter we want to describe the similarities found in the back-end configurations of these devices.

MAC Addresses

As was stated earlier, for every vNIC that gets created and assigned to a virtual machine, a unique MAC address is created. This MAC address gets stored in the VMX file for the virtual machine in which it is created. VMware utilizes several mechanisms when verifying the uniqueness of the MAC addresses that are assigned. The first, and most obvious, mechanism is the use of unique 3 bytes

Organizationally Unique Identifiers (OUIs). These OUIs ensure a VMware vNIC receives a MAC address that is completely unique from any other network card vendor. VMware has the following OUIs registered:

```
00:0c:29
00:50:56
00:05:69
```

Unless you have machines that have been upgraded from ESX 1.5, there is a good chance that you will not see the 00:05:69 OUI in use on any virtual machines.

The second mechanism for ensuring each vNIC receives a unique MAC address is by utilizing the UUID of the virtual machine. Each virtual machine has a unique UUID number that is based on several factors. An algorithm is calculated against this UUID and the remaining 3 bytes of the MAC address are generated. Even when utilizing this algorithm, VMware cannot guarantee the uniqueness of the MAC address. To combat a MAC address conflict scenario, ESX performs an integrity check and if a conflict is detected, a new MAC is generated. ESX performs integrity checks until a unique MAC address is generated. Once generated, the MAC address is written to the VMX file of the virtual machine the vNIC is configured for and will not change unless the path to the VMX file for the virtual machine changes.

VMware has designated that MAC addresses beginning with 00:0C:29 are automatically generated by ESX. These are the values that are generated utilizing the algorithm mentioned previously. MAC addresses that fall within the range of 00:50:56:00:00:00 and 00:50:56:3F:FF:FF are reserved for manually configured MACs. In a typical configuration of an ESX host and virtual machine, the following lines are found in the VMX file of the virtual machine, which define the MAC address of the vNIC. In this example, the virtual machine in question has two virtual NICs configured:

```
ethernet0.addressType = "generated"
ethernet0.generatedAddress = "00:0c:29:98:7f:e2"
ethernet0.generatedAddressOffset = "0"
```

```
ethernet1.addressType = "generated"
ethernet1.generatedAddress = "00:0c:29:76:6b:34"
ethernet1.generatedAddressOffset = "0"
```

In the event that a manual MAC address entry is required, VMware allows us to modify the VMX file and input our own MAC address that falls within the pre-defined range of 00:50:56:00:00:00 and 00:50:56:3F:FF:FF. In order to change the MAC address of our ethernet1 adapter in the previous example, make the following changes to the VMX file:

```
ethernet0.addressType = "generated"
ethernet0.generatedAddress = "00:0c:29:98:7f:e2"
ethernet0.generatedAddressOffset = "0"
ethernet1.addressType = "static"
ethernet1.generatedAddress = "00:50:56:00:00:01"
ethernet1.generatedAddressOffset = "0"
```

When manually setting the MAC address of a virtual adapter, the MAC chosen should be documented and referenced every time a new MAC is required. This will guarantee that the same MAC will not accidentally be entered twice. Manually setting the MAC address in this fashion guarantees that it will not change, even if the path to the VMX file is modified.

Of course, what would be complete within ESX without VirtualCenter completely changing the rules? The same inconsistency applies for MAC address allocations that are automatically generated for virtual machines. When the vmware-ccagent is installed on an ESX host, the automatically assigned MAC address range changes to conflict with every rule mentioned above. The following range is the standard for automatically generated MAC addresses when VirtualCenter is utilized in an ESX environment:

```
00:50:56:80:00:00 to 00:50:56:BF:FF:FF
```

In addition to the MAC range changing, we also see a slight variation in the VMX file of the virtual machine, letting us know that VirtualCenter has played a role:

```
ethernet0.addressType = "vpx"
ethernet0.generatedAddress = "00:50:56:98:3c:4a"
ethernet0.generatedAddressOffset = "0"
```

Physical NICs / pNICS / VMNICs

Physical NICs of an ESX system are those that are dedicated for use by the virtual machines. Each ESX system will typically have several of these "VMNICs" to assist with balancing the network load or provide redundancy to the solution. We will discuss some of these load balancing and redundancy methods later in this chapter. What we want to achieve here is define a clear understanding of the pNICs of the system and how to optimize their performance for the virtual machines that are configured to use them.

As with all hardware components, ESX compatibility should be verified with VMware's System Compatibility Guide. We have found that the VMkernel does not have a lot of flexibility when attempting to utilize NICs that are not listed in the compatibility guide. To ensure supportability by VMware, we recommend that you reference the following document:

`http://www.vmware.com/pdf/esx_systems_guide.pdf`

One last item to mention is that network adapters that will be assigned as VMNICs should all be the same vendor and model whenever possible. This ensures compatibility for all VMNICs on a system and ensures all VMNICs have the same capabilities for virtual machines. This recommendation excludes eth0. Often times, specific hardware vendors will either have an Intel or a Broadcom NIC integrated into the system board of a host server. This should not impact your decision on which vendor is utilized for VMNIC configurations.

Speed and Duplex
Speed and duplex settings for VMNICs are extremely important due to the fact that the network performance of your virtual machines depend on their proper configuration. The major determination for configuring faster VMNIC connections is the amount of total bandwidth that all of your virtual machines generate and receive. There is

typically a close correlation between total bandwidth and the amount of virtual machines that are configured on the server. When sizing your VMNIC connections, you need to consider both incoming and outgoing traffic of your virtual machines.

Similarly to eth0, the backup strategy plays a major role in sizing the VMNIC configuration of an ESX server. If your backup strategy does not change when utilizing ESX – meaning backup agents are still installed on each guest operating system – the VMNIC configuration needs significant consideration. At this point, you are no longer sending large amounts from a single server down a high speed link, and need to make the proper considerations for multiple systems. Scheduling of backups will play a major role in ensuring the proper throughput is available for your virtual machines. If your backups are performed using REDO logs from the service console, and without utilizing backup agents in the local operating systems, it may be possible to run several virtual machines on a 100Mb connection without issues. When you start building ESX systems that contain more than 10 virtual machines, gigabit Ethernet becomes increasingly more important. Unfortunately, there are no set rules as to whether gigabit Ethernet is required. Analysis of your physical servers must be performed over time and the data must be utilized to determine the bandwidth needs of the solution.

While working with multiple clients we have determined our own "default configurations" that we attempt to utilize when possible depending on the ESX systems in the client's environment. Please note that these configurations are extremely basic and do not take special VLAN configurations into consideration. We will discuss these VLAN options later in this chapter.

Processors	100Mb	Gigabit	VMs
2	2	0	6-8
4	0	2	16-20
8	0	4	30-35

Please note that the chart above only shows our default recommendations. We actually consider this our bare minimum when we layout designs for clients. There is no consideration above for eth0, which will be an additional NIC beyond those listed.

Configuring speed and duplex

Configuring the speed and duplex for VMNICs can be easily performed in the MUI under the Network Connections configuration
screen. When a change is made utilizing the MUI, the new configuration takes effect immediately. The connection status and negotiated speed will be displayed within the MUI, making it easy to determine the proper configuration for the desired speed and duplex.

In addition to utilizing the MUI, there is a way to modify the
/etc/vmware/hwconfig file to statically set the speed and duplex settings of the VMNICs. Before this file can be properly configured, the
bus and device number of the adapter must be determined.
Additionally, we must know the NIC vendor for each adapter that is
installed in the system. To determine this information, we need to
open /etc/vmware/hwconfig and look for lines similar to the following:

Adapter Vendor
```
device.0.5.0.name = "Intel Corporation 82543 Gigabit
Ethernet Adapter"
device.3.4.0.name = "BROADCOM Coproration NetXtreme
BCM5703"
device.3.5.0.name = "Intel Corporation 82557
[Ethernet Pro 100]"
```

VMNIC Mapping

The devices can be mapped back to their VMNIC ID by looking for
the following lines in the configuration file:

```
devicenames.000:05.0.nic = "vmnic0"
devicenames.003:04.0.nic = "vmnic1"
devicenames.003:05.0.nic = "vmnic2"
```

The above lines tell us the bus and device numbering for each of the
VMNICs that are configured in the ESX system. Armed with this
information, the speed and duplex settings can be configured by
adding configuration lines to the /etc/vmware/hwconfig file. Each
NIC vendor has unique options for configuring speed and duplex,
which are extremely similar to the options that were utilized for configuring eth0. Assuming each of our VMNICs is a different vendor,

the following lines can be added to our configuration file to set the adapter to 100Mb/Full Duplex:

```
device.esx.0.5.0.options = "speed=100 duplex=2"
device.esx.3.4.0.options = "line_speed=100
full_duplex=1"
device.esx.3.4.0.options = "e100_speed_duplex=4"
```

When /etc/vmware/hwconfig is modified using a text editor, the settings will not take effect until the next reboot of the ESX host. If you need speed and duplex settings to take effect immediately, the MUI must be utilized. Manual modifications of the /etc/vmware/hwconfig file should be used for automation purposes only.

Monitoring VMNIC Performance

ESX provides several tools that can be used to monitor the utilization. Vmkusage is an excellent tool for graphing historical data in regards to VMNIC performance. Vmkusage can be utilized to graph daily, weekly, and monthly traffic trends. VirtualCenter also provides graphing capabilities.

The second tool that can be utilized for performance monitoring is esxtop. It is a command line tool that is extremely similar to the top tool that is utilized to monitor performance of Unix and Linux operating systems. Esxtop will show, in real time, the following statistics for each VMNIC:

- Packets Sent per Second

- Packets Received per Second

- Megabits Sent per Second

- Megabits Received per Second

Further information about the in depth use of these tools can be found in Chapter 8 where we discuss the monitoring of ESX. It should be noted that VirtualCenter cannot be utilized to monitor the performance of individual VMNICs. VirtualCenter is only capable of watching the throughput that the entire system is utilizing and the throughput of a specific virtual machine. It cannot be utilized for trend analysis for your VMNICs.

Virtual Switches

The final, and most advanced, component of ESX networking that is handled by the VMkernel is the virtual switch. A virtual switch is a logical component of ESX that acts identically to a physical switch and is used to map a vNIC back to individual or groups of VMNICs for network connectivity. In addition, virtual switches can be configured in a "private" mode that has no connectivity to the physical network, but still allows virtual machines to communicate.

Whether you are configuring your virtual switch in a public or private mode, there are several functions that are identical. Each virtual switch can be configured to support 32 vNICs. Traffic that flows between any two vNICs on the same virtual switch will actually transfer over the system bus and will not traverse the network (assuming VLAN tagging is not being utilized, but more on that in a moment). When laying out your network design, this should be considered, as it is often advantageous to have network intensive applications talking directly to each other. When information is transferred in this manner, no network resources are impacted. All processing in this scenario is handled by processor 0 of the ESX host system.

When configuring virtual switches within ESX, a required field for the configuration forces us to specify a name for the switch. We recommend that this value be something that can help in determining how the switch is configured. There is one simple rule, which is "The first character for a virtual switch name should not be a number." There have been issues in the past in which starting the name of a virtual switch with a number has erratic behavior, especially when attempting to remove or rename it. Some examples of good virtual switch names that we have used at various client sites are as follows:

- net_10.0.0

- DMZ

- Production

- VMotion

By looking at the name of the virtual switch, we should be able to determine the subnet of any virtual machine that is configured on those switches. This is increasingly important when deploying virtual machines. A good naming standard will allow us to easily deploy virtual machines and know exactly how they will interact on the network. When VMotion is utilized in an ESX environment, there must be a separate virtual switch created which must contain one NIC at a minimum. Since there is typically only one virtual switch per ESX host that is utilized for VMotion, a simple virtual switch name should suffice. If you attempt to change the name of a virtual switch after it has been created, you must power off all virtual machines that are using the switch.

Public Virtual Switches

Public virtual switches are easily the most utilized virtual switches in an ESX environment. In a public virtual switch, anywhere from 1 to 10 VMNICs may be bound, providing connectivity to the physical network for virtual machines. When utilizing a single VMNIC, it is important to remember that there will be no redundancy in the network design for your virtual machines. Also, when utilizing gigabit Ethernet adapters, only 8 VMNICs may be bound to a single virtual switch.

Figure 4.4

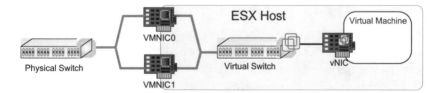

In a default configuration, all VMNICs are configured in a redundant bond that load balances virtual machines across all VMNICs in that bond based on vNIC MAC addresses. We will discuss this load balancing mode and other similar configurations later in this chapter. In addition to configuring load balancing methods, each virtual switch may be configured to handle VLAN configurations in different ways. By default, all virtual machines become extensions of the VLAN that the VMNIC switch port is configured for. ESX provides mechanisms to handle VLANs in different manners. Alternative VLAN configurations will also be reviewed at a later time in this chapter.

Configuring in the Console

It is possible to define public virtual switches by modifying 2 files within the COS. Creating the switches in the console is typically tied back to troubleshooting or system automation. The first thing we need to do is define a bond configuration within the /etc/vmware/hwconfig file. Once the bond is configured with the proper VMNICs, a virtual switch needs to be defined in /etc/vmware/netmap.conf that references this bond. To perform the first configuration, we want to add the following lines to /etc/vmware/hwconfig:

```
nicteam.vmnic0.team = "bond0"
nicteam.vmnic1.team = "bond0"
nicteam.vmnic2.team = "bond1"
nicteam.vmnic3.team = "bond1"
nicteam.vmnic4.team = "bond1"
nicteam.vmnic5.team = "bond1"
nicteam.vmnic6.team = "bond2"
```

In the configuration above, we have created 3 bonds (We DO NOT have virtual switches yet). The first virtual bond contains two VMNICs, the second contains 4 VMNICs, and the third bond contains a single VMNIC. Armed with the information added to hwconfig, we can proceed to create our virtual switches.

Now that we have our bonds configured, we can open /etc/vmware/netmap.conf and actually create our virtual switches. The available options for creating a virtual switch contain two variables; a name and a device. The name represents the Network Label as defined in the MUI. The device variable references a pre-defined bond configuration from the /etc/vmware/hwconfig file.

```
network.0.name = "VSwitch1"
network.0.device = "bond0"
network.1.name = "VSwitch2"
network.1.device = "bond1"
network.2.name = "VMotion"
```

```
network.2.device = "bond2"
```

By combining the two configuration files we have 3 virtual switches. In the above example, we have defined two virtual switches for use by virtual machines and a third for the specific purpose of utilizing VMotion in the virtual infrastructure. Manually modifying the above files will NOT automatically activate new virtual switches. If a virtual switch is not created using the MUI, the vmware-serverd (or vmware-ccagent if you are using VirtualCenter) process must be restarted.

Private Virtual Switches

The main difference between public virtual switches and private virtual switches lies in the fact that private virtual switches do not have a connection to the physical network. In a private virtual switch, all traffic generated between virtual machines is handled by the CPU, as there is no other way for this traffic to travel between virtual machines. Private virtual switches provide isolation and can serve several purposes such as testing AD schema changes with a namespace that is identical to production, or building a DMZ environment in a box.

Figure 4.5

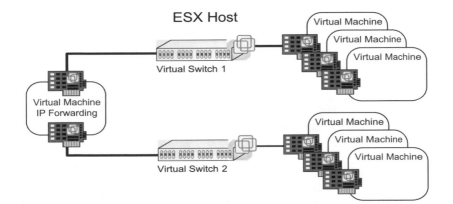

Virtual machines that are connected to a private virtual switch must be configured for the same subnet in order to communicate with each other. Multiple private virtual switches can be created within an ESX host to provide a multiple subnet environment. ESX does not provide routing capabilities internally across virtual switches. The only way that virtual machines that are on different virtual switches can communicate is by configuring a guest operating system with IP forwarding enabled. Guest operating systems must then have either static routes defined or default gateways configured that point to this "gateway" server to communicate across subnets.

Configuring in the Console

Configuring a private virtual switch manually by modifying configuration files is significantly easier than configuring public virtual switches. Since private virtual switches do not need to map back to VMNICs, there is no need to touch the /etc/vmware/hwconfig file. We can add two simple lines to /etc/vmware/netmap.conf to create a new private virtual switch:

```
network3.name = "Private Switch 1"
network3.device = "vmnet_0"
network4.name = "Private Switch 2"
network4.device = "vmnet_1"
```

Like public virtual switches, private virtual switches that are created manually will not become active until the proper processes are restarted.

Load balancing modes

VMware ESX provides two methods for load balancing the traffic generated by virtual machines. Both methods, in addition to providing load balancing for traffic, also assist in providing a redundant network design. There is also a third method of redundancy in which a pNIC within a virtual switch may be configured in a standby mode, which will also be discussed.

MAC Address

MAC Address Load Balancing is the default load balancing mode for ESX. This method does not require that any additional switch configuration be made to the physical switches that ESX is connected to, making it the best candidate in terms of network infrastructure compatibility. In this load balancing mode, the VMkernel has full control over which pNIC in a virtual switch publishes the virtual machine's MAC address to the physical switch infrastructure. By only allowing one pNIC to announce a MAC address for a virtual machine, there are no "duplicate MAC" issues on the physical switches that prevent the virtual machine from properly communicating. This also gives us the capability to create virtual switches that span across multiple physical switches, which increases the redundancy of the overall design.

In the event that the loss of a network link is detected at the pNIC that is currently running the virtual machine, the VMkernel automatically re-ARPs the virtual machine's MAC address down an alternative "known-good" path. It should be noted that this is not something that takes minutes; this failover typically occurs within 10 seconds. We have performed testing that shows this failover happening with anywhere from 0 to 4 ICMP timeouts. After the failed link is restored on the pNIC, we have found that there is typically a larger outage of about 10-15 ICMP timeouts. This is due to the Spanning-Tree protocol that is enabled on most switches. We will discuss a way to limit this timeframe shortly when we discuss physical switches.

While MAC Address Load Balancing may be the easier of the two methods to set up, it is not the most efficient at load balancing traffic. The VMkernel uses an internal algorithm to determine which pNIC in a virtual switch a specific virtual MAC address gets announced through. It is not possible to manually configure which virtual machines communicate down specific paths of a virtual switch. What this means is that the VMkernel simply tells a specific pNIC to handle the traffic for a virtual NIC without regard to the amount of traffic being generated. We have seen instances on ESX where one pNIC is generating significantly more traffic than any other within a virtual switch. When we do ESX designs in the field we do not utilize MAC Address Load Balancing to actually load balance traffic; it is used as a redundancy method and we use it when we know we have the appropriate network capacity within a virtual switch to handle an N+1 configuration. If we lose one pNIC in a virtual switch, we should still have the appropriate capacity to provide the virtual machines with the throughput they need for operation.

IP Address
The second method that ESX is capable of providing for load balancing is based on destination IP address. Since outgoing virtual machine traffic is balanced based on the destination IP address of the packet,

this method provides a much more balanced configuration than MAC Address based balancing. Like the previous method, if a link failure is detected by the VMkernel, there will be no impact to the connectivity of the virtual machines. The downside of utilizing this method of load balancing is that it requires additional configuration of the physical network equipment.

Because of the way the outgoing traffic traverses the network in an IP Address load balancing configuration, the MAC addresses of the virtual NICs will be seen by multiple switch ports. In order to get around this "issue", either EtherChannel (assuming Cisco switches are utilized) or 802.3ad (LACP - Link Aggregation Control Protocol) must be configured on the physical switches. Without this configuration, the duplicate MAC address will cause switching issues.

In addition to requiring physical switch configuration changes, an ESX server configuration change is required. There is a single line that needs to be added to /etc/vmware/hwconfig for each virtual switch that you wish to enable IP Address load balancing on. To make this change, use your favorite text editor and add the line below to /etc/vmware/hwconfig. You will need to utilize the same configuration file to determine the name of the bond that you need to reference in the following entry (replace "bond0" with the proper value):

```
nicteam.bond0.load_balance_mode = "out-ip"
```

Standby Mode
As mentioned earlier, VMware provides a third redundancy method for ESX. There is no load balancing associated with this option. This scenario is typically utilized when gigabit switch ports are available, but in short supply. When connecting the pNICs, one link is run to a gigabit switch port while the other is connected to a 100Mb port.

Figure 4.6

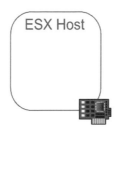

As you remember, the default load balancing method is MAC Address based, so running two different connection speeds could cause network performance issues if the slower connection gets virtual machines that are more network intensive assigned to it. When using IP Address load balancing, there is no priority given by the VMkernel to the faster connection, so the same rules apply; the slower link can easily become saturated significantly faster than the high-speed connection. If using two different speeds, VMware provides an option that may be set that will force all traffic to utilize a specific pNIC within a virtual switch.

We can easily configure the gigabit connection to be "home link" for the virtual switch. Upon failure of the home link, the backup link will automatically activate and handle the virtual machine traffic until the issue with the high speed connection can be resolved. When performing this failover, ESX utilizes the same methodology as MAC Address load balancing of instantly re-ARPing the virtual MAC addresses for the virtual machines down the alternative path. To make this configuration, add the following line to /etc/vmware/hwconfig:

```
nicteam.bond0.home_link = "vmnic1"
```

The above command assumes that your /etc/vmware/hwconfig file specifies bond0 as the virtual switch you wish to modify and that vmnic1 is the fastest connection in a two-port virtual switch configuration. It should also be noted that configuring a home_link for your virtual switch will disable all other forms of load balancing, as this effectively disables one of the pNICs of the virtual switch unless a failure condition occurs.

Beaconing

Beacon monitoring is a method that ESX can utilize to determine network connection failures beyond the switch ports that the pNICs of a system are plugged in to. (See Figure 4.7) The idea here is that ESX Server will send beacon packets from one pNIC to other pNICs on the same virtual switch. The beacon packets will then traverse the network through the switch infrastructure to the other pNICs on the virtual switch. If there is no response from beacon packets, this means there is a network disruption somewhere upstream. The server will note there is a connection loss after it fails to receive a specific number of broadcast beacons in succession. This number (called the beacon failure threshold) is configurable and absolute, meaning if you configure the beacon failure threshold to five, you have to lose five beacon broadcasts in a row for the failover to occur. If you only lose four, then the fifth is received, then lose another four, failover does not occur.

Using beaconing is only effective when the pNICs of a virtual switch are connected to different uplink switches. If the pNICs are only connected to a single uplink switch, then beaconing does you no good since you are adding beaconing overhead to traverse a path between switch ports on the same physical device. Using beaconing on a single physical switch will tell you nothing more than the fact that the device or its ports are still active, which ESX server will handle by default, without beaconing.

Unless you absolutely need to have ESX monitor your up stream network I would veer away from it. Beacon monitoring sometimes detects network failures that are not really happening. This happens when upstream switches stop beacon packets from reaching other pNICs on the virtual switch. This in-turn causes the server to declare a switch failure when really nothing has failed. It becomes really interesting once the failover occurs because traffic from the original primary pNIC may still be transmitted upstream (because there is no failure) and the upstream switches may receive duplicate packets from both pNICs

Figure 4.7 Beaconing

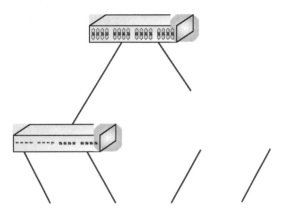

Virtual Switch

Physical Switches

While technically physical switches are not a direct component of ESX, we feel it is important to discuss some of the design options surrounding the configuration and use of a redundant network switch infrastructure. As you now know, VMware provides two methods of load balancing for configuring their virtual switches, both of which inherently provide redundancy when connected to multiple physical switches. For this reason we recommend that virtual switches with more than one VMNIC be plugged into different physical switches. Due to the nature of the load balancing configurations of ESX, all uplink switches must be capable of configuring the same VLANs to the ESX hosts.

The Spanning-Tree protocol has been known to cause delays in re-establishing network connectivity after a failed link returns to service. It is not uncommon to see 15-20 ICMP requests fail when a VMNIC within a virtual switch re-establishes its connection after a failure. To minimize the impact of the Spanning-Tree protocol, there are two things that can potentially be configured at the physical switch. The first option is disabling the Spanning-Tree protocol for the entire physical switch. There is an extremely good chance that this is not possible in most environments. The alternative, and most likely, solution to resolve some of these issues would be to enable Portfast Mode for the ports that the VMNICs are connected to.

Every hardware vendor is unique and has different ways to configure various settings. We recommend working with the vendors closely if there are questions in regards to a specific configuration that is required for VMware compatibility.

VLAN configurations

As has been mentioned in several locations in this chapter, there are several ways to integrate VLAN configurations into a virtual infrastructure. VLANs allow us to configure systems that are not connected to the same physical switches, and are possibly in different physical locations, to communicate as if they were on the same network segment. There are three different ways that ESX allows us to configure VLANs within a host. Each method has a different impact on how our virtual switches are configured and how our guest operating systems interact with the network. In addition, there are advantages and drawbacks to each method.

External Switch Tagging (EST)
EST is the default configuration for all virtual switches within an ESX host. In this mode, all VLAN configurations are handled by the physical switch. This does not require any configuration on the physical switch other than properly configuring the ports that the VMNICs of the ESX host are plugged into for the proper VLAN. This configuration is no different than if a physical server were being plugged into the network that required a specific VLAN configuration.

In the following diagram, we have two virtual switches, each consisting of two VMNICs. The physical switch ports that the VMNICs are plugged into are configured for a specific VLAN. By design, ESX ensures that a particular VLAN is presented all the way to the virtual machine. The only way a virtual machine can communicate on the network is if it is assigned an IP address that falls within the subnet range that defines the specific VLAN that it is connected to.

Figure 4.8 External Switch Tagging

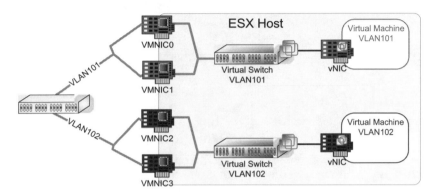

Advantages to Using EST

• Easiest VLAN configuration (No additional configuration necessary)

• Supported in every version of VMware ESX

Disadvantage to Using EST

• Amount of VLANs that may be configured is limited by the number of pNICs installed in the host

Virtual Switch Tagging (VST)

VST consist of allowing a virtual switch to handle its own VLAN tagging. By configuring the uplink switch to explicitly tag packets with the 802.1q specification, all control of VLAN configurations is handed over to the VMkernel. The processing of 802.1q tags is handled by the network adapter hardware, so overhead from these tags never hits the VMkernel and has no impact on virtualization processing. In this configuration, each physical switch port that connects to a VMNIC is configured in a trunk mode. After the trunk is established, specific VLANs are presented down the trunk to the uplink "switch" which, in the case of the diagram below, is ESX's virtual switch.

Figure 4.9 Virtual Switch Tagging

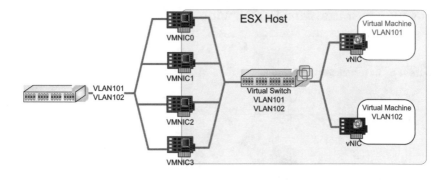

Once the virtual switch receives the VLAN information from the trunk it needs to have the capability to assign vNICs to specific VLANs. In order to achieve this, port groups must be configured within ESX. Since a virtual switch does not have physical ports that we can assign specific VLANs to, we need to utilize port groups as a reference to a particular VLAN. Port groups are configured on a per virtual switch basis. Each VLAN that is being announced down the trunk to the virtual switch must have its own port group configured before virtual machines can be utilized on the published VLAN. There are only two values that must be configured when creating a port group; the "Port Group Label", which serves as a name, and the VLAN ID itself. It is best practice to set the Port Group Labels to "VLANX", where X is replaced by the published VLAN's ID.

Once the decision to utilize VLAN tagging and port groups has been made, special considerations need to be made when configuring vNICs for virtual machines. Once a trunk has been established, we will no longer be able to map vNICs back to a virtual switch. Since the virtual switches are no longer connected to a particular VLAN, the guest will not be able to properly communicate on the network. Instead, we must point the vNIC to the Port Group Label that was defined for the VLAN that we would like the guest to reside in. Using the previous diagram, we have one vNIC that would point to the VLAN101 port group. The vNIC for the other system would point at the VLAN102 port group.

You will need to review your switch vendor's documentation to ensure 802.1q VLAN tagging is a function of your specific switch model. Each physical switch also has different configuration steps for properly configuring 802.1q; so again, documentation should be consulted for the proper configuration. One thing to note is that port groups cannot be configured with the "Native VLAN" for a switch. This Native VLAN is utilized for switch management and does not get tagged with a VLAN ID, and therefore is dropped by ESX. The default value for Cisco switches is 1, so any value between 2 and 4094 should work without issue.

Using VST also changes the way in which we recommend configuring virtual switches. One of the main reasons we recommend creating multiple virtual switches is so multiple VLANs can be utilized within a single ESX host. VST removes this restriction and allows a seemingly unlimited number of VLANs to be accessed through a single virtual switch. For this reason, if VST is to be utilized in an environment, we recommend configuring a single virtual switch that contains all VMNICs in the system. This provides additional redundancy and throughput to the virtual switch, but simplifies the management of an ESX host by allowing us to configure port groups only once per ESX host. If VMotion is utilized in an environment, we still recommend that this be a standalone virtual switch and that it be configured in EST mode.

Advantages of Using VST

- A single virtual switch can utilize multiple VLANs, removing the dependency on multiple virtual switches and VMNICs to support multiple VLANs

- Once 802.1q trunks are established, adding new VLANs to ESX is a simple process

- Decreases the amount of network connections for ESX hosts that will support multiple VLANs, potentially freeing up high-speed switch ports

Disadvantages of using VST

- May not be supported by all network infrastructures

- Configuring trunk ports directly to servers is a new configuration in most environments, and is not always welcome

Virtual Machine Guest Tagging (VGT)

The final mode for configuring VLANs for virtual machines is virtual guest tagging. In VGT mode, the virtual switch no longer reads 802.1q tags, but instead forwards them directly to the virtual machine. The guest operating system is then responsible for properly configuring the VLAN for the vNIC of the virtual machine. There is extremely limited support to this configuration. In fact, in the current state, there is no way to configure a windows operating system within ESX using this method. The only way this can be configured is if a Linux guest is running. Most 2.4 and higher Linux kernels have VLAN tagging support built in. The only time this configuration can be utilized is if a particular virtual machine requires access to more than 4 VLANs. This number is based on the fact that a single virtual machine may only utilize 4 vNICs.

Figure 4.10 Virtual Machine Guest Tagging

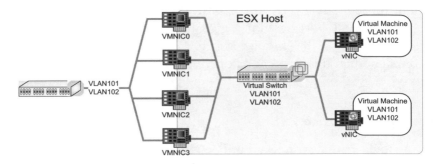

In order to configure VGT within ESX a global configuration change needs to be set that disables the capability to utilize VST for the entire host. We strongly recommend against using this configuration, and if 5 or more VLANs are required for a system, that it be reconsidered as an invalid consolidation candidate for ESX. If you wish to ignore all warnings and attempt this anyway, the following line must be added to /etc/vmware/vmkconfig:

```
Net/VlanTrunking = "0"
```

This change will not take effect until the ESX host has been rebooted.

VMotion Networking

When VMotion is a factor in an ESX design, there are a few configuration options that need to be considered. VMware makes the strong recommendation that all VMotion traffic occur on its own VLAN and that all connections be gigabit. These are simply recommendations from VMware and not requirements. Due to several circumstances including gigabit port availability, pNIC availability, and using unmanaged switches for connecting ESX to the network, we have configured VMotion in a variety of manners. Please note that these are simply a substitute when the recommended environment is not possible. If all components are in place, there is no reason why VMware's guidelines should not be followed.

One thing that we have noticed is that gigabit networking is still not widely available in most datacenters. This causes certain challenges when taking 16 windows servers and consolidating them onto a single piece of hardware with minimum performance impact. When VMotion comes into the picture, it introduces additional complexity. We have configured several ESX systems to use VMotion over a 100Mb connection. While the speed of this may be a little slower, we have yet to see a VMotion failure because the 100Mb link cannot keep up with the changes being made to a system. Instead of taking 30-60 seconds for a VMotion, the timeframe is pushed up closer to 90-120 seconds for low-utilization servers and several minutes for busier servers.

During our travels we have also found that blades are still trying to get a strong foothold in the virtualization market. One of the significant challenges with blades is the amount of network connections that may be assigned to a single chassis. In most cases, the maximum is three, which is also the minimum requirement for a redundant network design for ESX without taking VMotion into consideration. There are several tricks to get around this in a blade scenario, which we will describe shortly in this chapter. One workaround is to utilize the virtual switch that is used by the virtual machines to handle the VMotion traffic. In this case, we cannot recommend that VMotion migrations be done during production hours due to the potential impact on the virtual machines when contending for bandwidth. This solution actually breaks two of the best practices for VMotion as defined by VMware: configuring a private VLAN and not utilizing a dedicated virtual switch for VMotion traffic. This, again, is not an optimal solution, but when you have limited network connectivity in a system, it allows VMotion to function.

Blade Networking Options

The increasing popularity of blade servers as an ESX platform introduces various challenges to the networking configuration, especially when VMotion is involved. A "best practices" installation of ESX calls for at least 3 network adapters: one for the COS and two redundant VMNICs in a virtual switch for virtual machine use. In this default configuration we are already at the maximum capacity for network adapters in a blade chassis. We need to get creative if we wish to integrate VMotion into this solution. There are two different network configurations that can be utilized in this instance. We recommend that you review the advantages and disadvantages of each before attempting to make a design decision for blade configurations.

The first option is to utilize the virtual machines' virtual switch to also handle the VMotion traffic of the network. Careful analysis of network traffic needs to be performed before making this determination, as VMotion migrations can potentially impact the network performance of the configured virtual machines. When configuring VMotion within VirtualCenter you would simply state that you wish to use the virtual machines' virtual switch as the VMotion network.

Figure 4.11

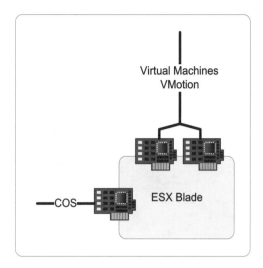

Advantages to Sharing Virtual Machine Traffic and VMotion Traffic

- COS traffic can be on a different VLAN if necessary

- No additional configuration within ESX required

Disadvantage to Sharing Virtual Machine Traffic and VMotion Traffic

- VMotion traffic can potentially impact production virtual machine performance

The second available option is utilizing the vmxnet_console driver of ESX to share eth0 and a VMNIC to handle COS and virtual machine traffic while utilizing a dedicated NIC for VMotion. As you can probably guess, significant system configuration needs to be performed before this solution can be properly utilized. This configuration utilizes a special driver that maps eth0 to a bond of VMNICs. The following steps are an advanced configuration and should only be attempted on development servers. The configurations should be performed directly from the console as there is a chance that the host will lose all network connectivity during the configuration.

Figure 4.12

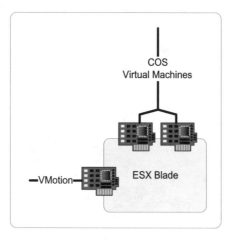

The following steps assume no virtual machines have been configured on the ESX host:

1. Modify /etc/modules.conf to comment out the line that
    begins with "alias eth0". This will disable eth0 on the next
    reboot of the ESX host.

2. Run vmkpcidivy –i at the console. Walk through the current
    configuration. When you get to the network adapter that is
    assigned to the Console (c), make sure to change it to Virtual
    Machines (v). This should be the only value that changes
    from running vmkpcidivy.

3. Modify /etc/vmware/hwconfig by reconfiguring the network
    bonds. Remove any line that begins with the following: (In
    this case, "X" can be any numeric value.)

    ```
    nicteam.vmnicX.team
    ```

    Once the current bond has been deleted, add the following
    two lines to the end of the file:

    ```
    nicteam.vmnic0.team = "bond0"
    nicteam.vmnic1.team = "bond0"
    ```

4. Modify /etc/vmware/netmap.conf to remove and recreate the required virtual switches. Since we are working under the assumption that this is a new server configuration, remove any lines that exist in this file and add the following 4 lines:

```
network0.name = "Production"
network0.device = "bond0"
network1.name = "VMotion"
network1.device = "vmnic2"
```

This will establish two new virtual switches once the system reboots. The first virtual switch will consist of VMNIC0 and VMNIC1 and will be utilized for virtual machines. The second virtual switch consists of only VMNIC2 and is dedicated for VMotion traffic.

5. Modify the /etc/rc.d/rc.local file to properly utilize the vmxnet_console driver to utilize a bond for eth0. Add the following 2 lines at the end of /etc/rc.d/rc.local:

```
insmod vmxnet_console devName="bond0"
ifup eth0
```

6. Reboot the server.

When the server comes back online, we will have a pretty advanced network configuration. The COS will actually be utilizing a redundant bond of two NICs as eth0 through the vmxnet_console driver. Virtual machines will utilize the same bond through a virtual switch within ESX and have the same redundancy as eth0. VMotion will have the dedicated NIC that VMware recommends for optimal performance.

Advantages of using the vmxnet_console Driver

• Redundant eth0 connection

• VMotion traffic will not impact virtual machine performance

Disadvantages of using the vmxnet_console Driver

• Difficult configuration that is difficult to troubleshoot

• eth0 must reside on the same VLAN as the virtual machines

Now that we have discussed a wide array of storage and networking configurations for an ESX environment, we can take a closer look at the details involved in designing our guest environment. A solid infrastructure design combined with a stable guest layout is critical to a successful VMware ESX implementation.

Chapter 5

Designing the Guest Environment

So far, most of this book has focused on the architecture and mechanics behind VMware ESX Server. We've described (sometimes in excruciating detail) the smallest components that make up ESX and the virtual environment. In contrast, this chapter focuses on the guest environment itself. This is somewhat important seeing how it's the whole reason anyone uses VMware in the first place.

In this chapter we'll look at how to create a VMware strategy for your organization and how to determine which servers in your environment will become guests in the ESX Server farms you create. Then, we'll dive directly into creating the guest virtual machines, the different ways of doing it, how to manage things like golden masters and ISOs, and strategies for configuring resource allocations for the virtual machines.

Creating a Strategy for VMware

Until a few years ago, the only people in an IT organization who had used (or even heard of) VMware were generally the developers and engineers. These original users of the VMware products used VMware Workstation and in some cases GSX Server to implement virtual machines for testing and lab development.

VMware allowed these IT pros to create quick test beds for new scripts, applications, or even to try out a new OS within their organization. Eventually, some IT departments started using VMware to host large portions of their test environments. However, even in these cases, most CIOs or CTOs still had not heard of the product. Those that had only had a passing knowledge of it.

As the practice of using virtual machines for testing grew, people started to notice (and so did VMware) that most of their other production hardware was underutilized. Most servers were over engineered from the start to save on upgrades later. In addition, more and more servers were required for everyday business, and it seemed like each new application on the network required its own dedicated server—even if all it did was run a batch job a couple of times a day.

In addition to this general production server underutilization, IT organizations also started to notice other things. The first thing they noticed was that the time they were spending provisioning, putting together, racking, configuring, and managing servers was becoming a larger part of their day. It used to be that organizations ran the same servers for long periods of time with very little change. Most management was on the application side or simple server maintenance and monitoring. Now it seems that almost every day brings a new application requiring any number of new servers—even while the old servers on the network never seem to be completely decommissioned.

As companies and datacenters grow larger, they begin to notice that the vast majority of their production servers are underutilized. Try this little exercise if you don't believe this: Walk into your datacenter and pick a rack of Windows servers. Out of the rack pick three of the servers at random. Open up the console on these servers and run performance monitor for 20 minutes on each. Look at Overall Processor Utilization and Physical memory in use. If you want, throw in a network and a disk counter. I'll bet that not one of the three is at or near a 90% utilization on any one of those counters. In most cases, when I have done this (not including Citrix environments), the servers are all less than 50% utilized on all of those "Core Four" resources.

Now we as engineers and architects think this is a good thing. This is because we know that if they are not near capacity, then the performance is as good as it can be on the server and there will be few if any complaints from the user about performance for those applications. The problem here lies in the fact that you may have a datacenter with several thousand processors in it all at an average of 30% utilization. Thirty percent! Think of that. That's like buying a car you can only drive two days a week, then having to buy two or maybe three more of those cars to fill up the rest of the days of the week.

One thing to remember about processing is this: Any server that is not running with 100% CPU utilization is "wasting" time executing idle threads. Whether you have 30% utilization or 80% utilization, there are still available CPU cycles.

Every idle tick that is processed is time when the processor is doing nothing and is waiting for you to send it more instructions. Why not use this capacity? A server at 80% is just as fast as a server at 30%— it's just waiting to be used.

It's easy to understand that VMware can help with this. The real question is how can it help your specific organization? The answer depends on where your organization's pain points are. There are basically a few different strategies for VMware. Some of these can combine and morph into smaller tactical solutions, but the basic concepts can be found in one of these three situations:

- Using VMware for test and development environments

- Using VMware for underutilized production servers

- Using VMware for ALL servers in your environment

Let's examine each of these strategies, what they entail, and the benefits and drawbacks of each.

Using VMware for Test and Development Servers

This is kind of like saying, "let's use our old hardware for test servers." Almost no one can argue with this strategy. Using VMware for a test environment is really a no-brainer. Within any size organization a single VMware ESX server can be a huge benefit to the test environment.

VMware's ability to host a large number of underutilized servers on a single piece of hardware can reduce hardware costs for your test environment by 50-75%. In addition, the ability to make a Virtual machine disk un-doable is a huge benefit. Imagine the following scenario:

A developer in your company wishes to test a new application install he has created. It works on his workstation but he hasn't tested it on any server builds yet. The catch is that each time he runs his test he has to see if the install was successful or not, and if not, he needs to start with a fresh build. Using a VMware test environment, the developer can test his install and if it has failed, it can be back to a fresh image in under a minute.

Let's take this development environment a little further. If this same developer needs to test his install against various types of server operating systems and configurations, he would ordinarily require one server of each type or else he would be forced to rebuild the server using the OS or configurations for the next test. In a VMware environment, this developer can have numerous servers all running on a single piece of hardware provisioned for just these tests. He can finish his testing sooner, utilize less of the IT staff's time, and in turn can decommission or delete the servers he used for testing if he no longer needs them. (Try doing that with a $6000 asset assigned to a specific cost center!)

Let's look at a real world example of this from one of our large clients. Before VMware, this client struggled to keep up with all of their development and test servers for their core business application. They had close to 100 test and development servers alone. After we took a look at these servers, we realized that 90% of them sat completely idle doing nothing at all on a given day.

After some calculations we determined that they could repurpose about 80 of these servers if we brought in two eight processor servers for VMware. This client was also undergoing a major expansion in their Citrix farm, and the 80 "extra" servers were a huge benefit to have from a cost savings perspective.

You're probably wondering what happened to the other 20 servers. Those 20 were used for system stress testing new applications. Since those 20 were identical to the existing production Citrix servers, we decided that we would leave these physical servers alone in order to be able to accurately test system changes (as far as performance goes) on duplicates of the production hardware.

When deciding to use VMware in your test and development environments you first must answer a few basic questions and do some discovery in your environment:

What will your production systems look like?

A test environment for a company whose production environment is hosted completely on VMware will look completely different than a test environment for a production environment consisting entirely of physical servers.

For now we won't get into the advantages and disadvantages of hosting production servers on ESX. (That comes later in this chapter.) Instead just take a look at your strategy for your production environment.

If you're introducing VMware into a test environment and your production environment will be built out of completely physical servers, then you should start by determining how many of the test/development servers are used or are going to be used for performance and stress testing. Once this number is known, you can basically rule these servers out of the VMware environment. When stress testing or gauging the performance of an application or server, you want to exactly duplicate the production environment. A performance test against a VM for an application being hosted on a physical server is basically useless.

However, the remaining servers are your VMware candidates. These servers are generally used for testing the functionality of new application code, service packs, OS upgrades, etc. These are called the "functionality" test servers because they'll be used to test the functionality of the system after a change.

These servers have just become your targeted guest operating systems. Once you have identified them, you can create a quick cost/benefit analysis showing the costs of physical servers for this environment versus virtual servers. We generally find that in test environments, the cost of virtual servers is about one third to one quarter the cost of physical servers. If the majority of your servers are idle 90% of the time, this ratio may even be higher.

Advantages of using VMware for your Test/Dev Environment

- Cost effective use of hardware

- Large portions of your production environment can be replicated on a few servers

- Lower cost of hardware for the entire test environment

- Faster rollback during testing

- Faster deployment of a new test platform

- Test VMs can be decommissioned and even deleted after they are not needed

Disadvantages of using VMware for your Test/Dev Environment

- Requires that your staff have (or learn) some basic VMware skills

- VMs are not good for load testing if your production environment is completely physical

As you can see, the advantages of using VMware in your development or test environment easily outweigh the disadvantages. On top of that, the second disadvantage can be completely mitigate by simply keeping an few pieces of hardware for load testing if you plan on maintaining physical production servers.

Using VMware for Underutilized Production Servers

VMware is also often used for production servers that have very little in the way of hardware requirements. A number of companies are beginning to realize that the strategy of application isolation (giving each application in the environment its own unique server) has left them with numerous servers that utilize very little of the physical hardware available. Often times you can look at a production server that hosts file shares for users or even the backend data for a specific department and will notice that the server is barely being used.

In this scenario, an IT department would utilize ESX Server to host multiple production servers. This allows them to retain unique servers for their applications while reducing the overall hardware requirements across the board.

This type of thinking in any other aspect of business is unthinkable, so let's look at the following scenario to see if it sounds familiar:

The accounting department in your company requests a new server for an application they've decided to implement. The application vendor states they require their own server (typical!) but that resource requirements are not very high for this server. Well even if the application only needed 300Mhz of processing power, you can't even buy that processor anymore. Instead you have to buy a machine with a 3GHz processor and since you have certain company standards you throw in mirrored SCSI drives and a gigabyte or two of memory. Now you have a server that you paid $6000 for that you're using 10% of.

In most cases even production servers are underutilized. Since we as IT professionals have been trained to make sure that the system is responsive to the end user, we've been conditioned to think that less utilization equals better performance for the user. To us it is a "good thing" when a production server runs at 20 or 30% utilization and is only using half of its physical memory. The problem here is that we (or the businesses we work for) have basically been paying for lots and lots of hardware that isn't being used. Imagine if every server in your environment ran at 50% utilization on all its resources. Now imagine that you could magically cut the number of servers in half by moving processing time, memory, etc. from one group of servers to another. You would be seen as the IT genius of the year. Why? Because it makes business sense.

All of this basically means that businesses have x% of available server resources not being used and still continue to purchase more of these same resources. It's like a company owning two buildings in downtown Chicago, both of which are only 50% full. Sure they plan to grow but they only plan to add 10 or 20% more people over all. Should they go ahead and buy a third building? Of course not. This (in business) makes no sense, but for some reason we as IT professionals have been taught this is how we do things in the Wintel world. (Part of the blame must go to the hardware vendors here, but that's another story.)

Combining numerous logical servers onto a physical piece of hardware is no longer a good idea, it's a "must do". Environments of any significant size can see a major cost savings in hardware by just putting some underutilized servers onto a single ESX server. In most large environments, the pay back for ESX is about 6 months depending on the rate of server deployment per month. For one client, the ESX payback was seen in 12 weeks, and that included factoring in consulting costs to architect the environment.

So how is it done? You can begin by looking at existing servers in your environment and even servers that are being requested. Estimates are made about the server's utilization and that helps us determine the number of guests per processor. Later in this section we'll dive into the detailed process of evaluating potential guests but for now you should understand that you will have to estimate requirements for new servers and evaluate existing servers' utilization in your environment.

Often your "newer" servers can be re-used as ESX hosts for a number of your other servers. In this strategy existing dual and quad processor servers can be re-purposed as ESX hosts. Their original operating system is migrated to a VM and other VMs are then loaded onto the "new" ESX server. This allows you to implement a server consolidation strategy with a reduced outlay in new hardware costs.

Advantages of using VMware for Under Utilized Production Servers

- Cost effective use of hardware
- Existing hardware can often be reused as ESX hosts
- Lower cost of hardware for the entire environment
- Faster deployment of new VM servers
- Fewer production network ports required
- Fewer production SAN ports required

- Less time spent provisioning and tracking hardware in the environment

- Less hardware to manage and support in the environment

- Ability to move VMs from host to host as performance dictates

- Ability to do maintenance on physical hardware without interruption to VMs

Disadvantages of using VMware for Under Utilized Production Servers

- Requires that your staff have (or learn) VMware skills

- Some software vendors do not officially support VMs

- Can require in-depth knowledge of VMware to troubleshoot performance problems

- May require you to invest in some SAN infrastructure to provide space for VMs

Using VMware for all of your production servers

While this may sound like a leap for some of us, it's really not that far fetched. VMware offers a lot of benefits aside from its major one of being able to share hardware.

When a business decides to use VMware for "all" their production servers, they rarely actually get every server on the network hosted on VMware. But the theory for such a deployment (or attempting such a deployment) is as follows:

Since very few servers on the network are truly utilized 100%, this means that a dual processor web server with 65-70% utilization still has cycles left. While in a consolidation model this server may not fit your requirements for migration into ESX, it still has hardware resources available. Let's assume that you wish to move all servers into the ESX environment. If this is a true business goal, then you could move the web server onto a quad or eight-way ESX host and still have room for other VMs. You can then select VMs for coexistence with this server that require very little in the way of resources.

This will allow you to get your maximum number of VMs per processor even though one of the VMs uses a high amount number of resources.

The general idea behind using VMware for all of your production servers is twofold:

- You can use your hardware to its maximum extent and realize all of the benefits from that

- Disaster recovery (DR) becomes extremely simple for the entire environment

Generally when people move all (or a vast majority) of their servers to VMware, it's because most of their servers are underutilized or they have a DR plan that relies heavily on the portability of virtual machines. In either case, they begin to truly use VMware to its fullest potential. Determining if this works for your environment will depend on whether most of your servers are underutilized or if you need that VM portability for DR or other purposes.

Advantages of using VMware for All or a Majority of Production Servers

- Cost effective use of hardware

- Existing hardware can often be reused as ESX hosts

- Lower cost of hardware for the entire environment

- Faster deployment of new servers

- Fewer production network ports required

- Fewer production SAN ports required

- Less time spent provisioning and tracking hardware in the environment

- Less hardware to manage and support in the environment

- Ability to move VMs from host to host as performance dictates

- Ability to do maintenance on physical hardware without interruption to VMs

- Facilitates DR for the entire Environment

Disadvantages of using VMware for All or a Majority of Production Servers

- Requires that your staff have (or learn) VMware skills

- Some software vendors do not officially support VMs

- Can require in-depth knowledge of VMware to troubleshoot performance problems

- Requires a more complex and expensive SAN infrastructure

What Makes a Good Guest?

Depending on what strategy your company has chosen for VMware will define what servers will become guests in your environment. If you have chosen to move all but the most resource intensive servers (visually picture a quad processor Exchange server running at 85% all the time or a Citrix server), almost every guest in the environment is a "good" guest. If you have decided that the test and development environments will all be hosted on VMware, then all test and development servers besides the ones used for stress testing will make "good" guests

Deciding which servers to place in the VMware environment during a consolidation is part skill and part an exercise in simple resource calculations. During the review of your server infrastructure, a decision will be made regarding each server to determine if it will continue to be physical or will be migrated or built as a virtual machine. This decision should be based on two factors:

- The physical resource requirements for the server

- The number of users or amount of activity the server will support

Often times these two factors are tightly interrelated and increase or decrease at the same time. A good example of this would be a simple database server: Being a database server by itself does not rule out the possibility of being hosted in VMware. If the database server will be built (or is being used) for a small number of users (say 40 or 50), it is likely that its hardware requirements will be extremely low (possibly lower than the resources a standard single or dual processor server may provide). In this case the server may be an ideal VMware candidate.

Turn this example around to a database server that will start with 40 or 50 users but eventually service hundreds or thousands of concurrent end users. This server's/application's requirements may require more processing power and memory than a standard dual processor server may be capable of. In this case, the major benefit of moving the server into a virtual environment (to save money on hardware by allowing server resources to be shared by multiple servers) will be undermined since the candidate will most likely consume a large portion of a single host's resources, leaving little if any room for other virtual machines.

The "ideal" candidate is a server/application that requires few physical resources (processor, memory, disk, etc.) but must be its own "stand alone" server, meaning the application it hosts cannot be logically combined or shared on another server. By looking at the server's true resource requirements, you can determine if it would use (on a normal basis) less of the hardware resources than a single physical server will provide. In most cases, physical servers are over engineered by a large margin to allow for growth (or just because you can only buy current technology, i.e., current processor speeds). This over-engineering generally applies to all resources including processor, disk, network, and memory. With VMware, this over-engineering is not necessary since resources can be maximized and resource share allocations changed as server requirements mandate, thus maximizing the use of all of your hardware.

Figure 5.1. Candidate Matrix

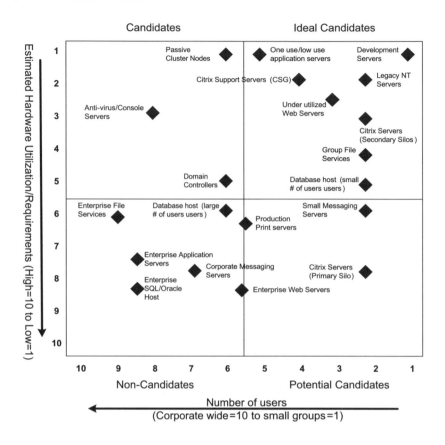

Deciding which servers are a good fit for virtualization is not always cut and dry. Based on some industry best practices and assumptions on utilization, we've developed the chart seen in Figure 5.1. This chart creates a "rule of thumb" for server types. Obviously there are exceptions to every rule, but the basic principals of comparing user load and hardware utilization will apply whenever you select a VMware candidate.

So what should I look at on a potential Guest?

When a decision is required on whether or not a server should be provisioned as (or migrated to) a virtual server, several criteria should be considered. In each case the amount of use, potential hardware utilization, number of users, and any other special hardware requirements will have to be reviewed before a decision is made.

Supported Guest Operating Systems

The first criterion to be looked at is whether the potential guest operating system is supported or not as a VM. As we said earlier in the book, VMware presents physical hardware through a virtualized "layer." While this hardware is presented as "generic" hardware, it still requires specific drivers and functionality (just like any other hardware out there).

VMware provides drivers for its virtual hardware for a number of operating systems that it supports. The supported list of operating systems for ESX 2.5 includes:

Windows Server 2003 (all versions)
Windows XP
Windows 2000 (server versions and Workstation)
Windows NT 4.0 (Server Versions and Workstations)
RedHat Enterprise Linux 2.1 and 3
RedHat Linux 7.2 +
SuSE Linux Enterprise Server 8 and 9
SuSE Linux 8.2, 9.0, and 9.1
NetWare 5.0+ Server

Since VMware ESX is an Intel server-based solution, you'll notice a trend in the operating systems it supports. All the operating systems in the list are native Intel-based operating systems. ESX server does not virtualize the hardware to a point that other processor architectures can be presented to the guest. Instead, it truly allows the guest to access the "real" hardware through a more generic type of interface.

"Core Four" Resource Utilization

One you determine that the potential guest operating system is supported, you'll need to examine the amount of physical resources required by the guest. These are resource we like to call the "Core Four".

These core four resources are the processor, memory, disk, and network requirements. As with any Intel server, the most common bottlenecks with VMware are processor and memory. However, disk and network bottlenecks can easily occur in VMware environments if you're not careful.

Since a single physical server will host multiple VMs, a hardware bottleneck can negatively impact multiple systems. By estimating resource requirements ahead of time, it's possible to not only determine if the potential guest will fit the VMware model, but will also allow a VMware administrator to determine which host will support the guest in order to maintain a good "mix" of high and low utilization virtual machines on each ESX host.

Processor

As discussed in Chapter 2, the physical processors on the ESX Server are shared amongst all the guest operating systems being hosted. By default, shares of the resource are distributed evenly between all guests (more on this later in this chapter). This sharing allows VMware to divide available processing time between all the guests evenly, assuming that all guests request an equal amount of processor time (which often isn't the case).

In almost all environments, guests will require different amounts of processor time from the host from second to second. As a guest requests processor time, the host allocates it from the available processor resources on the system. Assuming there is available processor time (idle time), the processor cycles are made available right away. If the processors on the host are 100% utilized, the host reverts to the guest resource shares to determine the priority in which to respond to guest requests. The amount of shares allocated to the guest (all guests being equal by default) determines which guests are "more important" when there is contention for the requested resource.

Share/resource allocation is discussed in depth later in this chapter, but when selecting a guest operating system, it is important to understand the basic way resources are divided.

When determining whether a candidate should be a virtual machine, it is important to estimate the actual requirements from the processor side. The most important metric to estimate will be the processor's average utilization during working hours. The second most important will be its variability—the amount (and duration) of spikes in utilization. Later in this section we'll create two examples to use during the decision process but for now we'll create a general rule of thumb based on the chart below:

Figure 5.2. Processor Usage

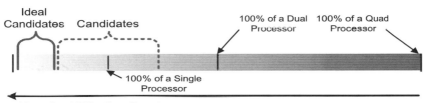

As this image shows, the most effective use of a host's processors comes from virtual machines that would have only used a percentage of their available processor resources. In addition, this assumes a 1:1 ratio when comparing the potential speed of a physical server's processor to that of the ESX host processors. If an evaluation is being done for a physical to virtual migration, and the physical server candidate is using older hardware, that needs to be factored in.

As an example, assume that a candidate machine has dual 550 MHz processors. In addition, this candidate averages 80% processor utilization during working hours. Assuming the ESX host is using 2.8 GHz processors, this candidate still falls well within the cost effective guest model using the equation below:

Figure 5.3. Processor Equation

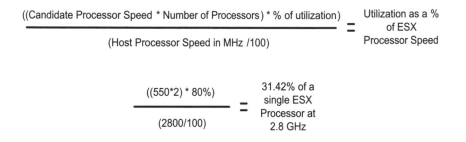

As you can see, even though this dual processor server is currently utilized at 80%, when compared properly to the faster processors, it equates to only 31% of a single processor at today's speeds. Of course this equation is simplistic and does not take into account the use of SMP, cache differences, and different processor architectures, however it can still be used to help identify a candidate and help to determine that candidate's placement in the ESX environment.

A good rule of thumb for the ESX environment used for server consolidation is to assume an average of 4-5 virtual machines per processor. This means that during work hours, each virtual machine should (by default and in a perfect world) utilize 20-25% of one of its host's processors. The reality is that virtual server utilization will fluctuate up and down, just like normal servers. This normal fluctuation will allow servers to spike and use resources as needed, then share or return those resources to other VMs throughout the day.

The amount of fluctuation in a server's processor utilization is the second aspect that should be examined. While the running average will give you a good baseline number, it may not tell the entire story. Using the example of a server that averages 30% on a daily basis, we may assume that it is a perfect fit for VMware (assuming all other resources are also in line). But if the averaged is derived from an hour of 20% utilization followed by a solid 10 minutes at 100% utilization, we may experience a problem. In normal operations servers will spike their processors for short durations; this is normal and not considered a problem. When a guest or potential guest is noted to consistently utilize all of the processor time available, it may not be a good fit for the VMware environment and the applications or its work load should be examined more closely

Memory

Much like processors, host memory is shared amongst the guest operating systems. Unlike processors, though, memory is not as dynamically shared as processor resources are. In ESX Server, each virtual machine is assigned a certain amount of memory that will be presented to the guest operating system. When the virtual machine is booted, the memory presented is directly mapped to physical memory on the ESX host. Once the guest operating system is running, ESX then begins to share the memory (this process is called transparent page sharing). In addition to physical memory and page sharing, ESX Server also maintains a swap space that will allow you to over allocate memory to your VMs. In a production environment where performance is critical, you may want to limit the use of this swap space, as memory pages for the VMs will be swapped from physical memory to the swap file as needed. This swapping process can degrade overall virtual machine performance.

The concept of memory sharing is important because it will allow us to make more realistic estimates of the required amounts of memory per virtual machine. The basic concept is that like operating systems have a large amount of data in memory that is identical. This identical data (or identical pages) can be shared between virtual machines. Assuming that the most common type of data is all 0's (memory pages not yet written to/used) then almost every virtual machine (at least upon boot) will be able to share some memory. Additionally, the more consistent the operating systems are on any given host, the more memory will be shared between them. Commonly you will see between 5% and 40% savings in memory because of this. A good rule of thumb for ESX server is about a 20% savings on average.

When examining a potential guest's memory requirements, it's important to ascertain the true memory requirements. Much like processors, we tend to overbuild for memory assuming that (a) we do not want to buy and install more memory if the server ever needs it, and (b) such an upgrade could cause down time and problems with the server. Using these two assumptions, most of us over build physical servers in order to prevent the need to upgrade later and simply because "memory is cheap".

In ESX Server, memory is often a tight commodity. One of the most common bottlenecks in most server consolidation environments is memory. With that in mind, a guest or potential guest should be looked at to determine the memory requirements for the following:

Component	Good Rule of Thumb
Operating System	128 to 384 MB
Anti-Virus and other software	30-50MB
Web and low end applications	32-128 MB
Medium intensity applications	128-512 MB
High intensity applications	512MB-1.5GB
Total VM Memory	256MB to 2GB

These numbers may look low to some engineers, but they're probably not. The reason for this is that engineers are taught to over-engineer a majority of servers they build. This is not to say that all servers fit this mold, but a large number do. The servers that do are potential VMware consolidation candidates.

In order to ascertain what your server will require (if we have to estimate, since there are no physical servers like the proposed guest), you should determine the software company's minimum recommendations for its application. From that, extrapolate some room for growth and determine if the candidate's true memory requirements are below 1.5-2.0 gigabyte. If so, the server may still be a candidate. If not, and if the server will truly use two or more physical gigabytes of RAM, then the server may utilize too many resources and possibly rule itself out (depending on your VMware strategy).

The assumption in most VMware designs is that each virtual machine will be configured with 512MB to 1.5GB of RAM. Like any other resource in ESX, the sharing aspect of the architecture allows us to over allocate resources that are on the physical server and go higher than this average on some servers. This means that a server with 16 GB of RAM could possibly host 19-20 virtual machines with an average of 1GB of RAM each without ever touching the VMware swap file (once a 20-25% memory savings and the memory used by the console operating system is figured in).

It's important to note that you don't have to overbuild a VM. The ability to increase the amount of memory on a VM is a very simple process. The change can be made via the administrative console and then the VM is virtually "powered off" and then back on. That's it! When the VM boots, the new memory is presented to the guest VM and allocated from physical memory, so there's no need to over-engineer.

Disk

The third resource of the core four is the disk or storage subsystem. Having high disk requirements do not rule out a candidate per se, it just requires some specific configurations. Disk utilization may be a concern, but often the limiting factor is not for disk IO but instead for the amount of space or type of drives required by the server.

ESX presents disk controllers to the virtual machines as a BusLogic or LSILogic SCSI interface. Through that interface, the virtual machines have access to their own unique drive which is really a .VMDK file. This file (stored normally on a high speed SAN) contains what the guest operating system sees as its physical disks and partitions. Operating Systems and applications are installed in the guest (and really into this VMDK file).

Often the amount of storage increases proportionally to the number of users utilizing the server. Additionally, the number of users accessing a specific server also increases the server's overall utilization. Assuming utilization (processor and memory) is higher than normal, but still acceptable as a guest, you should then review the storage requirements for that server.

In consolidation designs, each virtual machine is often given a fixed disk size. This size is generally in the 8-16GB range. Enterprise class servers may have a huge amount of disk I/O, meaning VMware may not be a feasible solution due to the impact the guest will have on disk throughput and possibly the cost of SAN disk. If SAN / storage space above the default VM size has already been figured into the cost of the server, and disk I/O is not a concern, then there is no reason not to make this candidate a VM assuming it meets all other criteria.

Network

Even though it's part of the Core Four resources, network connectivity is not usually a bottleneck in VMware designs. However, like the other Core Four resources, Network interfaces are shared amongst virtual machines. In the most consolidated environments, the design assumes 8-10 virtual machines per gigabit network connection. Allowing VMs to have equal shares and time on each network interface still creates an environment where each VM has at least a 100MB network connection.

With this in mind, the potential guest operating system should not be one that requires large amounts of bandwidth (assuming that large amount of bandwidth equates to the need for more than 200, 300, or maybe even 400 MB/sec of network connectivity). While this amount of bandwidth does not rule a candidate out, it requires that you place the VM on an ESX host that has a number of VMs with lower bandwidth requirements or one that has additional dedicated network cards.

Other Hardware Requirements / Server Roles

There is no "concrete" rule that dictates which types of servers can or cannot become VMs. However, there are some general rules of thumb you can apply when it comes to specific hardware required by servers and certain functions that are not as well suited to VMware. A good example of this is a fax server. Fax servers generally require special hardware such as PCI-based FAX cards. Since ESX supports a virtual hardware environment that's shared among multiple guests, support for a FAX card in an ESX server is not a good idea.

In addition to specialty hardware, there are other server functions that are not ideal for VMware due to its inherent architecture. We have found (and heard of others experiencing the same issues) that specific types of servers often hurt performance on a host even if the guest OS/VM is not using much of the core four resources. Servers that should be kept out of VMware environments include servers that require:

- A large number of kernel operations

- IDE drives

- USB / Firewire drives

- Parallel / Serial port devices (although VMware has limited support for these devices)

- Custom PCI devices

Avoiding Servers with a Large Number of Kernel Operations

One thing that's unique about ESX is the way it handles kernel calls to the processor from a guest operating system. Processor architecture is a little beyond the scope of this section, but let's review it for a second.

If you're a "Windows" person, you'll recognize terms such as "kernel mode" and "user mode" (or maybe "kernel-" or "user-level access"). These are Windows terms for access levels within a processor. In the modern Intel architecture, there are four access levels (or rings) labeled "0" through "3." Basically, Ring 0 allows full access to the processor and Ring 3 is the most restricted access. In the Windows world, we refer to Ring 0 as "system access" (like kernel mode) and Ring 3 as "user access."

In the VMware world, the ESX VMkernel runs at Ring 0. This means that kernel calls (or kernel operations) bound for the processor from guest operating systems have to be interpreted, transferred to Run Level 0, then back to the guest. The issue here is that as kernel/system calls increase, performance on the ESX host declines, even if the overall utilization of the server's core four are still low.

So what types of calls are we talking about? The most common is TCP connections. Actually, lots and lots of TCP connections. Servers that are continually creating and breaking down TCP connections may decrease host performance. Common servers that show this type of behavior are listed below:

- Proxy/ISA servers

- Web Servers hosting lots of static HTML content

- SMTP Mail Gateways

- Firewalls

Imagine a server that does nothing but create and break down these types of TCP connections hundreds of times a minute while using little of the other resources. This would create "load" on the host without affecting the core four as you would expect.

It's important to note that we're not talking about some little web server on your network for a handful of users or a mail gateway that only processes a couple of hundred e-mails a day. Instead, we're saying to be wary of servers like this that will handle an enterprise or large environment load.

IDE Drives
Servers that require IDE drives (other than the ability to mount a CD-ROM) will most likely not be a fit for VMware. ESX server does not support IDE drives for storing VMDK files or for direct access by the guest operating systems.

USB / Firewire Devices
By default, USB and Firewire devices are not supported for guest operating systems in VMware ESX. If a server requires a USB accessory or uses a USB device licensing key, it will most likely not work as a VMware candidate.

USB devices may be used by the guest in certain circumstances. To use a USB device with a VMware guest, the device must be attached to a network USB "hub". These devices are manufactured to allow a USB peripheral to be connected to a basic "hub" that is, in turn, connected to the network. Often they require a manufacturer's driver be installed in the guest to access the hub and thus the end device. While this configuration may not be optimal, it is possible and should be examined when making the decision to virtualize a potential guest.

Parallel / Serial Port Devices
VMware has the ability to map a guest operating system's parallel or serial device to the host's physical devices. The drawback here is that

there are a limited number of these devices on any given host. While the requirement for this device for a specific guest (such as a security or license dongle for an application) does not rule the potential guest out of the virtual world, the physical limitation of the number of devices available should be considered.

PCI devices

Specialized PCI devices required by some servers may not be supported within VMware. The most common of these non-supported devices are PCI cards for FAX servers. As a general rule, a server that requires a special PCI card for specific functions is not a good candidate for virtualization.

However, more "mainstream" PCI devices, such as SCSI adapters or network cards, are usually supported. In order for this to happen, the PCI device must be "ESX Compatible" and must have drivers that allow guest machines to see it as if it were a native device. Ordinarily, though, these devices would be made available as virtual devices to the virtual machines.

ESX-compatible network cards can even be "pinned" to a specific virtual machine, essentially isolating them from the other virtual machines. While this is not optimal since it limits the amount of sharing that can take place, it's a great technique to use when a guest requires a large amount of bandwidth or when security requirements dictate.

Summary

As you can see, determining when a candidate fits in the VM world is not always cut and dry. We've found that when examining numerous production servers, the vast majority are "underutilized." This is not to say that they are all running at 5% processor while only consuming 256 MB of memory, but it is not uncommon to find production servers running with 20-30% or less processor utilization with only half of their physical memory in use. It's easy in these situations to determine which servers "fit" and which ones don't.

Once you've decided on your VMware strategy and begun selecting guests, you'll probably be anxious to get the first VMs running in your environment. Before you jump too far into your deployment, there are several other items about the guest that you should be familiar with. In this section, we'll discuss "master installations" (or "golden masters"). Then, we'll move onto ISO CD-ROM image use in the ESX environments, before closing with specific VM configurations. Discussing this information now ensures you have more than a cursory understanding of VMs before jumping into your guest designs and plans.

Master Installations

Virtual machines are no different than physical machines in that deployment is made easier if you use a set of master installation images. Regardless of what physical hardware ESX is installed on, the hardware platform presented to the guest operating systems does not change. (Think about this for a second!)

This helps to minimize the number of different images you need to maintain for your environment. A general rule of thumb that most IT departments use is to create one image per operating system per hardware platform. This means if you plan on deploying four different operating system versions to two different physical systems in an environment, you would need eight images. VMware ESX simplifies this by removing the hardware dependency, resulting in less master installations and fewer images to manage.

What is a master installation?

A master installation is nothing more than a completely configured operating system installation that is up-to-date on service packs and security fixes.

Master installations typically contain the support applications such as antivirus software, management agents, or backup software. Master installations can then be imaged and "deployed" to new servers, greatly reducing the time, cost, and likelihood of error when deploying multiple servers simultaneously.

You most likely have master images for various operating systems and server hardware in your current environment. If so, resist the temptation to simply "ghost" them and use them for the master image in your ESX environment. Ghosting traditional servers can get you into trouble with SCSI and network drivers, and it probably won't save you any time in the long run. It's often much quicker to mount your operating system CD-ROM in a virtual machine and to perform the standard installation from there.

As mentioned before, you should create a master image for each operating system to be deployed in your environment, even when operating systems are of the same release. (Windows 2003 Standard and Enterprise Editions, Redhat Enterprise Linux ES and AS, etc.).

Why Master Images are Needed

There are many reasons why people use master images in VMware environments, but the most obvious is for server provisioning. Server build processes that would normally take several steps for each new operating system can easily be rolled up into the master image. This cuts significant amounts of time from the server provisioning process. Although similar diagrams have been utilized in the past, the simplified example in Figure 5.4 illustrates this point extremely well.

Figure 5.4

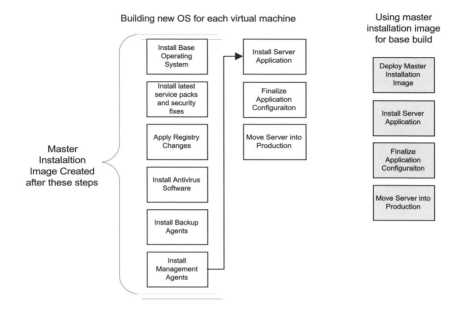

As you can see, we've managed to condense a nine-step process down to four steps. Realistically, there are a lot more steps that can be integrated into the master image than are displayed above. Even with our example, however, we've significantly decreased the complexity of server deployment.

Utilizing master installation images can also help keep a networked environment secure. We've seen too many cases where someone grabs the first Windows 2000 CD that they find to do a server installation. As soon as the installation process configures the networking components, we receive a phone call from someone in the security group telling us there is an infected computer on the network! After hunting down this server that we've never heard of, we realize a coworker is configuring a new server build with an original Windows 2000 CD and never installed the most recent service pack or virus protection software. While deploying new guests from a master image will not completely protect us, it leaves us in a much better position in terms of security than fresh installations for each new machine.

The final major benefit of master installation images is that they provide a standardized platform for your server environment. As images are deployed from the master image, you won't have to worry whether a specific registry hack was applied or whether you properly changed the administrator password. With a standardized image, you have confidence that the operating system that was deployed was built in a certain way, eliminating extraneous troubleshooting steps if something doesn't work as planned.

Storage

The strategies used to store your master installation images will directly impact how you deploy them. Typically, the images should be stored in a separate VMFS partition that every host in the environment has access to. This way, even if farms of servers have segregated disk pools from other farms, they will all still have direct access to the installation images. This prevents the images from having to traverse the network each time a host needs to provision a new virtual machine. Instead, they're transferred over the SAN which allows much higher transfer rates. SAN storage and configuration is discussed in detail in Chapter 4.

Advantages of a SAN Repository

• High-speed deployment of images

• No network utilization

Disadvantages of a SAN Repository

• Every server must have an additional LUN configured

• May impact disk performance on disk-intensive hosts

• All servers must be local to VirtualCenter management console

If a deployment tool such as VirtualCenter is used, you can also consider another storage option. This typically comes into play in configurations without SANs or enterprise-sized environments consisting of a large number of ESX hosts. It entails configuring VirtualCenter with an image repository on its local file system. Using this configuration, every server does not need direct SAN access to the same repository LUN. Any image deployed via this method will need to traverse the network, so configuring your VirtualCenter management console with a gigabit Ethernet adapter is highly recommended.

Advantages of a Network Repository

- Lower disk utilization

- No shared SAN requirement

- Can deploy images to remote locations

Disadvantages of a Network Repository

- Image deployments must traverse the network

- May require firewall rules to allow communication

- Typically slower deployment, especially when not utilizing gigabit ethernet

Checkpoints

When building a master installation image, you want to note steps which present a risk to the system integrity, especially with your first set of images for ESX. Such steps could include the installation of an untested management agent, registry changes, or even application installations. Even with the experience that we personally have with ESX and creating images for many different scenarios, we're not sure how every application available is going to act with VMware. In these cases, we take advantage of ESX's "undoable" disk mode which is explained in the next chapter. (To summarize, this allows us to set a checkpoint, and if an installation fails or causes a blue screen we can instantly revert back to before we began the process.) Alternatively, if the operation we were attempting to achieve completes successfully, we can permanently apply our changes and move to the next step.

This checkpoint process should be used several times throughout the build-out of your master installation images. This prevents a particular process or misconfiguration, especially during one of the final build steps, from forcing you to start over from the beginning. The native undo feature of VMware should be used as a time saving mechanism during your builds since it allows functionality we typically aren't afforded on physical hardware. It's not uncommon to have upwards of 15-20 checkpoints throughout the master installation build process.

What to put in a Master Image

When building a master image, several decisions need to be made as to what the image should include. Obviously we wouldn't have an image if it didn't contain the proper base operating system. (Keep in mind that you'll want a master installation image for each operating system version that you want to install. For example, you may wish to have both the Standard and Advanced versions of Windows 2000 for deployment.) Once the base operating system is laid down and configured, the first thing you should do is upgrade to the appropriate service pack and apply the latest hotfixes.

Once your based operating system is installed and patched up, the next thing you should install is the VMware tools package. Installing the VMware Tools will configure the proper drivers for the system, making the remaining steps a lot easier to complete. The following drivers get installed by the VMware Tools:

*   Video driver

*   Mouse and keyboard driver

*   Memory management driver

*   Network adapter drivers

*   Updated SCSI drivers

One of the most tedious steps in building any server can be the customization done through registry entries or file permission changes on individual system files. While a lot of this can be scripted, it still has the potential to be a tedious process, verifying everything was properly modified. By performing these changes once in a master installation image we can ensure that every future deployment has the proper settings. (Of course permission changes that are based on domain-level accounts can't be set until after the image is deployed and the server is added to the domain.)

As for applications themselves, you'll have to determine on a case-by-case basis whether a particular application can be added into the master image. It really depends on how the application reacts to a server whose name or SID changes (which will happen after your master image is deployed). While some applications in Windows may be "sysprep-aware," others will not re-register new server names properly and may have to be moved to the post-build section of your server deployment process. These types of applications are typically applications that must talk back to some form of management console.

Of course even applications that are capable of handling such changes are still susceptible to issues. When you deploy a master image, every image is built with the same name. Having the same system name constantly connecting with different IP information during the first boot can cause some management applications to have issues with duplicate entries, etc. You need to be careful with the following types of applications and perform the proper testing before determining whether they can be built as part of the master installation image:

- Management Agents (Candle, Net IQ, BMC)

- Anti-Virus software (Symantec, McAfee)

- Backup Agents (TSM, ArcServe, Netbackup)

- Other applications that must communicate back to a central management console or database (SMS, Citrix MetaFrame)

Finalizing Your Image

Once you have your base operating system and applications configured, you'll want to finalize your image and configure it in a state that will allow for the easiest deployment. For Windows master images, this typically involves running the appropriate Sysprep application.

The exact version of Sysprep that you need is dependent on the operating system version. Windows 2003 provides the Sysprep tools on the installation CD in the deploy.cab file under the "support" directory. For Windows 2000 images, you can download the proper files from Microsoft via:

```
http://www.microsoft.com/windows2000/downloads/tools/
sysprep/
```

Once Sysprep has been run, your system will be in a state that is perfect for imaging. The next time the system is powered on, it runs the "New Server Installation" wizard that is typical of all new Windows operating system builds. It prompts for server name and IP information. (The exact options that this setup wizard uses can be controlled in a configuration text file, allowing you to enforce uniformity across your environment.)

After your master image is all set, you'll need to move it to its final resting place. The exact method of doing this will depend on your image repository infrastructure described previously. If you're storing your VMware images in a SAN repository, your image should already be in the proper location to be rapidly deployed. Since every server in your environment can see the SAN repository, there is no reason to move your image to a new location. Deployment of images in this fashion will be explained in the next section called "Managing VMDK Files."

Images that are stored using a deployment tool such as VirtualCenter must be properly imported. This process will vary depending on which tool is being used to provision new operating systems. Since this process must be performed over the network, it may take some time to complete depending on the amount of network traffic between the ESX host server containing the master VMDK file and the deployment application's management console.

Summary

With proper planning, you can cut a significant number of steps out of your server provisioning process. This not only speeds up deployment time for new server instances, but also provides many benefits of a standardized image for your infrastructure. By keeping your images up-to-date as new security and operating system fixes become available, you can ensure the integrity of your network environment by not deploying new servers that are vulnerable to the newest virus.

ISO Images

When designing and implementing your VMware solution, you'll undoubtedly end up utilizing several ISO images. (This is not to say that all of these images will be specific to VMware.) The majority of ISO usage comes in the form of a guest operating system and application installation media. Dealing with ISO images is far more convenient than working with individual CDs. Gaining physical access to a host server is not always a simple task in production environments. ISO files are also far less likely to grow a pair of legs and walk away than a CD would be. Creating and storing a set of ISO images will provide quick access to the operating system and application components when you need them.

What is an ISO file?

An ISO file, in the simplest terms, is a single file that contains an "image" of a physical CD-ROM disc. The name is derived from the ISO 9660 file system standard created by the High Sierra group in 1988. It represents a standard CD layout that hardware platforms are capable of reading. An ISO file can be created by several different utilities and is an exact copy of the physical CD that was used as its source, including any information that makes it bootable.

Creating ISO Files

As mentioned before, there are several utilities you can use to create ISO image files. Most of the major CD burning packages distributed with CD or DVD burners have the capability to create ISO images. If CD recording software is not available, there are several commercial programs for Windows that will allow you to create ISOs. Some of the more popular applications are Undisker (www.undisker.com) and WinISO (www.winiso.com).

Most distributions of the Linux operating system, including the version packaged as the ESX console operating system, include native tools to assist in creating and manipulating ISO images. The "dd" command allows you to pipe standard input from a file or directory and export the standard output to a file. Using this definition, we can run the following command to take the contents of a CD-ROM drive and export it to an ISO file:

```
# dd if=/dev/cdrom of=/vmimages/filename.iso
```

Since this command will work with every available version of Linux, it can be run on a standalone workstation. (You can then copy the ISO file to your repository.) Alternatively, the command can be run locally on the ESX host without the need to transfer files over the network.

Storing ISO Files

A folder full of ISO images takes up quite a bit of disk space. ISO files are not compressed when they're created, so they end up being the exact size of the CD-ROM itself. We need to take the amount of image files that will be stored on an ESX host into consideration when planning the disk partition layout. VMware, (as well the authors of this book), strongly recommend that a separate partition be created for storing these image files. It has been our experience that there is usually an image created for each operating system that will be running as a guest within ESX (several images for some Linux distributions). Although these images typically are not used once the golden masters are created, it's best to leave them in place. Murphy's Law will often dictate that as soon as you delete your ISO images, you will need them for one reason or another.

The images themselves should be placed in subdirectories, especially in cases of a Linux distribution which could have as many as four CD images associated with it. The naming convention of the directories and files should make it easy to determine exactly what an image is at a quick glance, such as in the layout in shown in Figure 5.5.

Figure 5.5

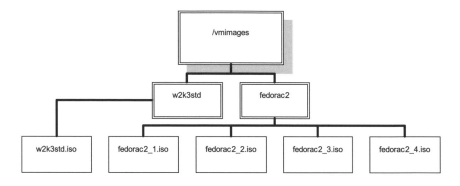

Copying ISO Images to ESX Server

Once an ISO image has been created, there are several different ways to get it transferred to your ESX server for use depending on your source operating system and ESX security settings.

From Windows

On a default ESX Server installation, the server is set to "High Security" which only leaves encrypted communication methods open. If this setting is changed to enable the FTP server locally, we can use any Windows FTP client (including the command line) to transfer our ISO files to the ESX console operating system. Be careful, though. Windows has a nasty tendency to want to transfer everything in ASCII mode by default in its FTP client. Therefore, you need to ensure you change this to binary mode before copying the file to ensure file integrity on ESX. This can be done by simply typing "bin" at the FTP command line after a connection is established.

When security is left at the default value, the only way to transfer files to the console operating system is to use the SSH protocol. Since Windows does not have native support for SSH, you need to download a third party utility to move your files. Fortunately, there are open source applications freely available that allow you to turn Windows into a SCP (Secure CoPy) client. One application in particular, WinSCP (http://winscp.sourceforge.net/eng/index.php), provides all the functionality required for performing file transfers between a secured ESX host and a Windows operating system.

From Linux (Or another ESX Host)

Like Windows, Linux has a built in command line FTP client that is used in a nearly identical fashion. Unlike Windows, Linux knows to use binary transfer mode by default, but it does not hurt to verify the transfer mode before you start copying files. With Linux, you may need to type the word "binary" in its entirety to switch transfer modes.

Linux also has a native command line SCP application that you can utilize to securely copy your files to ESX. While it doesn't provide a graphical representation of the local or remote file system, it's still an extremely powerful tool. To properly utilize the application to copy an image from Linux to ESX, you can use the following command:

```
# scp /tmp/sourcefile.iso username@remotehost:
/vmimages/osname/destfile.iso
```

If this is the first time you're establishing an SCP or SSH session with the remote host, you will be prompted to accept an authentication key, which it is safe to do. The command above provides all the information, including credentials, to connect to the remote host.

Since the console operating system of ESX is based on the Redhat 7.2 distribution, the same Linux methods will work if you need to copy an ISO image from one host to another. This is often times easier than trying to either store large amounts of ISO images on a desktop or recreate an ISO and copy it to a new ESX host whenever it is required.

Using ISO Images

Once we have our images copied to a remote ESX server there are several things we can do with them. They can be accessed directly as if they were a CD-ROM on the console operating system, or they may be configured for virtual machine use.

Mounting ISO Images via the Console Operating System

The console operating system can mount an ISO image and treat it as if it were a physical CD. This is convenient when attempting to install a management or backup agent from CD media and the datacenter storing the ESX host is not easily accessible. An ISO could be created for the installation media and installed on the remote host without ever touching the server. To mount an ISO image on the console operating system, you can use the following command:

```
# mount -o loop /vmimages/w2k3std/w2k3std.iso
/mnt/cdrom
```

Once mounted, the ISO image acts exactly as a physical CD would. The installation process of an application from an ISO image is usually faster than that of a physical CD due to faster read times from a hard disk. When the installation is complete, you should "unmount" the ISO image. This frees up your /mnt/cdrom mount point and frees up some system resources. Make sure nothing is accessing the ISO image, including the console, and run the following command:

```
# umount /mnt/cdrom
```

It's important to note that the command to unmount an ISO or CD is "umount," without the first "n". Also, if you're browsing the contents of a mounted volume when you try to unmount it, you will generate a "Device is in use" error.

Mounting ISO Images from within Virtual Machines

The main reason we're interested in copying ISO files to an ESX host is so that they can be used by a virtual guest operating system. ESX allows us to map our ISO image to a virtual CD-ROM drive of a guest machine. This is required for our first set of golden masters that we create and may be necessary for any third-party support applications we want to install. We can map this virtual CD in one of two ways.

MUI

By drilling down into the hardware section of a particular machine in the MUI, we can edit the CD-ROM properties. The default setting for a newly-created machine is to map to the physical device /dev/cdrom of the host system automatically at power on. It's a best practice to disable this device from automatically connecting since it consumes resources that can be utilized elsewhere.

To map an ISO image to the particular guest, change the device from "System DVD/CD-ROM Drive" to "ISO Image". When designating the location of the ISO, it's important to remember that the path is relative to the console operating system—not the system you're connecting from. Once the configuration is saved, you should be able to immediately utilize the newly-mapped ISO image in the designated virtual machine. Mapping of a CD-ROM drive to an ISO or physical drive can be performed at any time, regardless of system power state.

Remote Console

Using the Remote Console follows the same principals as the MUI, but is quite a bit easier to use. Like the MUI, the CD-ROM mapping can be changed no matter what power state the virtual machine is in. After drilling down to the CD-ROM drive in the Remote Console, you can either type in the path of the ISO file, or utilize the browse button to locate the appropriate image.

Common Issues with ISO Files

The authors of this book spent significant time on the VMware Community Forum and have found a surprising number of issues in which there are problems using an ISO image inside a virtual machine. After doing some research, we've come up with a few things you can quickly and easily check to avoid long headaches.

Checking File Integrity using the MD5 Algorithm

Since ISO images tend to be fairly large files, when transferred over the network they are susceptible to damage from things such as network latency or system resource utilization. It does not take much for a file to get corrupted during its copy process. Fortunately, there's an easy way to verify the integrity of the file on both the source and destination system using the MD5 algorithm

One of the first ISO images that most people encounter is the image downloaded from VMware's website for the ESX installation media. When you successfully log into VMware's website to download ESX, you'll notice the md5sum located near the download link. After downloading the file, you'll want to verify its md5sum on the computer it was downloaded to before burning it to a CD. Depending on which operating system you downloaded the ISO image to, there are several ways in which you can check the md5sum.

Verifying the Checksum on Linux

Like most utilities that typically require third-party software for Windows, Linux natively supports checking an md5sum. With a simple command, you can collect the checksum of any file:

```
# md5sum filename
```

In the example of checking an md5sum of an ESX ISO image, compare the 32 character sum that is returned with the information provided by VMware to ensure that the file was downloaded without corruption. If the sums do not match, you'll have to start from scratch and attempt to re-download the ISO image.

Verifying the Checksum on Windows

There are several free applications that do the same thing for Windows that can be used to generate md5sum information from files. There is one application in particular, winMd5Sum (http://winmd5sum.solidblue.biz/), that has a "compare" feature integrated. This is extremely handy and prevents human error from trying to compare a 32 character key.

Figure 5.6

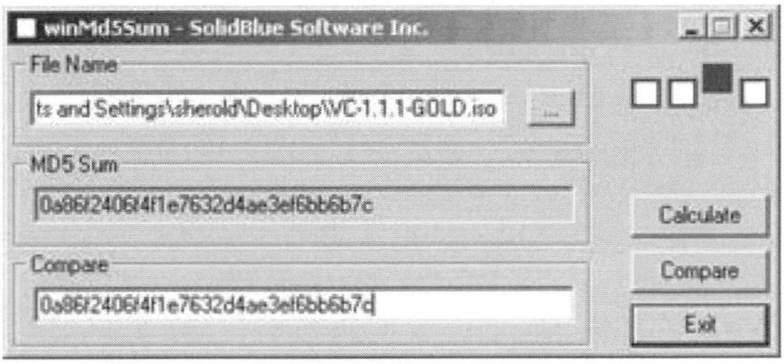

Verification

Every time an ISO image is moved, the md5sum should be verified. Even though you've probably never done this before, we cannot stress how much suffering this can potentially save you when dealing with your ESX host.

Booting From an ISO Image

The first time you power on a newly-built virtual machine, an NVRAM file is created. This is the file that stores the BIOS settings of the virtual machine. The default action of the virtual BIOS is to boot from the CD-ROM the first time it loads. Regardless of whether a bootable CD is actually found, the BIOS boot order is then changed to make the CD-ROM the last boot option. What this means is that if you fail to mount a bootable CD during the first power on, you'll have to go into BIOS and modify the order in which the system searches for boot devices. You'll usually recognize this issue by the fact that the virtual machine attempts to perform a network boot even though a bootable CD is mounted.

Guest Machine Networking

Now that you have a method to get your virtual machines installed and built, you'll probably want them to talk to the network. In fact, you may even want to control which of these servers can talk to the network, which are completely isolated from the network, and which are firewalled off from the other VMs and the network. This is where your control over virtual networking comes into play.

We'll start off by discussing some basic configurations and delimitations. Right off the bat, it's very important to separate the idea of physical NICs and switches from their virtual counterparts, and it's even more important to understand how the two interact (or don't interact) depending on configuration. (Physical NICs and their configurations were covered back in Chapter 4.) In this chapter we're going to look at the network from a guest VM point of view (and just touch on the physical aspect in case you skipped right to this chapter).

Physical Network Cards and Virtual Switches

While the physical network cards and their configuration are discussed in detail in Chapter 4, in this section it is important to understand and review some of the basics. In each ESX host, one or more physical adapters will be configured for use by the virtual machines running on that host. In most production configurations, at least two and as many as four to eight NICs are often configured as VMNICs. (The name "VMNIC" refers to the physical NICs on the host that are configured to be used by the virtual machines and not the console OS.)

No matter how many VMNICs you have, you'll have at least one virtual switch. You can imagine a virtual switch simply as a standard 32-port switch with the VMNIC assigned to the switch acting as an uplink from the virtual switch to your physical network.

Thinking along these lines, you also have the ability to use multiple VMNICs (physical network cards) in a bonded configuration which can then be associated with a specific virtual switch. This configuration provides redundancy (within the physical infrastructure) and allows for a higher amount of throughput from the VMs to the physical network.

We won't go into great detail on VMNIC configuration in this chapter. The important thing to understand here is that each VM you create is connected to a virtual switch, and that virtual switches can be associated with physical NICs to allow for network connectivity.

Virtual Switches

Like a physical switch, a virtual switch lets you connect a computer (in this case a VM) with a network card to the network. Virtual switches can be attached to the physical network via a VMNIC or NIC bond, or they can be completely virtual with no outside connection (only connected to the VMs running on the ESX Server).

To understand this, think of the virtual environment as a whole infrastructure with running machines, network connections, and switches. Let's look at Figure 5.7 (on the next page) as an example.

Figure 5.7

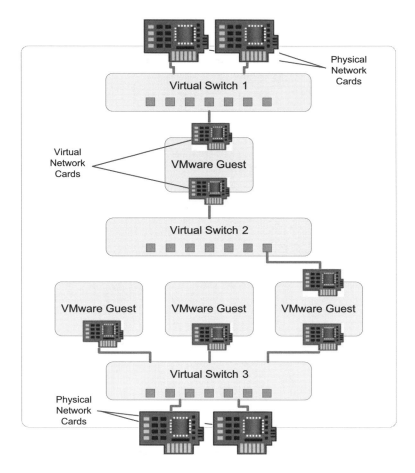

As you can see, the diagram shows a sample ESX host using multiple virtual switches. Notice that only Switch 1 and Switch 3 are "up-linked" to physical network cards. In this example, you can also see that the virtual machines utilize virtual network cards to connect to the switches. The way these cards are configured by the ESX administrator determines which switch they're connected to. In addition, you may also notice that Switch 2 is not connected to any VMNICs. Instead, this switch is completely virtual, moving network data between connected guests without ever being connected to the physical network. As you can see, virtual networking is not that different from normal networking. The trick here is to understand how these switches work and when you want to utilize multiple virtual switches.

ESX Server allows you to create as many virtual 32-port Ethernet switches as needed. Most people think that the NICs on the ESX server are "virtualized" and that the guests just use these virtualized NICs. This is not true at all. Instead, each VM has its own virtual NIC(s) that are then connected to a virtual switch. The virtual switch can then transfer traffic between virtual machines or link to external networks. This basically turns ESX's networking into an extension of the network it is plugged into.

Creating a Virtual Switch

Creating a virtual switch from within the Web Interface is a fairly straightforward process. While we won't show a bunch of screen shots showing how to do this, we will give you the basic steps and make some observations about the configuration options you will encounter.

The virtual switches and network connections configuration can be accessed as root under the Options tab | Network Connections selections. You can add the virtual switch by selecting "Add" at the top of the page. Once you do this, you'll be prompted to configure the new switch and should be aware of several configurable settings.

The "Network Label" is basically a friendly name used for switch identification. We like to name these in accordance with the network subnet the switch is plugged into. For example, if the VLAN or subnet is 10.1.17.0, then we name the switch accordingly. This type of naming has two benefits:

- It identifies the switch clearly and easily for everyone.

- It keeps a consistent naming convention across ESX hosts within a virtual farm infrastructure. While this may not seem important now, you'll find out throughout this book that in order to use functionality like VMotion, the ESX server hosts, their network labels, and the LUNs they see on the SAN all must be configured identically.

If the switch you're creating is not connected to the network, you should choose a simple name for it that fits within your design. Generally this will be called something like "Internal_0." This allows you to identify that it's an ESX-internally connected switch only, and with the 0 suffix you can add more of these internal switches as needed.

Once you select a network label, you'll then need to bind an outbound adapter to the new switch if you want it to communicate with the real external network. When binding to the physical NIC, you can select either an outbound adapter or a bond—these both have the same functionality, and they are both physical NICs connected to the physical network. The difference is that a bond is numerous physical NICs bonded together to provide fault tolerance and increased throughput (as covered in detail in Chapter 4).

At this point you may want to jump right in and create a new switch to get started testing the guests. If you're a bit nervous now that we have talked about naming conventions, designs, and requirements for virtual farms, you can relax knowing that you can always rename or edit a switch at a later time. Of course to make a switch change (like renaming it), you need to connect all your VMs to other switches first, but this is not a big deal.

What if I need more out of my switches?

You may be thinking that this default configuration is great for your lab, but that your production environment may have VMs on different VLANs all on the same host. Or maybe you want to configure load balancing or fault tolerance for your switches and VMNICs. While all of this is possible, it's a little off topic for this chapter and is covered in detail in Chapters 3 and 4. Chapter 3 helps determine the types of hardware you want, and Chapter 4 goes into the detail of configuring those NICs and virtual switches.

Virtual Network Cards

As stated previously, each virtual machine maintains virtual network cards. In fact, you have the ability to support up to four virtual network cards per VM. These cards, in turn, connect to virtual switches you create within ESX. You generally won't need more than one virtual NIC unless you are separating traffic to multiple networks for security or routing purposes. This is because the redundancy you may require for the server is handled at Virtual Switch/VMNIC level and not within the VM. A failure of a physical NIC (if bonded to another physical NIC) is transparent to the VM. The VM just continues to communicate with its virtual switch.

So what are these virtual NICs? The NICs are basically virtualized hardware provided by VMware. The two types of NICs that are supported are the "vlance" and the "vmxnet." The vlance is really an AMD PCNET-32 compatible piece of virtual hardware. This device is supported in almost all guest operating systems out there and the driver is readily available (even for DOS bootdisks) within the guest environment. The vmxnet device requires a VMware-specific driver. None of the guest operating systems have native support for this driver and it must be installed manually.

So why did VMware create two different kinds of virtual NICs? One provides support for pretty much any guest out there (vlance), and the other can be installed for better performance within your VM guest (vmxnet.).

Advantages of using the vlance virtual NIC

- Compatible with the AMD PCNET-32 devices
- Compatible with most operating systems
- Used by default during the install of a guest

Disadvantages of using the vlance virtual NIC

- Lower performance than the vmxnet device
- Has more CPU overhead than the vmxnet device

The vlance driver is a nice simple driver that will support almost any guests you try to install in ESX. It's downfall (if you can call it that) is that it requires a little more processor resources and is not as fast as the vmxnet device.

Advantages of using the vmxnet virtual NIC

- High performance device written to optimize network performance within a VM

- Recommended for use on gigabit segments and when using virtual networks

Disadvantages of using the vmxnet virtual NIC

- Will require a VMware supplied driver for the NIC to function

- May not support some guests' operating systems

If you're installing a VMware guest manually, the vlance network card is the default that will be used. Once the system is up and functioning, the most common way to install the vmxnet driver is to install the VMware Support Tools. Besides optimizing the video and mouse drivers for the VM, these tools also install the new network driver. You can then power down the virtual machine and change the network card type to vmxnet.

If you're planning on using golden images for your VM deployment (see the "Golden Masters" section of this chapter), you can install the tools directly into the images. This allows you to create the new VMs with the vmxnet network card and be assured that it will be seen by the guest operating system.

If you're more of a "hands on type of guy," you also have the ability to mount the VMware tools data like a CD and manually install the drivers. In a Windows guest you can disable the autorun feature of the CD-ROM drive, then from the guest console, select Settings |VMware Tools Install. This will mount the VMware tools image as a CD-ROM within the guest. From here you can browse for you drivers and install them manually. This is probably more of a pain than it is worth. The proper install catches all of the drivers and helps with the VMware tools service that does useful things like synchronizing the guest clock to the host clock, and installing all of the proper drivers.

Using Multiple Virtual NICs

People often ask us if it makes sense to use multiple virtual NICs in virtual machines. This question usually comes from engineers used to physical machines having two NICs for redundancy and wanting the same for their VMs. In this case, the answer to this question is "no."

A VM does not require two virtual NICs for fault tolerance. Instead, the single virtual NIC is associated with a switch that has its outbound connection configured to a bonded set of VMNICs. These physical NICs provide the redundancy for the entire virtual switch they're configured for. If one of the VMNICs should fail, the others in the bond continue to function as normal with no interruption on the guest side.

That being said, the only reason to have multiple virtual NICs in a VM is when you want to have a multiple connections to multiple virtual switches. If these switches are internally routed within the ESX or are "up-linked" switches configured with outbound VMNICs, multiple virtual NICs begin to make sense. Let's look at the Figure 5.8 (on the next page) to get a better sense of this.

Figure 5.8

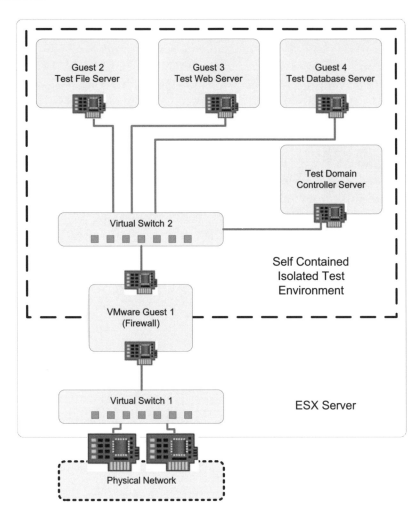

Figure 5.8 shows an isolated test environment. Notice that Guest 1 has two virtual NICs. One NIC is connected to Virtual Switch 1 and the other to Virtual Switch 2. In this case, Virtual Switch 1 is associated with a VMNIC 1 and can "talk" directly to the physical network. The second virtual NIC in Guest 1 is connected to Virtual Switch 2. This switch is an internal switch only. The remaining guest can only talk to other VMs connected to that switch. Since Guest 1 is a Firewall, it controls what traffic is routed to the Virtual Switch 1 and thus the physical network.

As you can see, the most common reason for using two virtual NICs in a guest is to create a firewall between the guest and the physical network. Another reason would be to have multiple virtual switches associated with different bonds on different subnets, allowing a guest that needs access to both subnets (multi-homed) to be connected to both with multiple virtual NICs.

MAC Address for Virtual NICs

One common question from engineers (and for network and security guys) is about what MAC addresses these virtual NICs use. Some people assume that the virtual NICs are piggybacking on the MACs of the physical NICs. This is not true. Each virtual NIC has its own unique MAC address—just like a physical NIC—and the MAC address you see passed through the switch is that of the NIC on the virtual machine.

Controlling Guest Resource Usage

Okay, so now you have some virtual machines that are using host resources and their networking is all set up.

As you run your environment, you'll probably like to control the amount of resources used and give preference to certain virtual machines. That is what resource shares and min/max settings are all about. The minimum and maximum settings are absolutes. This means that virtual machine X will never get less than Y amounts of memory or more than Z amount of memory. On the other hand, "shares" are a way to give preference to a guest operating system when the resource being sought is scarce. Let's examine each of these separately since they're two different ideas.

The Basics of Min/Max Settings

Let's start with a look at a virtual machine's Min/Max memory settings since they are the easiest to visualize and explain. You can find the minimum and maximum memory settings in the memory tab of the properties for a specific VM in the MUI. Let's assume you've configured a specific VM for 384MB of memory using the MUI with default settings. ESX Server sets the maximum memory to 384MB and the minimum to 0MB. This means that at any time, the VM may never have more than 384 MB of physical memory or less than 0MB of physical memory.

Assuming this VM is idle and other VMs require access to physical memory, this VM's memory can be redistributed to other active VMs all the way down to 0MB. This does not mean that the VM will see no memory! It just means that the reported memory to the guest (384MB) is not physical memory but instead swapped memory.

If you want to guarantee that the VM has a certain amount of physical memory at all times, you need to set a higher minimum. Let's assume you want to ensure some minimum performance level by guaranteeing a VM a portion of the memory you have allocated – maybe 192MB. You can set your minimum to 192 and the max to 384. This means that any memory above 192MB can be redistributed to other VMs when not in use. The original 192 MB will never be redistributed but instead will always be reserved for use by that particular guest.

Now let's apply this idea to the other resources on the server. Looking at the processor, you have the ability to set the min and max between 0 and 100% (the default is min 0 and max 100%). If you wish to allocate a certain amount of processor time to a VM, regardless of whether or not they will use it, you should set the Minimum above 0%. This will allocate that percentage to that VM at all times. The drawback to this configuration is that if you were to allocate 10% to the VM that is usually idle, you have basically removed 10% of an available processor's power from all the other VMs.

Conversely, you can set a maximum amount of processor utilization on any virtual machine. Let's assume you have a VM that runs a batch process once a day. During this process it max's its processor utilization for 20-30 minutes at 100%. You may decide that that you want to limit this VM's processor utilization to 50%, even if that means its batch job will take longer to complete. This is basically "processor throttling" at the host level for that VM. The VM will only be allowed to use 50% of a single processor and will reduce the impact on other running VMs on the ESX server. The drawback to that is that the batch process running takes twice as long to complete.

The trick here is to understand the consequences of setting maximums and minimums. Minimums guarantee a specific amount of a resource to the VM but deny that much of the resource to other VMs. Maximums deny the VM a portion of a resource while allowing other VMs more access to that resource.

For the disk and network resources, we don't have the same configurations for Min and Max as we do with memory and processor. Memory and processor are easily throttled and controlled while disk and network work under a different set of rules. Disk access is controlled by shares (discussed later in this section), and the network resource is controlled via traffic shaping (again, discussed later in this section). For now it's only important to understand the Min and Max theory.

Resource Shares (CPU and Memory)

Now that you understand Min/Max settings, we can begin to look at share settings. In the memory example from the previous section, we created a VM with a Minimum of 192MB and a maximum of 384MB. While this is fairly straightforward on its own, we need to look at what happens when the physical ESX Server starts to run out of memory. At some point, the ESX Server will have to decide which virtual machines take preference if multiple ones are competing for the same physical resources. This is where "share" settings come into play.

Shares of a particular resource determine how that resource above the minimum is redistributed to other VMs. Let's assume that our original VM is sitting idle and two other VMs are vying for physical memory. If both of these new VMs are configured with the exact same minimums and maximums as the original, a default share configuration would cause the remaining psychical memory to be distributed evenly between the two. However, you can give preference to one VM over another by increasing its share allocation.

In ESX Server 2.1 and higher, share allocation is always represented with some type of number. Using the simplest example (processor shares), we have numbers between (basically) 1 and 4000. The share settings seen in the MUI or in VMware's VirtualCenter allow you to set one of 4 possible configurations: low, normal, high, or custom. The first three settings are easy to visualize. The normal setting provides twice as many shares as low, and the high setting is twice as many shares as normal. Take a look at the following table to help equate these settings to numbers for easy visualization.

Share Setting	Shares (as a number)
Low	500
Normal	1000
High	2000

Now let's assume that processor resources on your ESX Server are in contention. (There are lots of VMs looking for processor time and very little to go around.) Of our three VM,s one is set to high (or 2000 shares) and the others are set to normal (1000 shares). In this case, the VM with the 2000 shares would receive as much processing time as the other two VMs combined. This of course assumes that no Min or Max settings are configured for any of the VMs. The share settings are there to basically determine where resources should go when a resource is under contention. If there is no contention, then all of the VMs receive their requested amount of the resources. This differs from the Min and Max settings that are there to guarantee a specific amount of a resource whether the resource is scarce or not.

When would I use Shares versus Min/Max Settings?

By default, each VM receives "normal" share allocations and Min/Max settings, so you're actually using them at all times even if you don't know it.

For each VM, processor Min and Max settings are 0% and 100%. Memory is configured with a Min setting of 0MB and a Max setting equal to the amount of memory that you configured for the VM. (As stated before, disk and network settings are a little different and don't necessarily have a min/max setting.

As for shares, each VM starts out with "normal" settings for each resource. For processors, this is 1000 shares per processor presented to the VM. For memory, it equates to 10x the amount of memory assigned to the VM. (384MB of memory would have 3840 shares.) These settings create an environment where all VMs split resources evenly. If you run an environment and want to guarantee that certain VMs get more resources, then you need to modify this behavior.

For example, if you mix production VMs and development VMs on the same ESX Server, you might choose to configure the development VMs for a "low" share setting to minimize the chance that their execution would negatively impact production VMs.

Another situation where setting VM shares is useful is when you have applications with varying levels of sensitivity on the same ESX host. If one production server (or its hosted application) is deemed "more important" or more "performance sensitive" than the others, its shares can be increased to ensure that its performance is better than the other VMs when resources get tight.

What about Disk and Network Shares?

As we mentioned before, disk and network resources are handled a little differently than processor or memory. On the disk side there are no Min/Max settings and the host determines usage purely by the share settings. Disk shares determine the percentage of disk bandwidth that a virtual machine is allowed to use. Like the other resources, all VMs receive equal access to disk resources by default. If there is contention on the disk resource and specific VMs are disk sensitive, you should increase the shares for that VM.

The network resources on your host do not use shares like the three of the four core resource do. Instead, ESX Server allows you to enable network shaping on a "per VM" basis. This shaping effects outbound network bandwidth only and can limit bandwidth according to the values specified by the ESX Admin.

Once traffic shaping has been enabled for a VM, you need to provide three values:

- *Average Bandwidth:* This specifies the average bandwidth the VM should be allowed to use

- *Peak Bandwidth:* Limits the bandwidth on the VM during traffic bursts

- *Burst Size:* The amount of data that may be sent out in a single burst (a burst exceeding the Average Rate)

Due to the nature of network traffic (inherently bursty and sometimes unpredictable), you need to configure these three setting to create an average that the server should be allowed, an amount of peak bandwidth to allow (during bursts above average), and a burst size that limits how much data can be sent during a burst (at peak bandwidth) before the server is throttled back to average.

As an example, let's imagine a VM that hosts a simple web server. This server is often used to view static pages but also provides large files that are downloaded by users. You want to limit this VM's average bandwidth to 2Mb. However, when a user downloads a large file you want the server to go to its peak bandwidth of 10Mb for a burst size of 1Mb (the average size of the file being downloaded). While this example doesn't fit every situation, it gives you an idea of what can be controlled as far as the VM's network is concerned. Once the server bursts above the 2Mb average, it will be allowed to use 10Mb until it has transferred a total of 1Mb of data. After this point the server is throttled back to its average bandwidth. In the real world very few people use these controls and instead opt to install more NICs or gigabit NICs in their servers.

Beyond Shares and Min/Max Settings

There are two more settings that you can use to tweak the performance of your environment, in addition to the share and min/max settings. These are called the "Idle Memory Tax" and "Processor Affinity" settings. While these do not have the impact that shares or min/max settings have, the knowledge of what they do and how to use them will allow you to create a better performing VM environment.

Idle Memory Tax

When share allocation for memory takes effect (i.e., memory is in short supply), VMware provides a mechanism to prevent a virtual machine from hoarding memory it may not be using. Just because a particular VM has four times the memory share priority of another, does not necessarily mean it requires it at the time allocation takes place. This is where the idle memory tax kicks in.

The Idle Memory Tax is a process that associates a higher "cost value" to unused allocated shares of memory. This higher cost is only applied to unused memory and not applied to memory that is actively in use within the virtual machine. This taxing process allows the virtual machine to release the unused memory for use on other guests that may require it.

In its default configuration, the ESX host may reclaim up to 75% of the idle memory from within a VM. This rate can be adjusted by modifying the "MemIdleTax" option within ESX's advanced options. Additionally, you have the ability to change the frequency at which ESX Server polls for idle memory. The default setting of 30 seconds can be changed by modifying the "MemSamplePeriod" in the advanced option section of the Web Interface.

This setting is left alone in most production environments since it is pretty aggressive as it is, and the 30-second polling intervals are generally fine. If you happen to have a number of VMs that require large amounts of memory every once and awhile, then you may get some boost out of this. Of course if they rarely use all the memory you've assigned to them, you should probably think about scaling back the amount of memory you've assigned to the VMs before beginning to change a system wide setting that affects all VMs such as this Idle Memory Tax.

Processor Affinity

In addition to setting processing thresholds using one of the methods described previously, you also have the ability to control which physical processor or processors each virtual machine may use. This control, called processor affinity, can be coupled with the other processor settings and gives you complete control of virtual machine processor usage.

Figure 5.9

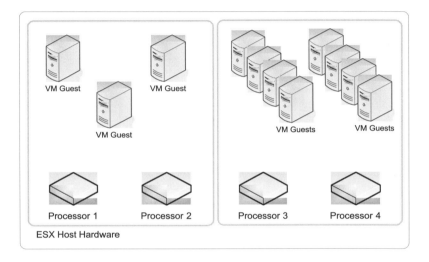

Processor affinity is not limited to specifying a single processor. By specifying a group of processors, you can tell ESX that it is allowed to allocate resources only from the selected processors, leaving the remaining processors inaccessible to the virtual machine. Critical application servers, such as database servers, may be the only virtual machines pinned to two processors on a host, while the front-end services may be running on the remaining six processors. This configuration can guarantee that the database has the required processing to support its guests.

So why would you use this? In most cases you won't. Processor affinity is generally configured to either troubleshoot a specific VM (dedicating it a processor and assuring it has all the resources it needs) or to ensure performance of a specific VM. Often times this is used to isolate resource-intensive VMs from the rest of the infrastructure.

Assuming you have a VM that is constantly spiking processor usage and requires that it not be throttled, setting processor affinity is a good way to isolate that VM and protect its performance while still protecting the performance of the remaining VMs on the host.

Managing VMDK Files

Before we can accurately describe a VMDK file, we should first review the VMFS file system. VMFS is covered completely in Chapter 4, but you can get by right now by just understanding the basics. VMFS is a proprietary file system developed by VMware that stands up to the high amount of I/O that is generated by ESX. All VMDK files created for virtual machines must exist in a VMFS partition for ESX to utilize them. To minimize overhead and optimize performance, VMware made VMFS a flat file system, meaning all files are located on the root of the partition. No subdirectories are allowed, so you have to ensure you incorporate a proper naming standard for your VMDK files.

What is a VMDK File?

Simply put, a VMDK file represents a physical hard drive that gets presented to your guest operating system. When connecting a new VMDK file to a virtual machine, the operating system sees it as a non-partitioned physical drive. This drive can be partitioned and formatted using a variety of file systems including NTFS and ext3. Up to 56 VMDK files can be assigned to any guest operating system, allowing for quite a bit of flexibility in creating a partitioning scheme in the guest operating system. When sizing a VMDK file, ESX has a limitation of 9TB per VMDK. If a server or application requires anything near this limit, it probably isn't the greatest of VMware candidates unless the disk utilization is extremely low.

Creating VMDK Files

There are several different ways to create a new VMDK file within VMware. For those that are patient and don't mind waiting to navigate the MUI, you can simply navigate into the hardware properties of any powered off virtual machine. You can choose to add a new hard drive device and go through the appropriate steps to create your new VMDK file. This method requires that you add the hardware to a powered off virtual machine. There is no way via the MUI to create a new VMDK file that is not attached to a virtual machine. While any VMDK that is created will typically immediately be assigned to a specific guest operating system, there may be a need to create a new VMDK that is a standalone file that isn't attached to any guests.

To do this, you'll need to use the console operating system to create a new VMDK file. The "vmkfstools" command is a VMware binary executable that's used to perform operations to VMDK files and VMFS partitions. (It will be described in further detail a little later in this chapter.) To create your new VMDK file, run vmkfstools in the following format as root in the console operating system. The "vmfs" in the command is the name of the VMFS partition that the new VMDK file will reside on.

```
# vmkfstools -c size vmfs:filename.vmdk
```

In the real world, this command can be used in several ways. Each of the following examples creates a new VMDK file that is the same size on the same VMFS partition.

```
# vmkfstools -c 4096M local_0:server1.vmdk
# vmkfstools -c 4096m local_0:server1.vmdk
# vmkfstools -c 4G local_0:server1.vmdk
# vmkfstools -c 4194304K vmhba0:0:0:8:server1.vmdk
```

Note that you can specify your VMDK size using kilobytes, megabytes, or gigabytes with the same result. Also, the "K", "M", or "G" can be used in either uppercase or lowercase lettering. Finally, note that you can use either the friendly VMFS name assigned to your partition or you can use the physical vmhba designation. Often times, it is easiest to use the friendly name.

VMDK File Storage

All VMDK files must be stored on a VMFS partition if they're going to run as or within a virtual machine on an ESX Server. There are actually two different VMDK formats that can be used with various VMware products. Monolithic format is the only format that ESX can use, and are the type of file that we've been referring to so far. However, there is another disk file format known as the COW format. COW-formatted file types are required for VMware Workstation and GSX Server. Up until recently VMware had utilized two different extensions that were utilized to distinguish these formats (DSK for Monolithic and VMDK for COW). Now, everything uses the VMDK extension. In any of the instances in this chapter that we are talking about Monolithic files, the legacy DSK extension may be substituted for VMDK. There are several noticeable differences between the two file types:

Monolithic Disk Files

- Contained in a single file

- Filled with zeros, sizing the VMDK file as their full size in the file system

- Can only be accessed in ESX

COW Disk Files

- Can be contained in a single file or may be broken up into 2GB files

- Can be configured to be only as large as the data contained within them and to dynamically grow as more storage space is requested

- Can only be accessed in Workstation or GSX Server products

One thing to note with any VMDK file is that the file system that they are stored on must be capable of handling the proper file size. With ESX, Monolithic files can only be accessed when running on a VMFS partition which, as we mentioned, can handle file sizes up to 9TB in size. Linux file systems such as ext2 or ext3 do not have the luxury of being able to handle file sizes larger than 2GB. This is why COW files may be broken up into several 2GB files instead of self-contained in a single VMDK file.

Converting Formats

It's important to note that disk files can easily be converted from one format to the other. A great use of this is if you create master images in VMware workstation environments. Once you've completed the configuration of your master image, you can copy your set of Monolithic files to the /vm/vmimages directory of an ESX server as COW files. When you need to deploy a new VM, locate the COW filename that does not have an incremental numerical value appended to the end. This file contains data about every file that makes up the physical drive. To import this file into a useable ESX format, you'll need to use vmkfstools in the following format: (The second line is a real life example.)

```
# vmkfstools -i sourceCOW.vmdk
vmfs:destMonolithic.vmdk
```

```
# vmkfstools -i /vm/vmimages/w2k3/w2k3.vmdk
local_0:server1.vmdk
```

This command will take some time to run, as it does a direct binary copy of the data stored on the Cow file into a new Monolithic file. All blank space on the VMDK file also needs to be written with zeros to make it useable by ESX. The size of the new Monolithic file will be the same size as the maximum disk size that was configured within the VMDK file.

When you created a new VMDK file within VMware Workstation, you were given the option to create it as either IDE or SCSI. You can only convert VMDKs that were created as SCSI drives, as ESX cannot handle IDE. You will receive errors if you try to import an IDE

VMDK and will either have to recreate your image or find another way to get your data from one server to another.

On the flipside, you can also take an ESX Monolithic file and export it to COW format. This can be done so the file may be used for testing in either Workstation or GSX. An export can also be used to minimize the size of your image files. Since the COW format is only as large as the data contained within the file system configured on the VMDK, it can save a significant amount of space when moving your images to a network repository. By default, when you create a template within VirtualCenter, it performs the Monolithic to COW conversion while storing the files. The command to manually export a Monolithic file to COW is extremely similar to the command to convert in the opposite direction:

```
# vmkfstools -e destCOW.vmdk
vmfs:sourceMonolithic.vmdk
```

```
# vmkfstools -e /vm/vmimages/w2k3/w2k3.vmdk
local_0:server1.vmdk
```

It's important to note that you do not want to convert Monolithic files to COW format and store them on VMFS partitions. We've personally run into nothing but problems when working with COW files located on a VMFS partition. It's a best practice to keep these stored on a standard Linux or Windows partition.

VMDK Access Modes

Within ESX Server there are four different disk access modes that a VMDK file can be configured for. These access modes determine how the data is written to the VMDK file and provide different levels of functionality.

Persistent Access Mode
This is the default access mode for all newly-created VMDK files. VMDKs in this configuration behave exactly like a drive on a physical machine would. Once you make a change to the file system, it's

permanently written to the VMDK file. It's recommended that unless there is a specific need to use a different access mode, that persistent be used, as it provides the best overall disk performance.

Nonpersistent Access Mode

VMDK files configured in a non-persistent mode discard all changes made to the file system since the point in time in which the access mode was changed to non-persistent. When the virtual machine is powered off (not rebooted), any changes that were made to the VMDK are ignored. This is handy in kiosk situations where multiple people have access to a machine through some form of remote connectivity. If someone were to delete key files, you can instantly return the system to its original state. Another situation in which nonpersistent mode may be convenient is for training classrooms. Several students may be given their own virtual machines as their lab to configure a specific system. They can install applications and reboot several times. At the end of the day, a simple power off of the VM will place the machines back to their original state.

When using nonpersistent access mode, it's best to completely configure the server then change the disk access mode to nonpersistent. This ensures you always go back to the expected configuration on the VMDK file.

Undoable Access Mode

Other than persistent mode, the undoable VMDK mode is probably one of the most utilized access modes. Undoable allows you to keep a log file of the changes made to your VMDK files (referred to as REDO files because of the file extension used to identify them). The VMDK puts itself into a "locked" state and no data is written to it as long as it is in an undoable state. The only changes are made to the REDO file. When the virtual machine is powered off, you're given three options as to what you wish to do with the data that has changed: commit, discard, or append.

Commit Changes

When you commit your REDO file, you're permanently applying all of your changes. The REDO log then starts to re-collect changes from this new checkpoint. If you utilize the undoable access mode to create checkpoints during an application installation or upgrade, you can commit your changes if your upgrade is successful.

Discard Changes
Discarding the changes being held in your REDO file will reset your VMDK file back to the state it was in when it was changed to Undoable mode. When an application installation or upgrade does not go as planned, you can instantly undo your changes by selecting discard. Even if your server receives a blue screen error due to a modification that was done to the system, your VMDK can be reset to its original checkpoint state. As mentioned in the master installation image section, it's not uncommon to create several checkpoints for this very reason.

Append Changes
Choosing to keep your changes will allow you to perform several actions before deciding whether to keep your changes or not. Many applications require a reboot as a part of their installation process. You often don't know how the system is going to react to these changes, so you may want to keep your redo log so you can properly test things before making your final decision. Once you're either satisfied with the results or you determine you need to back out your changes, you can choose either commit or discard on the next power down.

Append Access Mode
The append VMDK access mode acts identically to the "Append" option of the undoable mode. The only difference is that you're not prompted with actions to perform to the VMDK and REDO files. In order to permanently apply your changes, you need to utilize the vmkfstools command to commit the REDO to the VMDK. Alternatively, you can simply delete the REDO file to discard any of the changes you have made since changing access modes.

Manually Applying your Changes
As mentioned in the append description, there is a way to manually apply your changes from the command line. The vmkfstools command to commit your REDO file can only be run on VMDK files in append mode. There is another command that can be run, vmware-

cmd, which can be used to change your disk into and out of undoable mode while it's running. It is important to remember where the two different commands can and cannot be used. You can perform the following vmkfstools command to commit your REDO log and make the changes permanent to the VMDK:

```
# vmkfstools -m vmfs:filename.vmdk.REDO


# vmkfstools -m san_0:server1.vmdk.REDO
```

You will need to confirm that you wish to apply your REDO file to its parent VMDK file.

There is also a way that we can configure our VMDK file in a temporary REDO mode. What exactly does this mean? First, it does not provide a checkpoint of the system. This is a common misconception of using the vmware-cmd tool to switch the access mode of a running VMDK. If we create a REDO on a running VMDK and forget to apply our changes, they would automatically be committed when the system is powered off without prompts or warnings. Secondly, the VMDK file is locked in an unstable state. As we'll learn shortly, if a backup and restore of a VMDK file is done using the temporary REDO mode, your system will not be in a proper state for backup. If you wish to temporarily lock your running VMDK file and write changes to a REDO file without shutting down, you can utilize the following command:

```
# vmware-cmd filename.vmx addredo <SCSI_Device>


# vmware-cmd /vm/vmconfig/server1/server1.vmx addredo
scsi0:0
```

The vmware-cmd tool functions a little differently than vmkfstools in that you do not specify the VMFS partition and VMDK file that you wish to change the access mode of. You need to specify the configuration file and physical device as presented to the operating system. You can check the MUI or the contents of the VMX file to find out the exact device you need to modify.

To commit the REDO log to the VMDK file, you can do one of two things—shut down the guest operating system, or manually commit the REDO with the vmware-cmd tool. As mentioned earlier, as soon as you shut down a virtual machine that has a VMDK file that was modified with the above command, the changes will automatically be committed on power off. The next time the virtual machine is powered on, the VMDK file will revert to the standard persistent mode. If you wish to commit your changes to a running virtual machine without powering down, you can utilize the following command:

```
# vmware-cmd configfile.vmx commit <SCSI_Device>
<level> <freeze> <wait>
```

```
# vmware-cmd /vm/vmconfig/w2k3sas1/w2k3sas1.vmx com-
mit scsi0:0 0 1 1
```

You will notice a lot of extra options attached to the end of this command. The following breakdown details what these options mean.

Level
The level may have two values: 0 or 1. To understand the concept these values represent you have to realize that you can actually add more than one REDO log to a single VMDK file. By using the "vmware-cmd addredo" command twice, you can actually create up to two levels of REDO logs. You will have three files at this point; filename.vmdk, filename.vmdk.redo, and filename.vmdk.redo.redo. We're getting slightly ahead of ourselves here as the usefulness of this will be explained shortly, but it's required to illustrate the options of the vmware-cmd options. If you set the level to 0, the topmost REDO file is applied to its parent. In the example of two REDO files, the filename.vmdk.redo.redo file will be merged into its parent, which is filename.vmdk.redo. If this same command were to be immediately rerun, filename.vmdk.redo will get merged into its parent of filename.vmdk. At this point, the disk access mode will return to its normal persistent mode.

With a level of 1, the second to topmost REDO file is applied. It is only available when you have two REDO files on the same VMDK file. This applies the changes from filename.vmdk.redo into its par-

ent of filename.vmdk. The top level REDO file filename.vmdk
.redo.redo is then renamed to filename.vmdk.redo. The command
may then be rerun specifying a level of 0 to commit the final changes
from filename.vmdk.redo to filename.vmdk.

Freeze
The freeze option is only utilized if level 1 is specified. When the last
REDO file is committed, the system must pause while the commit is
occurring. It cannot happen in real time to the operating system. The
length of the pause depends on the size of your REDO files. By specifying a freeze value of 0 when you use the level 1 option to freeze
the second level of REDOs, the system is not frozen. The commit will
happen more slowly than if the system were to freeze, which can be
set with a freeze value of 1. Again, when you only have a single
REDO file, your system will freeze while it is committed and it will
ignore the option specified for the freeze value.

Wait
The wait option specifies how the command exits. If you set the wait
value to 0, the command prompt will immediately return to you
before the VMDK file has finished committing its changes. If option
1 is specified, you will not be given the opportunity to enter additional commands until the commit is completed. This is useful for
scripting the process of adding and committing REDO logs in a batch
process.

Why Did I Need to Read All That?
If you have made it this far, then you have gotten further than we did
the first time we began researching VMDK access modes. You may
be asking yourself "Why do I need to add a REDO log to a running
VMDK if I cannot revert my data, and why would I ever need to?"
The answer is somewhat simple if you put together the pieces of the
puzzle. The key here is that the importance doesn't lie in the fact that
the VMDK is writing changes to a REDO file as much as the VMDK
file itself is locked and changes cannot be written to it. Using some
advanced scripting through either bash or Perl, you can create a script
that will lock your VMDK file, back it up in its current state, and
commit the changes that have occurred since it was locked. Let's take
a look at the individual pieces in a chronological manner.

Adding the REDO File
The first thing that will occur in your script is you will add your REDO file. This locks your VMDK file and begins to track your changes inside another file. Your VMDK file is now in the prime state to be backed up using the console operating system's backup tool.

Adding a Second REDO File
Remember that when you commit the last REDO log, your system has no choice but to pause itself. Depending on how long your back-up took, you may have a very large REDO file that needs to be committed. On some systems, a large outage could cause severe issues. By adding a second REDO log, we are in a position where we can apply the changes of the first file without the system freezing.

Applying the First REDO File without a Freeze
Using the level 1 option, we can apply the filename.vmdk.redo file. As this may take some time to complete, we want to specify a freeze value of 0. This will ensure our system remains functional during the commit. Our second REDO file takes the name of the first REDO log file upon completion. We also want to ensure that we set the wait value to 1, as we do not want to begin committing our second REDO file until the first has been completed.

Applying the Second REDO File with a Freeze
The amount of time that it takes to commit the first REDO file should be nowhere near as long as it took to back up the original VMDK file. Thus, the second REDO file should be comparatively smaller in size. Because of this smaller size, there is less impact to the system during the freeze that must occur to commit it. Since we only have a single REDO file remaining, the freeze option is no longer available to us. Also, since there is nothing else to commit, we do not need to set the wait value to 1. After the second REDO file has been committed, our VMDK returns to normal persistent operation.

Some applications that are constantly changing at high rates may still encounter long pauses when the last REDO log is written to the VMDK. We can minimize the impact by recreating another second-level REDO file and jumping back to the previous step. By using scripting logic, you can have the system ensure the REDO file is smaller than a certain size or specify a maximum number of attempts to reach the size threshold before just taking the freeze hit and committing the final REDO file.

If you recall, when you change a VMDK access mode to undoable, you can revert back to the point in time that the access mode was changed. What happens when this occurs on a running system? If you restore the VMDK file onto a different ESX host, it will come up as if a hard power off had occurred. This should be strongly considered if you decide to attempt to backup your systems in this fashion. Some applications such as SQL or Exchange do not take kindly to having their systems shut down in an inconsistent state. As you'll find out in our data and disaster recovery chapters, this type of VMDK backup is recommended only for disaster purposes and should not be relied upon for daily backups of your virtual machines.

You should also be aware that utilizing a REDO file will have some virtualization overhead associated with it. VMDK files that must write all changes to a REDO file will have to check two different locations when reading information. ESX will first read the VMDK file, and then verify the data against the REDO file, which may have updated information. Carefully choosing the right disk access mode based on your usage scenario can be a powerful tool within ESX.

Resizing VMDKs

When you create your VMDK file, the size of the file is equal to the capacity of the hard drive configured. As we mentioned previously, ESX Server fills the VMDK with zeros to fill it to capacity so it is properly represented in the file system. Once you install your base operating system and server applications, you may realize that you did not properly size your VMDK. The vmkfstools command provides you with an option to expand the size of the VMDK file to a new size. The size specified is the new size of the VMDK, not how much you wish to increase it by. You will notice that the syntax used is identical to that specified to create a new VMDK file in both the size and target options.

```
# vmkfstools -X size vmfs:filename.vmdk

# vmkfstools -X 10240m local_0:server1.vmdk

# vmkfstools -X 10G vmhba0:0:0:8:server1.vmdk
```

It's extremely important to note that expanding a VMDK file will only make your physical disk appear larger to the operating system. Any partitions created on the VMDK within the operating system will remain the same size. You will need to use a third party partition tool such as Partition Magic if you wish to increase the partition size available to the operating system.

You can also use the –X option to make your VMDK smaller. You must be extremely careful with this option that you do not make your VMDK smaller than all the partitions created on the physical disk within the operating system. Doing so may leave your system in an unusable state and data loss may occur. You can use the same partitioning tool as above to make your partitions smaller within the guest operating system before attempting to shrink the VMDK file to prevent data loss.

Opening VMDK Files Outside a VM

There may be cases when a guest operating system becomes corrupted to the point that it cannot boot. In the physical world there are several different ways to attempt to remedy this situation:

• Reload a base operating system and restore the system data

• Remove the hard drives and attempt to restore the data on a different physical host

• Boot with an NTFS DOS disk and attempt to replace the corrupted file (assuming you can figure out which one it is)

While it may not initially seem like some of these options are available in ESX, all are in fact very possible. Deploying a master installation image is a fairly simple process in ESX. The backup agents may even be a part of the master image. The data can be restored from the last known good backup set and you can be on your way.

Since the physical drive of a guest operating system is nothing more than a VMDK file, you can connect a non-booting disk to another VM as a secondary drive by spending about 30 seconds in the MUI. You can then use the backup client of choice to restore your data to your original boot VMDK. Once the restore is complete, you can detach it from the "restore host" and reconnect it to its original virtual machine and properly boot.

Like ISO images for CD-ROMs, VMware also allows you to capture floppy images, often saved with an extension of FLP. You can create a floppy image of the NTFS DOS disks and boot into the system the same way you would with a physical server to have direct access to the NTFS data without loading the operating system.

In June 2004, VMware released an unsupported utility called the VMware DiskMount Utility. This utility allows you to mount a virtual disk file in a Windows operating system. It is compatible with Workstation, GSX and ESX disk files in both the Monolithic and COW formats. Since this book focuses on ESX, we won't cover GSX or Workstation VMDK files in depth suffice to say, "The DiskMount Utility works the same."

When things get extremely bad, and system resources on your ESX hosts are tight, you can copy your VMDK file to a Windows host. Using the VMware DiskMount Utility, you can mount your virtual device as a drive letter within Windows and access it directly through your guest operating system. The DiskMount Utility has a lot more functionality in a Workstation or GSX environment in which the VMDK or VMDK files already reside on the local operating system and do not need to be transferred over the network. The installation package can be downloaded from VMware's download site at http://www.vmware.com/download/. To mount a VMDK or VMDK file in your Windows operating system, use the following command after installing the DiskMount Utility package:

```
vmware-mount <Drive Letter>: <Path to VMDK or VMDK
file>
```

```
vmware-mount F: d:\vmimages\server1.vmdk
```

If you need to disconnect your mounted drive, you can simply type:

vmware-mount <Drive Letter>: /d

vmware-mount F: /d

Creating a Guest Virtual Machine Standard

Before we jump into the different ways to create the guest virtual machine, it's probably a good time for you to determine what your standard VM configuration will be. Throughout this chapter we've talked about numerous options and configurations within the guest. Now you should decide what the standard VM will look like in your environment.

While this decision may sound somewhat odd, you need to look at VMs just like a physical machine. Often new users of ESX will start creating new VMs without much thought to the virtual hardware they are specifying. We've heard of companies creating every VM in their environment using Virtual SMP and 2 GB of memory per host. Their thought was that it would increase performance, and if the guest did not use all the resources, they would be shared out to other VMs. Well, the problem is that the sharing of memory and calculations required to support SMP will increase the load on your ESX servers. This of course is what you are trying to eliminate. The most sound course of action is to create a standard VM configuration that will work for the majority of your servers, then deviate from that for specific guests that require different configurations.

So what should be in this template? Basically the hardware configurations and options you have seen throughout the entire chapter. You should determine the amount of memory per VM, the default shares of, and min / max levels of memory and processor each VM will get.

You may be thinking at this point that your servers are all different and will therefore need different configurations. This is not a problem. Just create several templates and use them accordingly. Below is a sample list of templates generally used in VM environments:

- Production Windows 2000/2003 Server

- Windows NT 4.0 Server

- Linux

- Windows XP

- Possibly a development template for each of these

As you can see it's a pretty short list. The idea is to create a set of standards from which to work with. This will help in provisioning and ensure you don't over allocate resources on you host just because you gave every VM on the machine 2GB of memory with a minimum of 1GB. If you were to do that on an ESX server with 12GB of physical memory, you would not be likely to start VM eleven or twelve.

You'll also notice that we've said there may be a different configuration between development and production servers. In this case you may allocate the same amount of memory but with fewer shares. Or you may decrease the amount of memory depending on the OS and how your developers work. In any case, your templates or standard configurations should take into account the hardware configuration of the ESX servers and only over allocate resources to levels at which you have tested and found acceptable for your environment.

The following is a list of items you should define in each of your VM standards:

Memory
Memory Min/Max
Memory Shares

Processor
Processor Min/Max
Processor Shares
SMP Configuration

Disk
Throughput/Shares

Network
Shaping enabled?
Number of VMs per VMNIC/Virtual Switch

Once you have a standard (much like any piece of hardware), provisioning and selection of virtual hardware options becomes much easier for your staff. Additionally, you're setting their expectations as to what to expect out of a VM and letting them understand that the days of development servers with 2 or 4GB of RAM are gone.

Creating your Guest Virtual Machines

By now you understand all the basics of the virtual environment. Now it's time to decide how you're going to create your guests. When all is said and done, there are three ways to create your guest VMs:

- Manually using the Web Interface

- Scripted / command line

- Using management tools like VirtualCenter

Each of these methods basically accomplish the same thing—they create a functioning and running VM. They also have a number of steps or functions that are identical, and depending on your requirements and you environment, you will have to determine which works best for you and fits your overall environment the best. To do this, let's review each option and talk about its strengths and weaknesses. Then we'll move onto how each one can be done.

Manual Creation of the VMs using the Web Interface

In a default ESX Server installation, this is the way you will create VMs. From the first screen of the web page you can start a web-based wizard that will create and configure a new VM along with creating the new VMDK file for that VM. This is the most common method of creation for new ESX administrators and smaller ESX environments.

Who should use this method? New environments will inevitably begin this way. Generally when the first ESX server is built, the very next thing people want to test is a running VM. The Web Interface allows them to create a VM very quickly and begin an OS installation within minutes. For test environments (testing ESX that is) and for smaller environments with no more than 3 or 4 ESX servers, this method is perfect.

Advantages of using the Web Interface to create VMs

• Available after initial install of ESX

• Wizard driven and requires very little (if any) training

• Is a relatively fast process and easy to accomplish

• Little to no "prep" work

• No additional infrastructure or software required

Disadvantages of using the Web Interface to create VMs

• Does not scale well as the environment grows

• You must look at each ESX server or keep a running list of their utilization to determine where to deploy the new VMs

• Does not make use of templates without some command line/shell use

Things like custom VM share settings and specific hardware settings must be manually configured for each VM even if using a template VMDK.

As you can see, this is the best way to get started with ESX. If you have a small environment or are just testing ESX, this method is right for you. The following steps will walk you through the simple creation of a VM and describe the configurations you may want to change:

1. From the Web Interface Status Monitor, select Add a New Virtual Machine.

2. You'll be prompted to select an OS Type, a Display name for use in the Web Interface, and a location and name for the VMX configuration file.

3. You will then be asked for a number of processors and the amount of memory. The default number of processors is always one and the default amount of memory varies depending on the OS.

    Note: At this point the VMX file is created. You will notice a slight pause before the disk configuration screen comes up.

4. You will then be asked to add a virtual disk. Here you will choose between three options:

    *   Blank (ESX will create a new VMDK file) is good when creating VMs by hand and creating new images
    *   Existing (ESX will look at its mass storage devices for a VMDK file you have placed there) is good for use when you have "master" images and are copying the VMDK files prior to creating the VM
    *   System/LUN disk (a raw "real" disk or LUN) is hardly ever used in the real world at this stage.

5. Once the type is selected you will have to either:

    *   Name the new VMDK, set its initial size, and define the location for its storage
    *   Browse for the existing VMDK file and select it; or
    *   Select the path to the disk or LUN you wish to use
    *   In addition, if you've used a VMDK file, you'll have to choose the type of disk as described in the VMDK file section of this chapter.

258 VMware ESX Server

6. The last step is to finalize the hardware for the VM. After finishing the wizard, you're brought to the hardware tab for that virtual machine. From here you can add additional disks, configure which switch the VM is connected to, and add any other hardware you wish.

As you can see this is not really a complicated process. All in all it takes about 30 seconds to finish and you could have a VM ready for installation or booting, depending on your configuration. While this process is not complex, it is still hands on. For most small environments this is perfect since there is no need for management tools or scripting. However, as your environment grows and requirements change, you may find the need to script this process (making it repeatable and removing the human factor) or to use provisioning tools which allow deployment from templates.

Using a Template VMDK File when Manually Creating a VM

Even if you manually create new virtual machines, you can still use template VMDK files. This is what most people do in small environments, even if they don't have VirtualCenter or any scripted installs. We'll take a detailed look at this in Chapter 9, but the basic steps are as follows:

1. Create a new VM using the steps listed above.

2. Create a blank disk.

3. Set the disk to the size you want your template to be. Don't overdo it, since you can always add a data disk if needed. This first disk is really for the OS and possibly application installations.

4. Install your guest operating system to this VM.

5. Once the installation is complete, install your VMware Tools and any other supporting software you may need (Anti-virus, management clients, etc.).

6. For Windows servers, run Microsoft Sysprep on the guest OS just as you would for imaging a regular Windows server or workstation.

7. Shut down the virtual machine at the end of the Sysprep process.

Once this is done, you can use this template to create other guests. To deploy a new VM based on this master image, simply copy the VMDK file (and rename it of course). Then, in Step 4 of the steps listed above, select an existing disk by browsing for your newly-copied VMDK file. Once you boot the guest, Sysprep will complete (most likely prompting you for thing like the computer name and IP address) and you will have a fully functioning guest.

If you need to update the template with new patches and whatnot, simply start the template VM, complete the Sysprep process, update the software required, then re-Sysprep and shutdown the machine.

Scripted/Command Line Creation of Virtual Machines

There may come a point in time that you want to script your installs. This is generally done because you need to create a number of similar VMs in a short amount of time or just because you like to script and feel its fun to spend time looking at code that is meaningless to anyone but you. In either case, you have that option with ESX Server.

VMware comes with a number of options for creating and interacting with VMs from the shell. In most environments that use scripts, the creation of the VMs are based on template VMDK and VMX files. The scripts are usually nothing more than commands that copy template VMX and VMDK files, then register the VM on the host and possibly even boot it. Let's take a look at the advantages and disadvantages of using scripting for guest creation.

Advantages of using scripts to create VMs

- Eliminates the "human" factor from VM creation

- Faster than wizard-based creation when you need to create tons of VMs

- Creates a repeatable process that can be later tied into other management tools or interfaces

- No additional infrastructure or software required

- Different templates with different shares and VM configurations can easily be duplicated

Disadvantages of using scripts to create VMs

- Requires scripting skills and a pretty deep knowledge of Linux or ESX Server

- You must look at each ESX Server or keep a running list of their utilization to determine where to deploy the new VMs

- You must weigh the time spent developing these scripts against the amount of time it would take to create your VMs

- Scripts may require changes or stop working when ESX server is upgraded. This requires extra testing prior to upgrades

Before you jump into vi and start writing, you should really weigh the benefit you get from writing a script. Consider the time it will take to create the script and test it and weigh that against the amount of time you will spend creating the VMs manually. We had one customer who didn't want to use a tool for deploying VMs but also didn't want to use the GUI. (He just hated GUIs.) He wanted a script. Of course he was only going to create one or two VMs a month, but this didn't matter to him. This guy ending up spending two weeks writing and testing this script, which ended up saving him three or four minutes each month.

The trick with this (like any scripting) is that there are an uncountable number of ways to develop your script. Some folks prefer using a simple shell script, while others denounce any scripts that aren't written in Perl. In either case you still have several tasks that need to be accomplished to create the most basic of installation scripts:

1. You must copy or create a VMX file.

2. You must copy or create a VMDK file.

3. You must register the VM with ESX.

4. You need to start the VM (Optional).

Of course there are many more options you can incorporate into your scripts in addition to these basics, including:

*   Sending an e-mail when the VM is created

*   Adding the VM information into a database for management and tracking

*   Modifying or hardcoding the MAC address in the VMX file

*   Assigning permissions to the VM on the ESX host

*   And anything else someone might ask you to do

Regardless of what you choose to do, scripting VM creation is fairly simple. The trick is to have the right templates in place and some scripting skills.

Creating VM Guests Using Management Software

Up until this point, very little has been discussed about the different management software available for VMware environments. Management software like VMware's VirtualCenter is often used in VM environments containing multiple hosts (often more than two or three). Up until this point in the book we've looked at ESX (for the most part) as a single server. In this section, we'd like to touch on the management tools and describe some of the basic features they offer for deploying guests' operating systems.

VMware's VirtualCenter adds a lot of flexibility to the deployment of your guests. The basic idea behind VirtualCenter is to take a holistic approach to your virtual infrastructure and allow you to look at (and manage) the entire virtual farm as a whole. This includes the performance of the ESX hosts in the farm and the utilization of the hosts and guests running within the environment. The real beauty of looking at your whole environment in one interface is that it lets you intelligently decide where your next VM guests should be deployed.

On top of that, the VirtualCenter tools allow you to create templates from existing VMs in the environment, schedule VM creation, and even integrate with Microsoft Sysprep. Once your templates are created, you can simply click the host you want to deploy a new VM to and either deploy the new guest immediately, or schedule the deployment for later. If Sysprep is being used, VirtualCenter will prompt you for the new guest's computer and IP address information and will complete the entire VM creation process. You can even have it power on the VM once it is all created, which is very cool.

The downfall of adding any management tool is that it introduces additional software, cost and infrastructure that you'll be required to support. While most management tools only require a console server, a database of some type, and storage space to store your templates, it's still something that needs to be considered.

Advantages of using management tools to create VMs

- Creates a single interface for managing and creating VMs on all your ESX servers

- Eliminates the "human" factor from VM creation

- Faster than Wizard based creation when you need to create tons of VMs

- Creates a repeatable process that requires little training

- Different templates specifying different shares and VM configurations can easily be duplicated

- Management tools allow you to review the environment's utilization easily, and pick the host to deploy to

- Allows for VM/Guest creation to be scheduled

Disadvantages of using management tools to create VMs

- Requires additional infrastructure

- Requires additional software and costs associated with the software

Is it worth it to spend the money for software, software maintenance, database space, and support and storage if you only have one or two

ESX servers? Probably not, if you're not going to use any of the other features that such a tool would provide. But if you plan to use features like VMotion or have more than a couple of servers you need to manage, VirtualCenter (or something like it) becomes almost a "no-brainer".

Chapter **6**

Managing the Server with the Console OS and web interface

Now that you can build a basic ESX server and have a way to install and use your Guest VMs, we need to discuss the basic management of the servers and guests on an ongoing basis. This chapter will take a look at some of the basic things you will need to manage, a number of common tasks that will be performed in the environment, and a few not so common tasks. Obviously no technology book can show you all the tasks for any specific operating system, so here we just want to introduce you to the common tasks that you need to be aware of, and to the tools that you can use.

Management Concepts and Tools

When looking at your ESX environment as a whole there are two basic items you will need to manage. The first is the ESX Server itself. Obviously a very important, though often overlooked, part of the equation. The second item is the management and monitoring of the guests. This item tends to get the focus in most small environments (often to the detriment of managing the host properly).

No matter which item you refer to here (the guest or the ESX server host), there are three basic ways to make changes or manage the environment:

- The web interface

- Through the ESX server console

- A management platform like VirtualCenter

Obviously each of these options have their place in the environment. There are certain items available through the Server console that are not available (or easily used) through the web interface. Or there are certain options, utilities, or functions only available through a management tool like VirtualCenter. Just like a mechanics tool box, which tools – or method – you use, will depend on what you are trying to accomplish. Here we will spend a little time with each option and go over some of the common tasks for both the ESX Server and its guests.

Using the Web Interface

The VMware Web Management User Interface (VMware calls this the MUI or VMI, however we refer to it as the web interface) allows web browser access to an ESX host for monitoring and management. A majority of your administrative VMware tasks can be performed using the web interface, with the proper access of course.

Depending on your security settings for the host, traffic between the client and the ESX server can be encrypted using SSL. This interface is a powerful tool and generally enough to manage small ESX environments. The problems with the web interface become apparent in larger environments since you must connect to each server individually to perform tasks. It basically becomes harder to use as the number of hosts in your environment increase. Below are some of the tasks you can accomplish using the web interface:

ESX Host Management
Reboot of host
Disk Management
Network Configuration
Advanced Settings for ESX
Resource Monitoring
Some file system management (though it is slow)
Physical Device allocations (seems slower and "clunkier" than the command line)

Virtual Machine Management
Virtual Machine Deployment
Power Functions for Virtual Machines
Configuring resource allocation for VMs
Configure hardware and network configurations for VMs
User Rights for VMs (Using file system security)
Resource Management/Monitoring

Basically, VMware built the web interface to make it easier to use and manage their product. The interface allows you to do almost all the basic management needed in an ESX environment and simplifies it so that even users with very little Linux or UNIX experience can operate their servers.

The drawbacks of the web interface become apparent as the environment grows or as you need to troubleshoot a server. The web interface was not made for troubleshooting and few tools are available in the interface itself. Most ESX admins jump directly to the ESX Console for any real troubleshooting.

Advantages of using the web interface for management tasks

- Contains most tools and options for basic VM administration
- Simple to use
- Come with ESX server (free)
- Allows for some basic file system access

Disadvantages of using the web interface for management tasks

- Allows for you to only manage a single server or set of VMs at a time
- Does not have intuitive or detailed tools for troubleshooting
- Does not allow for the scheduling of tasks
- Requires the use of Linux based accounts or PAM

Using the ESX Service Console

The Service Console may be used to perform any VMware function through a command line interface. This is generally where most ESX admins will wind up when troubleshooting or when making changes to configurations. Server configuration changes are typically made by editing .conf files or by echoing text to the /proc file system. ESX and Virtual Machine specific tasks may be performed using command line tools such as vmware-cmd or vmkfstools.

Monitoring of Virtual Machines may be done using commands like esxtop. The Linux Console is an extremely powerful tool, but also difficult to use if you are not familiar with linux. This should only be utilized by the experienced VMware administrators, as there is potential to severely damage the ESX host by typing an improper command or option. Much like the web interface, the console limits you to access/controlling a single server, though most work done at the console is to reconfigure an individual server.

Advantages of using the Service Console for management

- Best level of access to the console operating system and its configurations

- Allows you access to tools not available in the web interface

- Great for anyone that feels comfortable with the command line

Disadvantages of using the Service Console for management

- Requires a knowledge of linux in order to use

- Requires the use of Linux based accounts or PAM

Using a Management Utility

We realize that there are a number of management software platforms out there for ESX. Later in the book we will discuss the differences between software such as Platespin and VirtualCenter, but for now we place the focus on VirtualCenter and use it as a baseline.

Management software like VMware's VirtualCenter allows for a centralized management and monitoring solution for both the ESX server hosts and the Virtual Machines. The biggest advantage to any management software in this environment is that it "fixes" the issue of only being able to manage a single host at a time. While VirtualCenter (and other management tools) does not offer all of the functions available in the first two methods, it does make standard day-to-day tasks simpler and allows you to monitor and manage multiple systems and VMs at the same time.

In addition, VirtualCenter makes it easy to integrate Windows authentication to assign permissions to ESX hosts and the Virtual Machines running on them. Without the management tools, you would need to look at implementing the Pluggable Authentication Module (PAM) to even begin to an authenticate external authentication mechanism. Of course PAM can have its own issues and is not centrally managed. PAM will be discussed further in Chapter 7.

Below are some of the tasks that you can accomplish using VirtualCenter at an enterprise level:

- Virtual Machine Deployment (and deployment scheduling)
- Cloning of existing Virtual Machines
- Power Operations on Virtual Machines
- View historical performance data of both VMs and ESX hosts.
- Managing resource allocations for Virtual Machines
- VMotion Virtual Machines across physical hosts

Of course, with a detached management system like this there are still certain tasks that are host specific that cannot be done from VirtualCenter. In these cases you will still "revert" to the Service Console or the web interface. Almost all of these tasks relate to hardware configurations on VMware Host servers. Some of these operations include the following:

- Adding new LUNs to the host
- Advanced threshold options specific to a host (Advanced Options in the MUI or /proc entries in the COS)
- Virtual Switch Configurations

Advantages of using a management tool in your environment

- Simplest way to centrally integrate Windows authentication
- Allows for the monitoring and management of multiple hosts
- Offers options like VMotion, not available in other tools
- Easy to use for admins not familiar with Linux
- Allows for tasks to be scheduled quickly and easily
- Allows for easily applied security to VMs and groups of VMs

- Offers options like email and pager notification

- Offers additional performance monitoring capabilities

Disadvantages of using a management tool in your environment

- Adds additional cost to the implementation

- Host specific hardware and configurations must still be done with one of the first tools

As you can see each of these options can have their place in your environment. In a small environment – read a few servers – generally all an admin will need is the web interface and the service console. As the environment grows, it generally becomes necessary to implement management software like VirtualCenter. The advantages of simple, single point administration becomes a necessity. In addition, most organizations will not have a large number of ESX admins that feel comfortable with the Console. Instead, a few high level admins will manage the hosts and their configurations and a larger group of engineers and admins will have access to the management software interface to perform basic deployments and monitoring.

ESX Server Management Tasks

Now that you know about some of the tools you will be using to manage your environment lets look at some of the specific tasks you will be required to do. This section will focus on host specific tasks such as adding hardware or changing its configuration, adding users, etc.

Installing New Hardware

Installing new hardware in your environment does not have to be a complex task. If the hardware is support by VMware and will be used by the VMkernel - like additional Network cards for VMs or a new HBA for SAN connectivity –it is actually very simple. Now if you are installing new hardware for use by the Console OS – possibly an additional SCSI controller that is not supported by VMware but is supported by Linux in general – things get a bit more tricky.

Installing and configuring hardware for use by the VMkernel

While this will require downtime to install the hardware and a reboot of the server, it is not a tough task. Installing new network cards or scsi controllers into your server (from a physical perspective) is a simple task. The nice thing about the VMware COS is that configuring the software side of this might be even simpler.

VMware contains all the required drivers it needs for supported hardware. Assuming you are installing additional NICs or SCSI devices all you need to do is install the hardware, power up the server, then configure the hardware via the web interface or the service console.

Configuring new VMkernel hardware via the Web Interface

Once the hardware is installed and the server is powered up, login to the web interface as root. Once into the web interface, select the Options tab, then Startup Profile. Find the new device you have installed and select whether it will be used by Virtual Machines or the service console. Apply your settings and restart your server and you are set. This process really writes all its configs to a file in the /boot partition. Upon boot these files are read in and the VMkernel will setup the appropriate devices.

Configuring new VMkernel hardware via the Service Console

A second way to configure a new device is to use the service console and the command "vmkpcidivy". As the name shows, this is Vmware's utility for dividing up PCI devices between the console use and VMkernel/Virtual Machine use. Again, once the hardware is installed you will need to power up the server, and login to the service console as root.

From the console run the command "vmkpcidivy –i". The –i switch puts the command in interactive mode. We described this command in Chapter 2 in some detail, but for adding or modifying the hardware you can follow the information below.

After running the command you are presented with a list of your current devices and their configuration. To modify the existing configuration with the name of "ESX" you just hit enter when prompted. If you are testing a new configuration and don't want to overwrite the default you will have to type the word "new" at the first prompt and name the new configuration (esx-test would work fine). After that you are presented with an option to configure each piece of hardware, starting with the amount of console memory.

There are three possible values to use for allocating your devices: c, v, or s. These represent Console, Virtual Machines, and Shared, respectively. When you get to the particular device(s) you wish to modify, enter the proper value and hit enter. If you wish to use the current value that is shown in brackets just before the prompt, you can just hit enter and move onto the next device.

When you have gone through the entire list of devices and configured the new device you have just installed, you will be prompted whether you wish to apply the configuration changes or not. If you think you have your settings right, apply the changes then reboot the system for the changes to take affect.

It is strongly recommended that if you are unsure of the change you are attempting to make, that you create a new configuration with a proper temporary name such as "esx-test". When you create a new profile, the settings from your original profile are not remembered. You will have to pay close attention to each option presented to ensure your system comes up in a functional state after its next reboot.

Why is my hardware not detected after installation?

There are times when you will install a new piece of hardware and the ESX system simply "doesn't see it". First thing to do is verify that it is on the HCL. If it is, then we have a couple of steps for you. If it isn't, then you can still use these steps, but they aren't supported.

The kudzu command

The kudzu tool is basically a hardware probe used by Red Hat to probe for hardware changes. Kudzu probes the system for hardware changes and based on these changes modifies /etc/modules.conf. A sample modules.conf is shown below which is basically the configuration file for loading kernel modules in Linux. In our test case shown below we added a 3Com network card, and kudzu modified the modules.conf file to reflect that the new card is now seen as eth1 from the console.

To run kudzu:

1. Log in as root on the service console.

2. At a console prompt, run kudzu.

Example: modules.conf

```
[root@esx1 etc]# cat /etc/modules.conf
alias parport_lowlevel parport_pc
alias eth0 e100
alias eth1 3c90x
alias scsi_hostadapter cpqarray
```

The system may seem to sit there for a minute but after that you can check the modules.conf to see if any changes were made. To view the modules.conf, use the cat command like this: cat /etc/modules.conf. This will print the content of the file to the terminal window.

Checking Disk Space

One of the more common issues (or should I say resolutions) that are seen in the VMware support forums is a lack of disk space on the ESX host. Generally it involves the root directory but can involve other directories on the server. This is because the majority of new ESX admins don't know how to check their disk space on their new ESX servers.

To check the used space available on your file systems you can use the vdf command. Much like the df command in linux, the vdf command will show you space usage on VMFS partitions in addition to what the console sees.

Log in at the system console as root and use df at any directory.

```
# df [ENTER]
```

The system should return to you output like this:

```
[root@esx1 /]# df -h
Filesystem                Size  Used Avail Use% Mounted
on
/dev/ida/c0d0p2           2.4G  1.6G  772M  67% /
/dev/ida/c0d0p1           50M   12M   36M   24% /boot
none                      93M    0    93M    0% /dev/shm
/dev/ida/c0d0p7          9.6G  894M  8.2G   10% /vm
```

Notice how we seem to be missing the VMFS volume. Now look at the results from the vdf command:

```
[root@esx1 root]# vdf -h
FilesystemSize  Used    Avail         Use%  Mounted on
/dev/ida/c0d0p2 2.4G  1.6G    765M    68%   /
/dev/ida/c0d0p1 50M   12M     36M     24%   /boot
none            93M    0      93M     0%    /dev/shm
/dev/ida/c0d0p7 9.6G  894M    8.2G    10%   /vm
vmhba0:0:0:5     87G   56G     31G    64%
/vmfs/vmhba0:0:0:5
```

Configuring Time Synchronization

In the ESX architecture the guest service has the ability to sync the guest's system clock to the host's on a continual basis. The reason for this is that the system clock within VMs begins to drift drastically upon boot due to the way processor cycles are allocated to the VM. Some times this drift is dramatic (the loss of 5-10 minutes in a single hour is not unheard of). Well this obviously presents a problem if you are running VMs that are time sensitive or if the login to VMs is dependent on the time differential being within a certain threshold between the client and the authenticating source (like Active Directory).

Never fear, others have already solved this issue. There are two schools of thought/solutions to this problem.

Letting the VMs Sync to an External Time Source

In this configuration you disable the synchronization between the VM and the ESX and let another source (like Active Directory) keep the VMs in sync with the rest of the network. While this works for some machines, it can become burdensome if you run more than standard Windows VMs that are part of a domain. And VMs that are not part of a domain, or Linux or Netware VMs, may need to be configured differently.

In addition, the Windows time services often have limits as to how much of a change can be made to a local clock time. This, and the fact the a VM's clock can be skewed, constantly make it a fight for the services like the Window's Time Service to keep up. Below is a quote from VMware that I think says it all:

"Unlike a physical machine, a virtual machine is not always loaded and running on a CPU. A virtual machine's clock can't run when the virtual machine is not running. When the virtual machine gets to run on a CPU again, the virtual machine's clock needs to catch up to real time. The Windows Time service attempts to synchronize the virtual clock to an external time source on the network; it is not aware of the unusual clock behavior of a virtual machine, however, so it does not synchronize accurately. In some cases, the Windows Time service can do more harm than good."

Let's review the advantages and disadvantages of this configuration before looking at your other options.

Advantages of using AD or other time sources for synching your VMs

• Requires no Linux/ESX specific knowledge to configure

• Requires no additional configurations on the host

Disadvantages of using AD or other time sources for synching your VMs

• If VMs cannot use the same time source you may require different configs per VM

• Time drift is still possible, though less of a problem with no synchronization

- Incurs more administrative overhead in your VM creation and management

Sync the ESX server to your Authoritative Time Source

In this configuration you leave the Host to VM synchronization active and sync the ESX server to a designated time server. In some environments this may be your AD PDC Emulator and in others you may go ahead and sync it to the same atomic clock you sync your environment to. In either case I am in favor of keeping the host to VM synchronization active. This host to VM synchronization is done constantly through the VMware tools and works every time.

Advantages of Synching the ESX server and using Host to VM Synchronization

- Ensures all VMs are in sync with no individual VM configurations needed

- Can ensure that all clocks within your ESX farm are in sync

- Reduces or eliminates the possibility of significant time drift within the VM

Disadvantages of Synching the ESX server and using Host to VM Synchronization

- Requires some configuration on the ESX host

As you can see, with a little bit of configuration you wind up with a number of advantages. Personally I am a fan of synchronizing my ESX servers with whatever atomic clock my AD Forest is using. Configuring time synchronization for your ESX servers can be done simply with the following steps:

NTP configuration for ESX 2.1 and Greater

Configuring the server for time synchronization is not that hard, and there are probably a dozen different ways to do it. The recommended way from VMware is to use the ntpd service and configure it for synchronization to the authoritative time server(s) of your choice. Since we're from Chicago, the following example will use one of the time servers at DePaul University. But you can easily replace the name and IP with any time server you choose to use.   A firewall rule may be necessary in this case to allow the ESX Host external access to UDP port 123.

1. Determine the time server name and IP address you wish to use. For a list of available and open time servers please go here: http://ntp.isc.org/bin/view/Servers/WebHome

2. Next you need to edit the /etc/ntp.conf file. We will basically be adding two lines to this conf file. So open it up in 'nano' or 'vi' and add the following two lines to the "# -- OUR TIMESERVERS ---- section of the file:

```
restrict 140.192.21.132 mask 255.255.255.255 nomodify
notrap noquery
```
(this is all one line)

```
server 140.192.21.132
```

You need to have both lines in the file for each server you wish to add. The restrict line keeps the time server from being able to modify your time or even query it. There are also examples of these lines in the file, they are just commented out using the # character. If you want to copy and paste the lines instead of re-typing it, you can do that too, just make sure to un-comment them.

3. Once you save or write the file out, you may want to view it again to make sure your changes are there; a simple cat /etc/ntp.conf will show you the file for verification.

4. Next you need to add your name server to the /etc/ntp/step-tickers file.

    This file is empty by default. Here you should add the FQDN of your time server(s). In our case, we added mars.sg.depaul.edu in the first line of the file, and saved it. Again after saving you may want to view the file just for verification.

5. At this point you can configure the ntpd service to start automatically when the server boots. This can be done by setting the service to "on" in the appropriate run levels. The chkcon-

fig command can set the ntpd service to start within run levels 3, 4, and 5.

```
chkconfig --level 345 ntpd on
```

6. You can now start the service manually using the following command:

```
service ntpd start
```

This will start the service and perform the initial synchronization. If you have running VMs on the system now, you should see the "optional" steps listed below.

Additional / Optional Steps

While the previous steps will configure your server for time sync, VMware documentation offers some steps that may (or may not) be required in your environment.

- Add Time Servers to /etc/hosts: VMware documentation recommends placing your time servers in your /etc/hosts file in case of DNS resolution issues. While I really have not seen this as necessary in my environments, it is an option if you have a flaky DNS system.

- Check the time difference between the time server and your server: If you have a number of sensitive VMs running on your system, you may wish to look at the time difference between your server and the new time server before starting synchronization. A big change in system time could cause problems in your VMs.

  To check this offset, run the following command and determine if you are going to have a major time shift and what its impact will be before synching.

```
ntpdate -q time_server_name_or_ip_address
```

- Finally, you can set the hardware clock to the kernel time once you have the synchronization up and running. This can be done by running the following command:

```
hwclock --systohc --localtime
```

Changing IP Settings for ESX

While no one likes to go through the process of re-iping their servers, there is always that time that you will wind up having to. At this time VMware recommends that you manually edit the configuration files involved to change the Service Console IP address. Some in the community have concerns about changing the IP address of the server since the algorithm used to assign VM MAC addresses is based on the console IP address. While this was true with earlier versions, it has changed since version 2.1.2 (see the section later in this chapter on VM MAC addressing).

It is also possible to simply re-run the 'setup' command within a console session and change the network configuration from within a simple interface. While VMware's documentation and posts to the support forums does not show this as an option for changing the IP settings, we have done it numerous times and it has always been successful. So, right now it seems you will need to jump into a text editor (like vi) and do some manual editing of the following files:

```
/etc/hosts
/etc/resolv.conf
/etc/sysconfig/network
/etc/sysconfig/network-scripts/ifcfg-eth0
/usr/lib/vmware-mui/apache/conf/httpd.conf
```

It might be a good point in time to copy these files; either copy them with a new name or to your home dir so they can act as references if you happen to completely screw up one of the files. First login to the console as root (or su over to root if you need to) and copy the files listed above.

Changing the local hosts file
Next, using 'nano', `vi`, or some other text editor, edit the following files to match your new configuration:

```
/etc/hosts
```

Sample hosts file:

```
# Do not remove the following line, or various
# programs that require network functionality will
# fail.
127.0.0.1           localhost.localdomain localhost
192.168.1.20        esx1.ronoglesby.com
```

Changing the Default Gateway
Again use a text editor to change /etc/sysconfig/network

Sample:

```
[root@esx1 root]# cat /etc/sysconfig/network
NETWORKING=yes
HOSTNAME=esx1.ronoglesby.com
GATEWAY=192.168.1.1
```

Change the IP Address and Subnet mask
Edit /etc/sysconfig/network-scripts/ifcfg-eth0 and change the IPADDR lines and the NETMASK likes as needed:

Sample:

```
DEVICE=eth0
BOOTPROTO=static
IPADDR=192.168.1.20
NETMASK=255.255.255.0
ONBOOT=yes
```

Changing DNS servers and search suffix
Edit /etc/resolv.conf if you need to change your DNS servers.

Sample:

```
search ronoglesby.com
nameserver 192.168.1.99
nameserver 192.168.1.21
```

Applying the Changes

If you have only made changes to the /etc/resolv.conf, no further steps are necessary. If you changed other IP settings you will need to restart the networking for the Console OS.

```
/etc/rc.d/init.d/network restart
```

Once you've done this you need to use the "netstat" command to verify that your console services have restarted and are listening on the Console OS's network interface. You should see a listener on ports 80 (http), 443 (https), and 902 (VMware Virtual Console).

```
/bin/netstat --tcp --listening --numeric
```

Running Support Scripts

VMware has a service support script named /usr/bin/vm-support, which gathers up all the relevant files required for their support department to debug your ESX server. If working with support, you will be asked to run this script then send the support staff the resulting file:

To run the script, from the Service Console, type:

```
root>/usr/bin/vm-support
root>ls -lt esx*
-rw-r--r-- 1 root root 393426 May 5 07:55 esx-2004-
05-05.6327.tgz
```

The resulting files is named: esx-<date>-<unique-xnumber>.tgz, and it contains a couple of hundred files that support will use to debug your system. This is almost the ESX equivalent of a support forced blue screen in Windows.

Adding Users to the ESX Console

Like many of the functions with the Server, you can add users either through the web interface or via the console. With the web interface, you simply need to go to the Options tab within the interface and select the Users and Groups link. Once in the users and groups window, click Add for the users. This will prompt you for the new username, the home directory for the users (generally /home/username), and the user's password.

You can also select to add this user to a group at this point or wait until the user is added and add the user when you return to the Users and Groups list.

Using the Service Console to add users is fairly simple. Use the adduser command with a couple of switches and you are good to go. Here is a quick sample with an explanation:

```
[root@esx1 root]# adduser ron2 -p test123 -d
/home/ron2 -c "Ron Oglesby Test"
```

Using this syntax we see 'useradd [username] –p [password] –d [homedirectory] –c [comment]'. And that's it. Your user will be added to the ESX and is ready to go. If you wish to put them in a group you can modify them via the web interface or add the –g switch to the command above and specify the group name.

Changing a user's password

Generally changing a password is not a tough thing but understanding that most readers of this book are Windows guys we think it's pretty important to draw this out (For sure, since it's so simple!). Simply run the passwd command followed by the name of the user you are changing the password for. A sample is illustrated below:

```
[root@esx1 root]# passwd root
Changing password for user root
New password:
Retype new password:
```

```
passwd: all authentication tokens updated successful-
ly
[root@esx1 root]#
```

And that's it. You're done. If you feel that there is a large group of users using your root account or know the root account password, it's important to change it to maintain security. Imagine every member of your IT staff knowing the domain Administrator password and never changing. Not very secure huh?

For information on running restricted commands as users other than root, see Chapter 7 for the sudo command and its configurations.

Using vmkfstools

The vmkfstools command will definitely be one of your more commonly used commands from the console. This tool allows you to do everything from the creation of VMFS files systems to the expanding of Virtual Machine VMDK files. As its name implies, it the VMKernel File System Tools. If you need to convert an existing VMFS partition to a newer version, or simply name a VMFS partition so you don't have to reference it as vmhba1:0:0:5 this is what you will use.

Obviously there are more commands, options, and possibilities than we can list here. But each available option can be seen by simply running the command with no switches. In addition VMware has a solid article file system management using this tool located at: http://www.vmware.com/support/esx2/doc/esx20admin_fsmgmt_vm fsaccess_disks.html.

Example Syntax: vmkfstools <options> <path>

For those looking to jump right in lets look at some of the command's syntax and some examples. When using vmkfstools and specifying a VMFS filessystem you will need to specify the <path> portion of the command so that it is an absolute path that names a directory or a file under the /vmfs directory.

For example, you can specify a VMFS volume by a path such as 'vmhba0:0:0:5' which is the way the VMkernel sees the partition. Or you can use the volume label, like 'local_0', which really references the same partition, but is more user friendly.

So let's assume we are creating a new VMDK file on a VMFS volume we could use either of the following commands:

```
vmkfstools -c 4096m vmhba0:0:0:5:mf1.vmdk
```

or

```
vmkfstools -c 4096m local_0:mf1.vmdk
```

There are a number of additional switches that can be used with this command but they are generally not needed and should only be used if you are CERTAIN that you need to change the default configurations. Additional switches:

-b --blocksize #[gGmMkK] Default Block size is 1MB if not specified

-n --numfiles # Maximum number of files on files system, default is 256

Before we go through the sample commands, it is a good time to note that if the vmkfstools command is failing, and you don't know why, you should check the /var/log/vmkernel for warnings. Now onto some of the more commonly used commands.

Scanning a Fibre Adapter for new LUNs

When adding new Fibre based LUNs to your system often a re-scan is required on the adapter for the newly zoned LUNs to be visible. It is possible to accomplish this scanning in the management interface under Options > Storage Management or by running the vmkfstools with a "-s" switch and specifying the HBA. This should be performed on all HBAs that the new LUN has been presented to.

```
vmkfstools -s vmhba1
```

```
vmkfstools -s vmhba2
```

Once you have run the command you can run the 'ls' in the /vmfs directory to determine if the new LUN has been found.

Create a new file system on a new LUN

Here we create a new VMFS 2 file system on the first partition of target 2, LUN 0 of SCSI adapter 1. The file block size is 4MB and the maximum number of files is 32.

```
vmkfstools -C vmfs2 -b 4m -n 32 vmhba1:2:0:1
```

Switch explanation:

> -C --createfs [vmfs1|vmfs2]
>
> -b --blocksize #[gGmMkK] Default Block size is 1MB if not specified
>
> -n --numfiles # Maximum number of files on file system, default is 256

Name the newly Created File System

Here we will name the new VMFS file system to a more user friendly name. We recommend that you differentiate between local and san based VMFS partitions by using a prefix of 'local' or 'san', or at the least 'l' or 's'.

```
vmkfstools -S san_0 vmhba1:2:0:1
```

In this case the "san_0" is the friendly volume name and the vmhba1:2:0:1 is the VMkernel name.

Lists the files on VMFS

There are times when the ls command reacts slowly on VMFS partitions. In these situations you can use the –l switch of vmkfstools to list the contents of the file system including VMDK files, redo logs, and swap files.

```
vmkfstools -l vmhba1:2:0:1 or vmkfstools -l san_0
```

Set the VMFS mode (Shared/Public)

With VMFS volumes there are two basic modes for file level access: Shared and Public. Public (the ESX server default) uses less overhead and a file level based locking mechanism that allows only one ESX server to access a VMDK file at a time. Shared on the other hand is used in failover clustering in which two VMs require access to the same shared VMDK file (their shared storage for the cluster).

vmkfstools -F public local_0 ('public' can be replaced with 'shared')

It should be noted that this command can only be run when all VMs on that partition have been shutdown and the swap file (if any) has been deactivated.

Recover/Unlock a VMFS file System

At times you may find that a VMFS file system is locked. This can happen after an ESX server has crashed while accessing that file system. After verifying that no other ESX servers are accessing that file system you can 'recover' it using the following command.

vmkfstools -R san_0 or vmkfstools -R vmhba1:2:0:1

Note: You should only use this command if you are certain that no other ESX Server is still accessing the file system.

Managing the Guest

There are almost an innumerable amount of tasks that you will have to perform on guests within your environment. For this section we have focused on the more common tasks and the ways to accomplish them. Here we will review tasks like how to set permissions on guest within the ESX file system, create dependencies for VMs being powered on when a host powers up and review a number of different tasks that may not be done daily but will eventually be required in your environment.

Some of these tasks may seem simple to you (depending on your experience with ESX or Linux) and some may be completely new, in either case we hopefully will have introduced you enough to the guest environment to understand what you need to do once your system goes operational.

Adding Disks or Disk Space to VMs

Let's assume you have created a number of VMs all with single VMDK files. Due to how ESX Server creates VMDK files we recommend you create a single standard for most VMs as far as initial VMDK size. So following this assumption lets say that all of your VMs were created with a single 10GB VMDK. You then receive a request from one of the server owners for more disk space. In this situation you have two options:

Create a second VMDK: Basically create another VMDK file for the required guest and add it to the machine as an addition virtual disk. This is much like having two physical SCSI disks in the system, one for the OS and application and a second possibly for data.

Expand the Existing VMDK file: This option allows you to continue to use the existing VMDK and only expand its size. In this case you would use vmkfstools to expand the size of the VMDK, thus presenting the disk back to VM with more space available. Once you have resized the VMDK file you must then use a partitioning tools within the VM to either resize its existing logical partitions or create new one.

Creating a Second VMDK

You can create a second VMDK file in the web interface by simply powering off the VM and following these simple steps:

1. Edit the VM properties from the main web interface page.

2. Select the hardware tab and click "add a device" at the bottom.

3. Select the hard disk option.

4. Proceed through the Disk creation processes just like a new VM.

5. Power on the machine and format the disk as you would normally.

At this point the VM will see the disk just as another SCSI disk on the SCSI adapter already installed. You will need to format the drive and prep it for the OS you are using, but this is a rather simple and painless process.

As with most functions in VMware you also have the ability to create the VMDK file via the command line using the vmkfstools commands. While we will be looking at these commands a lot through this chapter, here we will just look at the syntax for creating a new disk.

To create a new disk using vmkfstools we need to know three things: the VMFS volume that it will reside on, the name we will give the VMDK file, and the size of the VMDK file.

In this case my VMFS volume is "local_0", the size of the disk if 4096 MB, and the disk name is data12.vmdk

```
vmkfstools -c 4096m local_0:data12.vmdk
vmkfstools -c <SIZE> <VMFS Volume Name>:<VMDK Name>
```

With the VMDK file create you can add it via the web interface by selecting existing VMDK file in step 4 listed above and selecting the new VMDK off the proper VMFS volume. Alternatively, you can edit the VMX file for the guest and add the following lines:

```
scsi0:1.name = "local_0:data12.vmdk"
scsi0:1.present = "TRUE"
```

In this case we have assigned the disk the SCSI node address of 0:1 and set its location to "local_o:data12.vmdk" the file that we just created.

Once the disk is attached to the VM and you boot the machine, you will now have to format and activate the disk just as you would physical hardware. Assuming you have a Windows 2003 Server as a VM you will have to go into Disk Management and Initialize the disk and create the partitions in order for you to use the disk within the VM.

Expand the Existing VMDK

Another cool function of the vmkfstools command is the ability to expand an existing VMDK file to make it larger. When using the –X switch with the command, you can specify the new size of the VMDK file, with its location and name, and the tool will expand the VMDK file to the new size.

Assuming I want to take a VMDK file named wintest2.vmdk and expand it to 10GB, I would power off the VM and use the following command:

```
vmkfstools -X 10240m Local_0:wintest2.vmdk
```

The syntax for expanding the disk is almost the same as creating the disk, only you will use the –X switch to eXpand instead of the –c switch to Create the disk. Notice that the X switch is capitalized and needs to be.

At this point you can power the VM back on and use the new disk space. It is important to note that the expanded disk does NOT change your partitions. Instead, all it gives you is an amount of unused space on the disk, just as if you had a large disk from the beginning and just didn't partition it all.

If you are expanding the disk because you have run out of room on a system partition, you will need to use a partitioning tool like Partition Magic to resize the existing partitions. If you are just adding an additional partition, you can pretty much use the space as you would any other unused disk space.

Managing Permissions on a Guest

Assuming you are not using a Management tool like VirtualCenter, you will most likely need to assign rights to your VMs on each individual ESX server you have. While it would be nice to assign these simply and easily through a GUI, that is really why VMware sells VirtualCenter. In stand alone ESX environments, rights to VMs are controlled by file system rights on the VM's vmx file.

This may be a good time to point out that if you are still using the root account for access to your server, and multiple users are using root, it's not really a best practice, or for that matter, a good idea. The ability to manage VMs, power them off and on, etc., does not require root level access on the server. So why use it? In addition, if everyone that uses the server uses root, then everyone has the ability to modify hardware settings, change resources shares, etc. On top of that, you loose any ability to audit or track changes since everyone is using the same account.

So what level of security is needed to manage a guest VM? It depends on what you wish the user to be able to do with the VM. Before we get too deep into this, we need to discuss (quickly) a little bit about file permissions in the Linux file system. Permissions on files in linux can be seen by running the command "ls –l" or "ls –l filename" in the directory which the file resides. The "ls" command is basically like a windows "dir" and the –l switch is the "Long listing format" that will show you the file and directory permissions. Below you can see the results of a ls -l in the mftest directory:

```
[root@esx1 mftest]# ls -l
total 96
-rw-rwx--- 1 roglesby root 1474 Oct 20 10:02
mftest.vmx
-rw------- 1 root root  8664 Dec  8 10:44 nvram
-rw-r--r-- 1 root root 21148 Dec  8 10:44 vmware-0.log
-rw-r--r-- 1 root root 20780 Nov  3 11:34 vmware-1.log
```

```
-rw-r--r-- 1 root root 22269 Nov 2 09:15 vmware-2.log
-rw-r--r-- 1 root root 4378 Dec 8 10:47 vmware.log
[root@esx1 mftest]#
```

Notice the first 10 characters in the line for the mftest.vmx file. The first character is the type of file, (-) for a normal file, (l) for a link or, (d) for a directory. In this case we are looking at the mftest.vmx file and you see a (-). The following 9 characters are the permissions for the file. These 9 characters are broken into 3 sets of 3. The first set of 3 contains the permissions for the owner of the file; the second set contains the permissions for the group associated with the file; and the third set contains the "others".

For this example I changed the ownership of the mftest.vmx file to the user roglesby and left the group at root. In the line you can now see that the first name listed is the owner and the second is the group.

So what do the letters in the line mean? Easy: R, Read; W, Write; and X, Execute. In this case the user (roglesby) has read and write permissions to the file, and the group has (root) has read, write, and execute permissions. The dashes (-) in the line show the permissions that the user or groups do NOT have.

Ok, so what does this mean to VMware and how do I change them? Well, what it means to VMware is that permissions on the .vmx file for the Virtual machine control access to that VM. See Table 6.1 below to associate file permissions to operations on the guest:

Table 6.1: VMX File permissions and guest rights

Permission	Access to the VM
rwx	Full control of the VM; all actions and modification rights
r-x	Control power states (start and stop) and suspend the VM; cannot modify configuration
rw-	Cannot control power states or run the VM; can change con figurations but cannot use the remote console of the VM
- (no r)	Can not see the VM

Generally the owner of the VM will be given at least r-x permissions to the VM. This will give them the ability to stop and start the VM and connect to it via the console. But this configuration will limit them when it comes to configuration changes.

So where do the group permissions come in? The user may not be the owner, but they may be part of a group. Let's assume I created the VM and I "own" it, however, I need to give another user (or groups of users) operator-type rights. I can create the file and become the owner, then change the group on the file to a group like "vmops" for my VM operators. In that case the permissions may look like this:

```
[root@esx1 mftest]# ls -l mftest.vmx
-rwxr-x---   1 roglesby vmops        1474 Oct 20 10:02
mftest.vmx
```

We'll talk about changing groups and owners in a minute, however right now you need to setup the permissions on the .vmx file the way you want it. To do this you have two options: the web interface or the command line. Personally I like the command line better, however the web interface is a one-stop-shop and easier for non UNIX/Linux guys:

To change permissions, groups, or owners of a file using the Web Interface:

1. Login as root or a user with writes to the files you wish to modify.

2. Select the manage files link in the upper right hand corner.

3. Browse to the directory and select the file you wish to modify.

4. Click edit properties and edit the permissions or change the users and groups as needed.

To change permissions, groups, or owners of a file using the command line:

1. Login to the service console (remotely or locally).

2. Navigate to the directory that the file resides in.

3. Use the chown command to change the owner or group (syntax below).

4. Use the chmod command to change the permissions (again, syntax below).

The "chown" command is fairly simple. When you run for this you will need to use the −c switch to "change" owner or group, then you need to tell it the new owner and group. Assuming the owner of the mftest.vmx file is roglesby, and will remain that way, and the new group is "vmops", the command would look like this:

```
chown -c roglesby:vmops mftest.vmx
```

Changing the file permissions can get a bit more tricky. File permissions are show in a letter format in a certain sequence but are changed using numbers. Nice huh? Can we make it any more confusing for newbies? Anyway, the numbers are decimal values based on the binary position of the permission you are changing. So, since the permissions are always in the same order – r-w-x – the binary equivalent of these positions are 4-2-1.

So if you want the owner to have full control, the group to have rx, and others to have nothing, you get the following:

Owner	Group	Others
r w x	r - x	- - -
4-2-1 = 7	4 - 1 = 5	- - - = 0

Understand it, yet? Ok, now that we know r=4, w=2, x=1, and - = 0, you can see that the values convert to decimals or in this case a three digit decimal value of 750.

To change the permissions on this file as shown, we would run the following command:

```
chmod -c 750 mftest.vmx
```

This will result in the following permissions on the mftest.vmx file:

```
[root@esx1 mftest]# ls -l mftest.vmx
```

```
-rwxr-x---  1 roglesby vmops       1474 Oct 20 10:02
mftest.vmx
```

Obviously, this is not for those who are uncomfortable with the command line. But if you are, it's really the easiest way to do it, and the best way to ensure that your changes were applied.

Hard Coding a VM MAC address

In some instances you may be required (or may want) to hard code the MAC address on your VMs. There are certain admins in the community that feel this is a must. Personally, we don't think so, but while there are a couple of reasons to do it, the environment that requires it on a large scale is pretty rare.

Reason for Hard coding MAC Addresses:

*   You are using DHCP to assign IPs and require static MACs

*   You need to be able to host more than 256 virtual NICs in suspended or running VMs on a single ESX host (the algorithm only allows for 256)

*   You have an enormous number of running or suspended VMs per server (like over 100) and even more that are powered off and are worried about conflicts

Beyond these you may be doing something at the network level that requires a fixed MAC. In any case you should understand a little about how the MACs are generated and how to work around it.

VMware basically uses an algorithm to create the MAC that is based on the VM's Universally Unique Identifier (UUID) – which is a 128 bit integer that is generated for each VM off the path to the VM's configuration file – and the host machine's SMBIOS UUID. This is obviously a good way to guarantee a unique ID and thus a unique MAC address. But at this point the host will check the generated MAC address against any running or suspended VMs. If a conflict is found, an offset is added and the verification process starts again.

Of course VMware has their own organization of unique identifiers in the mac – these are the first three byte prefix that identifies the NIC manufacturer – that ensure that VMs will not conflict with physical machines, but can (in some situations) conflict with other VMs.

Setting the MAC address in the vmx file:

To start off with you must use a MAC OUI from VMware that they reserve for manually configured MAC addresses. This OUI is 00:50:56. Using this OUI will ensure that any MAC you statically set will not conflict with the automatically generated MACs on the system. The remaining portions of the MAC should then fall into the hex range between 00:00:00 and 3F:FF:FF. This would give you a valid range of static MACs between 00:50:56:00:00:00 and 00:50:56:3F:FF:FF.

It should be noted that the 4th position in the MAC should not go above 3F in hex. The range above 3F is used by VMware workstation and GSX server and could cause conflicts. Now if you do not run GSX or Workstation, this may not be an issue, but should still be avoided to alleviate the possibility of conflict.

Finally once a MAC is chosen you should modify / add the following lines to the VM's configuration file:

```
ethernet<number>.address = 00:50:56:XX:YY:ZZ
ethernet<number>.addressType="static"
```

The XX:YY:ZZ positions being filled in by your new chosen MAC address and the <number> being the number of the Ethernet adapter being hard coded within the VM.

Shutting Down a VM (vmware-cmd)

While this is basically an easy task (power on, power off buttons, right?), we wanted to show you another way to do it outside of the web interface, and explain a couple of basic differences between shutting down and powering off.

When you use the shutdown or restart options from within the web interface, ESX sends the guest service a request to shut down or restart the virtual machine. The guest service receives the request then sends an acknowledgment back to the ESX Server. When using these commands (shut down or restart) you should immediately check the Users and Event page for that VM in the web interface to see if any user intervention is required. The Shutdown and Restart commands basically try to use the Guest OS's shutdown process, like clicking "Start | shutdown" in a Windows OS. But this doesn't always work, specifically when a logged on user has a "locked" console within the virtual machine. Sometimes the VM will hang at this point, requiring user input to a message or just hanging at the screen and not shutting down.

If you get a message in the eventlog for the VM stating "You will need to power off or reset the virtual machine at this point," you will have to launch the Console for that VM and use the Power Off or Reset option. You should equate the shut and restart commands with those issued within the guest OS and equate the Power Off and Reset commands with the power button on a physical machine. So by using the VM's Power Off and Reset "buttons", you basically perform a hard shutdown of the VM, just like powering off a physical server.

Shutting Down or Restarting a Virtual Machine from the Command Line

An easy way to shutdown a guest from the command line is to use the vmware-cmd utility. This utility has a huge number of functions (which we will look at in just a minute), but for now let's look at its basic syntax for stopping and starting virtual machines:

```
vmware-cmd <vmx file location> stop <mode>

vmware-cmd <vmx file location> reset <mode>
```

In this case I may be trying to shut down my FS1 server which seems to be hung and has a vmx file location of /vm/fs1/fs1.vmx, so my command would look like: 'vmware-cmd /vm/fs1/fs1.vmx stop hard'.

The mode setting is an option setting you can give when trying to stop or reset a VM. Its three available options are hard, soft, and try soft. Hard is basically like hitting the virtual power switch. Soft is attempting to use the shutdown option through the guest services within the VM. Try soft attempts to use the soft shutdown, then if that fails, moves to the hard.

Conversely, you can power up or resume a virtual machine using the vmware-cmd by using the "start" option for the utility and the path to the vmx file.

VM Power Mode Scripts

One of the interesting features that the VMware tools have is they allow you to configure custom scripts for different power states. When a VM starts up or shuts down, you can run a custom script; when you suspend or resume a VM, you can also run a custom script.

On Windows VMs, the VMware tool adds a default custom script for both the suspend and resume functions. These custom scripts are really nothing more than BAT files that are stored in the Program Files\Vmware\VMware Tools directory.

Below is a sample of the resume script:

```
@REM #############################################
@REM # DO NOT modify this file directly as it will
@REM be overwritten the next time the VMware Tools
@REM are installed.
@REM #############################################

"C:\Program Files\VMware\VMware Tools\VMip.exe" -
renew
```

The suspend script is the same command line only with a –release switch for the VMip.exe. Very little is documented on this exe but from what we can see it only has three options: release, renew, and get. The first two are pretty self evident. They attempt to release or renew the IP as a guest is suspended or resumed (thus freeing up IP addresses instead of allowing them to go their normal lease duration).

The –get switch seems to do nothing more than just return the IP address of the current VM. While this is really not exciting, the idea of the scripts themselves, are.

By creating your own power on, power off, suspend, or resume scripts, you can create your own custom shutdown and startup scripts for your VMs. These scripts could stop or start services on suspends, send e-mail notifications, write to log files, etc. All you have to do is write the script, then from the VM's console, open the VMware tools (from system tray) and set the scripts to run when the desired power state function is invoked. Cool Huh?

Using vmware-cmd

As you saw in the previous sections, the vmware-cmd utility is pretty slick. The basic idea is that it allows you to do almost anything with a vm from the console that you could do from within the web interface. While we won't show you samples of every option available for the utility, we can review some of its more used functions and a list of all its published options.

The basic usage for the command is as follows:

```
vmware-cmd <options> <Path/vmfilename> <vm-action>
<arguments>
```

There is also an optional –s switch that specifies that the command is for an ESX server and not a VM. You would use the –s switch when using vmware-cmd to do server specific tasks like registering a vm on an ESX host.

vmware-cmd Connection Options:
   -H <host> specifies an alternative host (if set, -U and -P must also be set)
   -O <port> specifies an alternative port
   -U <username>   specifies a user
   -P <password>   specifies a password

If you are logged into the server you wish to execute commands on, there is no need to specify any of these connection options. But if you are running commands remotely from another server, or wish to put them into a shell script for central use, you can use these switches to accomplish that.

To get all the available functions from within vmware-cmd, just run the command with the –h switch. However for a quick list of common ones, with an explanation as to what they do, see our table below:

Common Operations	What it does
getconnectedusers	lists the username and IP of users connected to a VM
getstate	gets the current execution state of the VM
start <powerop_mode>	powers on or resumes a VM
stop <powerop_mode>	stops a VM
reset <powerop_mode>	resets a VM
suspend <powerop_mode>	suspends a VM
getid	retrieves the VM id, also known as its "world"
getuptime	retrieves the uptime of the guest OS

While these are some of the more commonly used VM operations, there are also about another dozen that are available. Some of these options allow you to commit redo logs to your VMs, get product information, and even connect or disconnect virtual devices. For a full listing of the available functions, run vmware-cmd from a console prompt.

Chapter 7

Security

In this chapter many of the advanced security options available to ESX are discussed. After introducing the ESX security architecture, further details surrounding user management will be presented. The majority of the topics mentioned in this chapter revolve around providing a secure Linux operating system environment for the COS. For this chapter I (Scott in this case) enrolled the assistance of a good friend of mine to ensure the accuracy of the information provided.

Derek Milroy is a CISSP and GSEC certified consultant that has been implementing security in corporate environments as both an internal employee and a consultant for six years. Although he has implemented firewalls, IDSs/IPSs, and VPNs for various employers and clients, he focuses heavily on securing Microsoft and Linux hosts, network security monitoring, and forensics/incident response. I had the opportunity to work with Derek for a period of three years and didn't think twice about asking for his assistance in creating usable and accurate content for this chapter.

ESX Security Architecture

Any operations on the ESX server, either at the user level or root level, require that the user authenticate to an account database on the ESX host. VMware provides Pluggable Authentication Modules (PAM) to allow processes to authenticate to a variety of account databases. By default, ESX utilizes the standard console operating system account database through PAM. Once proper authentication is verified, the requested action is kicked off by the vmserverd process. Each of the different management methods (console, Web Interface, etc.) has a different way that it communicates with the PAM layer, as shown in Figure 7.1.

Figure 7.1 VMware Authentication

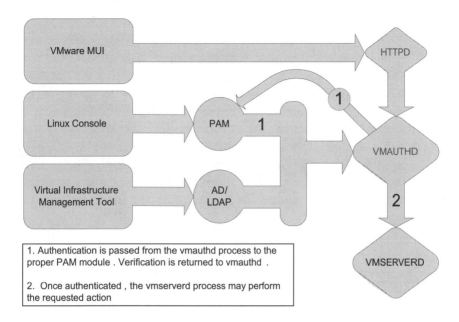

1. Authentication is passed from the vmauthd process to the proper PAM module . Verification is returned to vmauthd .

2. Once authenticated , the vmserverd process may perform the requested action

VMware MUI

The VMware MUI utilizes Apache to present web pages to a client browser. There are scripts incorporated into the MUI that prompt for authentication and send the information to the vmauthd process, which communicates with PAM. PAM then compares the username and password to the local database and either allows or disallows the login request. All traffic sent between client and host is encrypted using SSL by default.

Console operating system

Although the console operating system interacts directly with PAM, when the vmauthd process receives any request, it must verify that the user requesting the action has the proper VMware permissions. Like the MUI, the current user information is sent back to PAM to verify the user's permission to perform the selected action. After this final verification the vmserverd will perform the requested action.

VirtualCenter

VirtualCenter provides a Windows based login to the management console. Permissions for these Windows logins are handled directly by VirtualCenter and access rights are stored within its database. VirtualCenter will verify that the user has rights to perform the requested action and then send a request to the vmauthd as a service user account known locally to the console operating system. All users who manage the environment through VirtualCenter perform actions as a service account user on the backend. The root user is NOT used to perform the actions at the ESX level. Like the other two methods, this service account is passed back through PAM before vmserverd processes the request.

Default ESX Security

As everyone should know, ESX has three default security settings that may be chosen out of the box, and an option to customize which services are enabled on the system. We do not recommend choosing any option other than "High" security settings. This ensures no traffic is ever communicated with an ESX host in an unencrypted state. This also ensures no username or password information is ever sent in clear text over the wire. One concern many people have with this is the capability to copy files using FTP or communicating with the server over telnet. There are secure solutions for any need to communicate to an ESX host. We find ourselves regularly utilizing the following tools for interacting with an ESX host:

- *PuTTY* This is an absolute MUST HAVE application when working with ESX. It provides secure remote shell (similar to telnet) communications to an ESX host. The best part of the application is that it is free under the MIT license. Commercial applications are available such as SecureCRT, but PuTTY provides all the functionality you could need for ESX. A quick Google search of either application will point you to the proper download pages.

- *WinSCP* Another application that should be in everyone's toolbox is WinSCP. This application allows for secure file transfers over ssh. It should be noted that the speed of file copies using WinSCP between a Windows system and an ESX host will be significantly slower than standard FTP connectivity. If utilizing small files, this should not be an issue. One thing we have noticed is that there is often very little need, if ever, to copy large files such as VMDK files to a Windows system. The majority of VMDK file transfers we have seen are moved between ESX hosts. Again, a quick Google search will easily find the WinSCP home page.

- *scp* As just mentioned the majority of large file transfers, such as VMDK files, are performed between ESX hosts. As a review of Chapter 5, we can use the following command to transfer large files between ESX hosts (or between an ESX host and a Linux system).

```
# scp /path/to/sourcefile.vmdk username@remote-
host:/path/to/destination.vmdk
```

When utilizing scp to copy files you will get a progress bar and an estimated time for file copy completion.

- *NFS Server* Although ESX has the capabilities to act as an NFS server, we do not recommend that the functionality ever be enabled. We feel ESX is an appliance and should be treated as such. Unnecessary services should not be enabled. Other Linux/Unix systems can easily be NFS servers, and ESX has the capability to remotely mount these network shares. In addition, there is the capability to map to Windows NetBIOS shares. Instead of setting up an ESX host as a file server, turn it into a network client to access the files that it needs by mounting remote shares.

Password Encryption (Shadow)

There are three main files that are utilized for user account information on an ESX host. These are /etc/passwd, /etc/group, and /etc/shadow. The /etc/passwd file contains a list of configured users on the system. For each user a UID and GID number, a home directory, a default shell, and potentially a full user name will exist. Since the file system utilizes this /etc/passwd file to verify users and rights on files and directories every user must have read access of this file. The /etc/group file is similar to /etc/passwd. For each group that exists on the system an entry exists in /etc/group. Each group listed has a GID number assigned to it. At this point there may not be any users that are in any groups outside of their default group. After configuring custom access rights or enabling the wheel group later in this chapter you will see a list of users assigned to the specific groups as well. Like the /etc/passwd file every user must have read access to the file for file and directory permission listings with the ls command.

You may notice that directly following the user in /etc/passwd there is an "x" character. This character normally dictates the password assigned to the user. Since the shadow password option is enabled by default during the ESX installation all passwords are stored in an encrypted format in the /etc/shadow file. The root user is the only person that has access to read this file, so it is as secured as it can be on a Linux system. Inside the /etc/shadow file you will see the familiar list of user names. An * sign directly following the username in the file indicates an account that is disabled. Also included for each user ID in this file is the password encryption key, the amount of days since 1/1/1970 that have passed since the password was last reset, the amount of days left before the password expires, and the amount of days remaining on a password before a user is notified that their password is going to expire.

Using a shadow file for password encryption is an extremely effective method for ensuring the integrity of a Linux machine. We do not recommend attempting to change this authentication method if you plan on using a local account database for your authentication scheme. We will see a little later that there are external authentication methods available for use with a little configuration.

Firewall

A common misconception with ESX is that when you change security levels using the MUI, you change a firewall policy on the host. Most people are surprised by the fact that iptables is NOT installed on ESX as part of its default installation. When changing security levels in ESX you are modifying which xinetd services start with the system when it boots. The chosen security level will not impact additional applications like backup or monitoring agents that are installed on the system. As long as those services are properly running there should be nothing required at the Linux level to "open access" to those services. Since ESX comes in a secured state out of the box (in terms of configuration) we do not recommend that any firewall software be installed on the system, although it is possible to install and configure iptables.

Configuring User Access

Everyone who has read through the mounds of ESX documentation or has had the privilege of taking the ESX training classes is aware of how VMware configures user access to specific virtual machines. VMware uses a "Flagship" user account that creates and controls all virtual machines. The permissions model of an ESX host is relatively weak in allowing user-level access to control virtual machines and is one of the main reasons most people end up purchasing Virtual Center for their environment. We have a few alternatives that either compliment or replace VMware's recommended flagship account that allow for further granularity in allowing user-level access to your environment. Before we discuss these we should understand the various roles we can assign to users or groups.

Role-Based Access

ESX utilizes user and group permissions of files at the console operating system level to assign role-based permissions to virtual machine access. By assigning various read, write and execute permissions to VMX and VMDK files you can limit which users have the capability to view guests or control power functions within the MUI. While VirtualCenter replaces the roles and security native to ESX, it is important to understand the underpinnings of the ESX security model, especially in smaller environments where VirtualCenter may not be utilized.

By utilizing the console operating system, we can assign four different roles within ESX that can be used to manage both the host and the virtual machines. This level of access is based on both the permissions that are assigned to the guest's configuration file and the custom access we allow with various security customizations discussed in this chapter. Below you will see what these roles are and what access permissions must be assigned to open up the required rights. Each level of access is capable of performing the tasks of the roles above it. Details on the console operating system permission structure are listed in below the roles.

Read only

- No access to log into MUI

- May only view vmkusage statistics (Assuming vmkusage was set up properly)

- Assigned by giving no access on the world (other) rights to the VM configuration files

Guest OS owners

- Ability to log into MUI

- May only view virtual machines they own

- May control power functions of owned guest

- May use remote console feature of owned guest

- Assigned by giving r-x access rights to the VM configuration file

VMware Administrators

- May control power of all guests

- May use remote console feature of all guests

- May create and delete virtual machines

- May modify virtual machine hardware configurations

- May change access permissions of guests

- Limited access to console operating system by using sudoers file

- Assigned by giving rwx access rights to the VM configuration files

Root

- May create and remove users and groups

- May modify resource allocations for guests

- May modify all ESX settings, including network and storage configurations

- Full control over console operating system

- Assigned by default to root user upon ESX install

- Users must be in "wheel" group to escalate to root using su

Alternative to VMware's method

There is a significant reason why we would be interested in utilizing a different strategy than the flagship user account method within ESX. Ensuring we have an audit trail for access to a virtual machine is a requirement of most security policies. If all actions within ESX are carried out by a flagship user it is extremely difficult to determine who really turned off a Virtual Machine or has been creating guests improperly. In some environments this may not be an issue if only 2 or 3 people have access to perform this activity on an ESX host. I have worked in environments where as many as 10 people had the capability to create and modify virtual machines. Having an audit trail for user access to systems is a major portion of regulations such as Sarbanes-Oxley and should not be taken lightly.

vmadmins group

One way to combat the user level management challenges of ESX is to create a local Linux group called "vmadmins". Users that should have the capability to create and modify all virtual machines on the guest should be placed in this group. In order to pass audits on Sarbanes-Oxley it is important that each user have a unique ID and no local service accounts be utilized to login to the system and execute commands. Although we personally feel that ESX should be treated as a network appliance and have a different set of guidelines, it is a very grey line in terms of whether it is a Linux host and needs to fall under the appropriate support models. Personally, we can't remember anyone ever saying "Please lock down the F5 Big-IP to match our BSD Unix standards". The easiest way to create the vmadmins group and add users to it is with the following commands:

```
# groupadd vmadmins
# usermod -G vmadmins username
```

By using this method, there are several administrative steps that are added when creating a new virtual machine. Before any virtual machines are created, the permissions of the /home/vmware directory will need to be modified. If the /home/vmware directory does not yet exist, now would be a good time to create it. Use the following commands to create the directory and set the proper permissions for the vmadmins group.

```
# mkdir /home/vmware
# chgrp vmadmins /home/vmware
# chmod 2770 /home/vmware
```

The above commands will perform several actions:

- Create the /home/vmware directory
- Change the group ownership to the vmadmins group
- Give Read, Write and Execute rights to the user and group permissions
- Ensure all subdirectories and files created under /home/vmware will automatically have vmadmins assigned as their group owner

It is now safe to create a new virtual machine following the standard procedures. The only thing that must be considered is the location of the configuration file. To ensure all vmadmins can properly access the created virtual machines the following must be entered when prompted for the location of the configuration file. This will properly create the necessary subdirectory for the individual virtual machine and assign vmadmins as the group owner:

```
/home/vmware/servername/servername.vmx
```

The final step before powering on the new virtual machine is to ensure the proper permissions are assigned to both the VMDK file and the VMX file so that members of the vmadmins group can properly operate the server. In order to be able to connect to and modify the disk file, the vmadmins group must first be assigned group ownership of the VMDK file. This is achieved by executing the following command:

```
# chgrp vmadmins /vmfs/san_x/servername_0.vmdk
```

Once the proper ownership has been assigned, we need to give both the user and group owner of the file read and write access:

```
# chmod 660 /vmfs/san_x/servername_0.vmdk
```

Running the previous two commands takes care of the VMDK file that contains our data. There are three more commands that will assign the proper access permissions to the configuration directory and VMX file. These are:

```
# chmod 660 /home/vmware/servername/* -R
# chown root /home/vmware/servername/servername.vmx
# chmod 570 /home/vmware/servername/servername.vmx
```

This assigns read and write permissions for the user and group owner of the entire configuration directory, which is required for the proper level of control over the virtual machine. One this has been completed, we may now power on our new virtual machine through the MUI.

As stated before, this adds significant administrative overhead to creating virtual machines, but also provides a greater audit trail than having all administrators utilize the same logon ID per VMware's recommendations.

Setting up account policies

Linux provides us with several mechanisms to enhance the security of our user account policies. We have seen several instances in which a client's security group requires ESX servers to follow the same (or as close as possible) security restrictions as the existing Unix/Linux servers. Fortunately, VMware has the capability to tighten our policies utilizing PAM modules. There are several restrictions that we commonly see across the various environments we implement. Listed below are the various modules and what they allow us to secure. All of the options listed are utilized in the /etc/pam.d/system_auth file. The following is an example system_auth file that has been secured to meet some of the tightest security requirements. You may find that you will need to utilize complex passwords to find one that will be accepted by the system under the specified configuration. This file can be easily tweaked by referencing the following website, which has an extensive list of default PAM modules and how to utilize them. The ones we have utilized in our example are pam_cracklib, pam_tally, and a modification was made to pam_unix.

```
http://www.kernel.org/pub/linux/libs/pam/Linux-PAM-
html/pam-6.html
```

```
#%PAM-1.0
# This file is auto-generated.
# User changes will be destroyed the next time auth-
config is run.
auth    required   /lib/security/pam_env.so
auth    required   /lib/security/pam_tally.so
onerr=fail no_magic_root
auth    sufficient /lib/security/pam_unix.so likeauth
nullok
auth    required   /lib/security/pam_deny.so

account required    /lib/security/pam_unix.so
account required    /lib/security/pam_tally.so deny=5
no_magic_root reset

password  required    /lib/security/pam_cracklib.so
retry=3 type=VMware  minlen=9 difok=2 lcredit=0
```

```
password   sufficient   /lib/security/pam_unix.so nul-
lok use_authtok md5 shadow remember=5
password   required   /lib/security/pam_deny.so

session   required   /lib/security/pam_limits.so
session   required   /lib/security/pam_unix.so
```

pam_tally.so
The lines containing pam_tally.so are in place to lock out the user's accound after a number of failed logins. To unlock a locked account, you must use either of the following commands:

```
# faillog -u username -r
# pam_tally --user username --reset
```

pam_cracklib.so
The pam_cracklib module checks for password complexity. The following restrictions are in place on our preceeding example.

- Minimum length of 9 characters

- Dictionary database is referenced for password simplicity

- The first Uppercase, Digit and Symbol count as 2 characters, so it's possible to have a 6 character password of: Vmw4r! (making 6 characters the absolute minimum when requiring 9 characters)

- The new password must have at least 2 characters that are different than the old password

- Does not allow password to match username or real name

pam_unix.so
The pam_unix module will not re-check the password as long as it passes the pam_cracklib restrictions. It will still deny passwords that are being re-used in less than 5 change cycles

Note that in order to get the "remember" function of pam_unix.so to work properly you must create a "/etc/security/opasswd" file. This may be easily created with the following command:

```
# touch /etc/security/opasswd
```

VirtualCenter

Having just told you how various roles are assigned and how we can lock down a user's access utilizing policies, we need you to grab the nearest blunt object (old hard drives work well). If you intend to utilize VirtualCenter in your environment proceed to pound yourself in the head until you forget just about everything we just showed you. Once the decision to utilize VirtualCenter is made you need to make a commitment to utilize it for all day-to-day management of your virtual machines and user access to those guests. That being said, it is significantly easier to utilize VirtualCenter for the stated tasks. VirtualCenter has similar role based access rights as previously specified, but unlike the standard security model, permissions can be assigned at any level of the organization layout within the console. This allows for granular control over who can modify and control specific guests or groups of virtual machines.

VirtualCenter provides a role-based security model to ensure the integrity of your ESX hosts and virtual machines. Permissions may be assigned at any level in the tree diagram above, including the virtual machine level. There are four roles to which an AD User ID or Group may be assigned. Each role inherits the permissions of the role preceding it.

Read-only

Users with this role may view virtual machines, hosts, farms, and virtual group attributes—that is, all the tab panels in VirtualCenter with the exception of the Console tab. Read-only users cannot view the remote console for a host. All actions through the menus and toolbars are disallowed. A Read-only user can view the templates and scheduled tasks but not perform any actions with them.

Virtual machine user

Users with the Virtual Machine User role may connect with a remote console and view the states of virtual machines. They also have the capability to modify the power state of the virtual machines in which they are assigned. This role cannot modify the configuration of hosts or virtual machines.

Virtual machine administrator

Virtual machine administrators have full control, with the exception of being able to assign permissions, over the hosts and virtual machines within VirtualCenter. The following actions may be performed by members of this role:

- Connect/disconnect host devices(CD-ROM, floppy)

- Migrate with VMotion

- Clone virtual machines

- Remove and permanently delete virtual machines and VMDK files

- Create, import, and deploy templates

- Add and remove hosts from VirtualCenter

- Create, remove, or modify farms, farm groups, and virtual machine groups and their content

- Modify resource allocations and share values for virtual machines

VirtualCenter administrator

With this role, users may add, remove, and set access rights and privileges for all the VirtualCenter users and all the virtual objects in the VirtualCenter environment.

Restricting root access to ESX

As we know, the root user has full access to do anything to the ESX host once it has logged in at the console level. This can potentially be extremely dangerous when too many people in an organization have this level of access. Additionally, logging in as root removes almost all capability to audit who is actually performing actions on the ESX host. The root password should be heavily guarded and known only by the highest level ESX administrators in an organization. There are quite a few methods to ensure those who require access to run specific commands are capable of doing so while still maintaining a high level of security at the host level.

Disabling root over ssh

One of the first steps that should be performed to lock down an ESX system is disabling root access over ssh. This will NOT disable root access directly from a service console or by utilizing the VMware MUI. By disabling remote login utilizing the root account you are forcing users to login utilizing a different account, thus creating an audit trail for logging what they are doing.

To disable root access to a remote secure shell we must modify the sshd configuration file. Use the editor of your choice to open the file /etc/ssh/sshd_config. Scroll down until you find the following line:

```
#PermitRootLogin   yes
```

Change the line to match the following, paying close attention to removal of the "#":

```
PermitRootLogin   no
```

This change will not take effect until the sshd service is restarted. This can be performed with the following command:

```
/etc/init.d/sshd   restart
```

It should be noted that disabling root access over ssh will make it impossible to use scp or WinSCP to copy files to an ESX host as the root user as well. You will need to make the proper modifications to your directories to allow individual users or the vmadmins group to copy files remotely.

Using the wheel group

Preventing a user from remotely logging in as root does not prevent them from utilizing the su command to escalate their privileges. By default ESX allows all users configured on the system to utilize the su command. Fortunately, VMware has included a PAM module that allows us to limit the usage of su.

By utilizing the wheel group we can specify a list of users who are allowed to escalate their privileges to root. This involves two things; we must first add the proper users to the wheel group, and we need to modify the su PAM module to enable wheel authentication.

Using standard Linux user management commands we can add users who are allowed full access to the system to the wheel group. The wheel group exists on the system by default, and the following command will add the user specified:

```
# usermod -G wheel username
```

By default, simply adding a user to the wheel group will not do anything. The wheel authentication for su is disabled by default. We need to modify the /etc/pam.d/su file to enable this functionality. Using your favorite text editor, find the following lines:

```
# Uncomment the following line to implicitly trust
users in the "wheel" group.
# auth        sufficient    /lib/security/pam_wheel.so
trust use_uid
# Uncomment the following line to require a user to
be in the "wheel" group.
# auth        required       /lib/security/pam_wheel.so
use_uid
```

At this point we have two options. Uncommenting the line starting with "auth sufficient" will allow all users that are in the wheel group to utilize the su command without specifying the root password. While this may provide a convenience to your administrators, it removes a level of authentication typically required to allow full access to a system. It is our recommendation that if security is a major concern (and it should be with Sarbanes-Oxley and similar acts), we recommend uncommenting only the second option, starting with "auth required". This will allow users in the wheel group the capability to use su, but they must enter the root password to do so. When an invalid user enters a password, even if it is the correct password, or an authorized user enters an invalid password you will see the following output:

```
su: incorrect password
```

Configuring sudo

Now that we have locked down the capability to login remotely and have an access list as to who can utilize the su command to gain full root access, we need to open up the proper level of access for ESX administration. We need to make sure that administrators can still run the commands that are required without having to actually escalate their permissions to root. The sudo application provides us with a mechanism to allow specific users or groups to run specific sets of applications.

All sudo configurations are made in the file /etc/sudoers. This file should not be edited with your typical text editing applications. There is a utility provided called "visudo" that will modify the /etc/sudoers file in the proper format. This utility is used the same way as vi and should and it is not recommended that any other utility be utilized to modify the sudo configuration file.

Planning your sudo configuration

Before we dig too deeply into the /etc/sudoers file you should know that sudo is a fairly advanced utility. We will only scratch the surface with the security functionality it can provide us with. The configuration described here has been used by us at several clients and has yet to fail a security audit. If more information beyond what is described here is desired, please view the following website:

```
http://www.courtesan.com/sudo/man/sudoers.html
```

The first thing that needs consideration when modifying the /etc/sudoers file is how users are currently configured on the system. If you choose to follow VMware's method of configuring a flagship user you will want to build a user alias list. This entails adding one or more lines to the "User alias specification" section of the /etc/sudoers file.

If we managed to persuade you from using VMware's preferred method of user management on the ESX host and a vmadmins group has been created, it is not necessary to create user aliases. If you have a long list of users with access to the ESX host (which we strongly recommend against) a user alias configuration could be convenient if you wish to allow different groups of users different access rights to certain commands. If you have a large number of user alias groups to configure we recommend that you instead use Linux groups to control access. As you will see, allowing Linux groups to have access to certain commands is quite simple in the sudoers file.

The second thing that should be considered is a list of applications that ESX administrators should have the capability to run without impacting the overall integrity of the host. These typically consist of vmkfstools, vmkpcidivy, and other command line administration tools.

Modifying /etc/sudoers

As has been mentioned already, "visudo" must be used to modify the /etc/sudoers file. We have seen instances where nano managed to corrupt the sudoers file to the point that it can no longer be used. After running "visudo" we will see several sections in the configuration file:

- *Host alias specification.* We will not be making modifications to this section of the file. This section defines a list of hosts (by hostname or IP) that the commands may be run on. Our configuration files only exist on ESX hosts so we feel no need to limit this.

- *User alias specification.* This section allows us to provide a group of users that may be referenced in the "User privilege specification" section in the sudoers file. The groups of users created here may only be utilized internally to sudo and are *not* useable in other applications or for Linux-level security permissions. A list of VMware administrators can be created by adding the following lines in this section:

```
User_Alias  VMADMINS = sherold, roglesby, bmadden

User_Alias  VMCREATORS = dmilroy
```

- Cmnd alias specification - This section allows us to specify groups of applications that were chosen during the planning stages of sudo configuration. Command aliases are utilized in conjunction with User aliases to define rules in the "User privilege specification" section. The Command aliases that we typically use are defined by adding the following lines to the sudoers file. Remember, you can define any application you wish, but you need to be careful of assigning too much access, like giving users the capability to use vi, cp, or cat. Granting access to these commands will allow users to overwrite files, including system files, which is definitely not desired.

```
Cmnd_Alias  VMWARE = /usr/sbin/vmkfstools,
/usr/sbin/vdf, /usr/sbin/vmkpcidivy,
/usr/bin/vm-support

Cmnd_Alias  PERMS = /bin/chmod, /bin/chown,
/bin/chgrp
```

- User privilege specification - This section is where everything comes together and the rules we wish to create are defined. Here we specify which users can run which commands. We are also given some flexibility in defining how the sudo command reacts when a user attempts to run a protected command. The following are several examples from the User privilege specification section and descriptions of exactly what is happening:

```
root         ALL = (ALL) ALL
```

```
%wheelALL = (ALL) ALL
```

The above lines are allowing the root user, and any user who resides in the wheel Linux group, to run any command on the system. The first line is a default entry in the sudoers file. The second line must be manually added. The "%" in front of the wheel tells sudo that this group should be referenced as a Linux group in /etc/group.

```
VMADMINS    ALL = NOPASSWD: VMWARE, PERMS
%vmadmins   ALL = NOPASSWD: VMWARE, PERMS
```

While the two above lines are extremely similar, they do not do the same thing. The first line references the VMADMINS User alias specified in the "User alias specification" section of the sudoers file. The second line references the Linux group "vmadmins" as defined in the /etc/group file. Beyond the users that both lines define, they do the exact same thing. Each allows members of their respective groups the access to run any command specified in the VMWARE or PERMS command aliases from any host. In the above lines of code "ALL" specifies that the commands may be run from any host. In addition, members of the specified groups will not need to authenticate themselves to run the allowed commands. If the "NOPASSWD" tag were not included the users would be forced to enter their Linux passwords before the command would run. It is important to note that the password entered is NOT the password of the root user, but of the user that is attempting to run the command.

```
VMCREATORS  ALL = PERMS
```

The above entry is the most restrictive of any that we have specified so far. This allows users that are specified in the VMCREATORS user alias to run commands specified in the PERMS command alias from any host. Unlike the previous entries, users who attempt to run this command will have to enter their Linux passwords before sudo will execute the specified command. Once authenticated, sudo will remember a user's password for a set amount of time. If a user fails to enter the correct password 3 times an entry is logged in /var/log/messages that matches the following:

```
Feb  6 20:55:16 SMHESX01 sudo[17173]:  sherold : 3
incorrect password attempts ; TTY=pts/0 ;
PWD=/home/sherold ; USER=root ; COMMAND=/bin/chmod
```

If a user attempts to run a command that they do not have the permission to run they will be presented with the following message on the screen:

```
Sorry, user sherold is not allowed to execute
'/usr/sbin/visudo' as root on SMHESX01.sherold.home.
```

All successful and unsuccessful attempts to utilize the sudo command are stored in the "/var/log/secure" file. This makes auditing the system significantly easier by having all attempts in one location.

Now that we have defined the various sections of our /etc/sudoers file, let's put it together and show what our final file should look like at this point:

```
# sudoers file.
#
# This file MUST be edited with the 'visudo' command
#as root.
#
# See the sudoers man page for the details on how to
# write a sudoers file.
#
# Host alias specification
# User alias specification
User_Alias        VMADMINS = sherold, roglesby, bmadden
User_Alias        VMCREATORS = dmilroy

# Cmnd alias specification
Cmnd_Alias VMWARE = /usr/sbin/vmkfstools,
/usr/sbin/vdf, /usr/sbin/vmkpcidivy,
/usr/bin/vm-support (This is all one line)

Cmnd_Alias        PERMS = /bin/chmod, /bin/chown,
/bin/chgrp (This is all one line)

# User privilege specification
```

```
root    ALL = (ALL) ALL
%wheel  ALL = (ALL) ALL
VMADMINS        ALL = NOPASSWD: VMWARE, PERMS
%vmadmins       ALL = NOPASSWD: VMWARE, PERMS
VMCREATORS      ALL = PERMS
```

Enabling External Authentication

There are several whitepapers from VMware that have been published in regards to authenticating your ESX servers against an NT4 or Active Directory environment. This solution is convenient if many users require access to an ESX host system and account management is becoming an issue. VMware provides significant documentation on configuring your ESX host to authenticate users against their Windows account information. Instead of covering the process here we will discuss usage scenarios for this setup as well as some of the benefits and drawbacks of integrating ESX authentication into your Windows password database.

Uses

There are obvious advantages to integrating your ESX environment into your Windows authentication database. Utilizing a centralized database allows your ESX users and administrators to remember a single password. In addition, the challenge of synchronizing passwords across ESX hosts disappears. Typically, external authentication would be utilized in an instance where VirtualCenter is not used in an environment, since users will need to log in locally to perform any operation to the ESX environment. When VirtualCenter is utilized in a virtual infrastructure we recommend that it be utilized to do the things that it does best; one of which is centrally manage user authentication to perform day-to-day tasks. The most important thing to note about VMware's process for NT/AD authentication is that it ONLY enables access to the VMware services through Active Directory. It does not allow for console logins. The amount of people that absolutely need console level access should be small enough that local authentication can easily be used.

Considerations

Integration of ESX into Windows authentication makes managing large amounts of users significantly easier, but is not the best solution in every instance. Several things should be considered before attempting to configure your system to authenticate against a Windows database:

- SMB (NT4) is significantly easier to setup than Kerberos (Active Directory)

- If using a Native mode Active Directory you must use Kerberos

- An account must still be created for each user as a point of reference for the Linux operating system. Only the passwords are referenced on the backed database

- Windows 2003 Native Mode AD will not function with the packages included in ESX 2.5 or earlier. The Kerberos packages will need to be updated before this configuration is attempted

One final note that requires attention is that you should not have a "root" account in your Windows database. The packages included with VMware were not built with the "noroot' option, meaning they will still attempt to authenticate the root user back to Windows. Any user that has the capability to create or change the password of a root account in Windows can potentially have full access to the ESX host. This security consideration also extends to regular users. Anyone who has the capability to modify passwords within Windows will be able to access the VMs on an ESX host. When configuring Windows authentication, it is extremely important to remember that your ESX host is only as secure as your Windows environment.

Patching

Patch management is an important part of maintaining a secure and stable environment. It is important to closely review new patches for both your guest operating systems and ESX itself before moving them into production. All ESX patches should first be tested in a development environment and any issues or special precautions should be noted.

ESX

VMware provides an easy mechanism to determine the current build revision of the VMkernel as well as the various drivers utilized to control the system by using the /proc file system. As you can see from the output from the command below, we are using build 11548 of VMware ESX, which is version 2.5.0. When you log into the MUI, it will state the version of VMware ESX across the top. The information in the /proc file system is useful, as it will tell you the various driver versions being utilized, which will assist in determining compatibility with third party vendors. If a patch becomes available to fix a specific issue, the VMkernel build should change.

```
# cat /proc/vmware/version


VMware ESX Server 2.5.0 [Release.2.5.0build-11548],
built on Dec 10 2004
vmkernel build: 11548, vmkcall: 31.0 vmnix interface:
28.0 driver interface: 4.0 kernel: 32.0
vmnixmod build: 11548, interface: 28.0
vmnix kernel interface: 32.0
Loadable module version info:
 vmklinux   build 11548: Built on: Dec 10 2004
 nfshaper   build 11548: Built on: Dec 10 2004
 bcm5700    build 11548: 7.3.5(06/23/04)
 qla2300_607    build 11548: 6.07.02
 ips        build 11548: 7.10.17   build 728
 bond       build 11548: Built on: Dec 10 2004
 tcpip          build 11548: Built on: Dec 10 2004
 migration  build 11548: protocol: 4.1 vmk interface:
2.1
```

As patches for VMware become available, they should be reviewed based on need for fixed issues or new functionality. When VMware releases a security patch, there is probably a very good reason for it, and it should be applied. VMware appears to release minor releases of ESX every 9-12 months, with occasional maintenance releases in between.

When VMware releases a patch or update for ESX, it is always accompanied by an installation script. Running this installation script will perform the proper actions to apply the patch. If the patch supplied relates to the kernel of the console operating system or the VMkernel, there is a very good chance that a reboot will be required in order for the changes to take effect. Other patches that have been released may update a support application in the console operating system. These patches will typically take effect with a restart of the impacted service, which VMware's installation script should do automatically. VMware releases update information through an email list, and typically has patches for new vulnerabilities available within a reasonable amount of time.

Guest Operating Systems

As with a lot of things relating to VMware, the fact that a guest operating system is running virtually should not change standard procedures for management and maintenance. If a patching and update mechanism already exists for your Windows environment it will still function in an identical fashion when running on an ESX host. The simple fact of the matter is; VMware does not simplify or complicate the patch management procedures of the Microsoft Windows environment.

Server Monitoring and Management

This chapter will examine how you monitor and manage your VMs and ESX servers. We will take a look at how you examine the performance of the host and the guests running on it and examine the tools used for this.

Rules Of Thumb

Before we dive into the more scientific ways of looking at performance we felt it was a good idea to look at some general ESX Server sizing rules of thumb and to get everyone on the same page as to what to expect from VMware. While each and every environment is different and the requirements of the guests will even vary from guest to guest, there are a number of general rules that are used in the community to size ESX servers. Obviously these rules of thumb go out the window in some of the more out-there environments, but for general purposes they are used far and wide by VMware consultants in the field.

VMs per Processor rule of thumb

When using underutilized guests, the general rule of thumb is that you will be able to get about 4 VMs per processor. This number can very depending on the load of your VMs. In some cases you may have a 1:1 ratio of VMs to processors and in others you may be at a 6:1 ratio. Also if you are using VMware as part of a complete strategy for all production servers and not just for consolidation your number may be drastically lower than this. But instead of creating a flow chart here of possible combinations, let's quickly look at the variables that have an impact on your number of VMs per processor.

Quantity and Speed of Processors

The rule of thumb is based on underutilized VMs and today's processor speeds, not the DL380 G1 in your basement. Generally the newer Pentiums (2.8Ghz and above) will supply you with plenty of room to host a number of low utilization VMs. Obviously if you are running older 1Ghz processors you will be able to host fewer VMs, or if your VMs are running processor intensive apps your ratio of VMs to Proc will drop accordingly.

In addition, this is one place that hyper-threading and larger cache is a big benefit. Early versions of ESX didn't support hyper-threading, and the first version that did showed mixed results from a performance point of view. But with ESX 2.1.2 or better and a large cache, hyper-threaded processor will help performance. How much? Well it's a rule of thumb, and it depends on your environment and applications running within your VM, but generally anywhere from 10-15%.

Some engineers ask why we included number of processors in this section. Well one thing people often don't consider is the processor time used by the service console. In our ESX builds we often increase the minimum CPU assigned to the service console to 25% on duals and quads (default is 8%). On eight-ways we have been known to recommend 50% or possibly even all of processor 0.

Let's assume you have a dual processor server and an identically configured quad processor, both running ESX. As a percentage of a single processor, the amount of time used by the console OS will almost be the same or pretty close between the two. But as a percentage of overall time cycles available to the machine – 100% of 2 in the dual and 100% of 4 in the quad – the % of processor used overall in the dual processor servers is higher. Using the 25% COS number, and assuming 4 VMs for every 100% of single processor, you can see that on a dual processor server we may get 7 VMs – 3.5 per processor installed, but on a quad we should get about 15 VMs, or 3.75 VMs per proc installed. Obviously this is a small difference here, but when you are trying to decide between duals and quads it could be something to consider.

VM Configurations
The configuration of your VMs can also have an affect on the number of VMs you get per processor. One common mistake newbies to ESX make is to make all of their VMs utilize VSMP –dual virtual processors within the VM. Anyway, in its current form VSMP adds an estimated overhead of 20-30% per VM that is using it. The

VMkernel basically has to look for free processing time on two processors at once. This is much trickier than finding some open cycles on a single processor anywhere on the server. This overhead will eventually bring down the number of VMs you can host, since your server is spending more and more time looking for open processors cycles than it should (or should need to).

Basically you should only enable VSMP for a VM if two things are true: 1- you have an application (like Exchange for example) that is mutli-threaded and can take true advantage of the second processor and 2- you NEED the SPEED. I have an Exchange server running for my website that I have configured as a single processor VM. Sure Exchange can take advantage of two procs, but why add the overhead to my server when the workload is such that the VM can do it all on a single processor. Taking a VM that will run at 20-30% utilization and adding a second processor will not make it twice as fast. As a matter of fact we have tested this configuration with a well known web application for one of our clients and found that in our configuration the second processor only yielded about a 35% increase in performance. Of course at this point you would also need to determine if adding a second single processor VM, and its associated OS and software costs, would be more cost effective than the dual processor VM.

VM Workloads

After the speed of your processors the VM workloads are the next biggest factor in how many VMs you will get per processor. Often the quoted ratios of 4:1 or 5:1 make people think that a magic wand will appear that will make 4 physical servers that run at 80% all day run on a single processor without slowing down application response time. I have been to a number of customers that have basically counted all of the servers in their environment, took that number and do some of what I call 'ratio math' to the count, and next thing you know they have consolidated their entire 80 server environment into 5 quad servers. Sorry, it just doesn't work like that.

Now, the reason I make fun of the math is that the customer never looked at the current workload of the servers. The amount of processor already utilized on these servers, the speed at which those processors are already running, and of course the types of operations these servers are performing, all have an impact on the number of VMs you will get per proc. In Chapter 5 we went over the processor ratio 'strike zone' in some detail. If you wish to determine your 'ideal guest' or review the formula for maximum consolidation numbers, jump back to that chapter real quick.

Local Storage and HBA Rules of Thumb

While these may seem like two different topics, we like to group them together to cover everything 'local' to the server. Local SCSI disk and HBA configurations have a big impact on how your VMs will perform and eventually how successful your implementation will be. So to start things off let's look at a few good rules to follow when designing local storage for ESX:

*   If using local SCSI storage for VM disk files try to add a second RAID controller into your server. Dedicate this added RAID controller to the vmkernel and use it exclusively for VM disk files.

*   If you are storing disk files locally and can not add a second controller try to create two distinct arrays to split the console OS install from the VMFS storage for the vmdk files – if your controller has multiple channels, use them....

*   Determine the size of your local partitions and disks after you have determined the amount of memory you will use in the server and the amount of VMSwap file you create. This will ensure you have enough local disk to support the swap file.

*   Unless you are in a boot from SAN configuration do not store the VM Swap File on a SAN located VMFS partition.

*   As seen in Chapters 2 and 3, we recommend leaving some space on you local drives for a /vmimages partition. Make sure to size your drives appropriately to leave space for this location.

*   Try to limit the number of IO-intensive VMs per VMFS volume. VMware recommends a maximum of 32 of these 'IO intensive' VMs per VMFS volume, although you should do tests if you plan on more than 16 per volume.

- Use 15k RPM SCSI drives. The small difference in price can pay off in performance.

- Refer to the installation chapter for actual sizing of partitions.

As you can see there are a number of things to consider when thinking about storage and disk performance. It has been our best practice with VMware to always try and separate the COS from the VMs as much as possible. This is one reason we often recommend using local storage for the ESX install even when using blade servers. This leaves the HBAs dedicated to the VMs and makes troubleshooting easier later on.

So what about HBA's? Well a good rule of thumb is that you need to supply about a Gb of HBA speed for about 8-12VMs. This would mean that in a quad processor server you could have two single Gb HBAs and support 16-24 VMs. If your VMs do very little, and have very little disk activity, you may get more VMs. However if your VMs are very disk intensive, you may need more throughput.

Network Connectivity

Like HBAs in your ESX servers you will need to estimate the amount of network bandwidth used by your VMs. Once your VMs are up and running it's a fairly simple process to use the available tools to see which VMs use a lot of network bandwidth and which don't. However how many NICs do you need to get started? Well that depends on a few things: the number of VMs per host, the bandwidth requirements of the VMs, your fault tolerance requirements and your company's networking design.

Recently we were working with a client on their first implementation of ESX. It seemed to be a pretty simple design with 10 ESX servers, about 170 guest OSs and 3 TB of storage. At the beginning, the network design seemed pretty straightforward: 4 maybe 6 network ports; 1 dedicated to the console, 1 for VMotion, and 2 for the Virtual Machines.

Due to the client's network design the 4 port configuration went right out the window. In this environment the client did not allow

VLAN trunking. Trunking basically allows you to configure a single switch port for multiple VLANs. This in turn would allow for the large number of guests that were being migrated to VMs to retain their original IP configuration (another client requirement). So, even though we had enough throughput to support the VMs, the VLAN design, lack of trunking, and requriment to maintain support on ESX for multiple VLANs required that we use 6 nics with 2 NICs configured on each of 3 virtual switches. In this configuration each virtual switch would be configured for a different VLAN, instead of using trunking and port groups that would allow each virtual switch to connect guests to multiple VLANs. This just goes to show that bandwidth and fault tolerance is not your only reason for adding NICs.

Anyway, the general rules of thumb are pretty simple. Allocate at least 2 NICs for each virtual switch if you require redundancy. Then, based on simple math, determine if an average of 100MB per server is enough. If it is, then 2 GbE ports with a single virtual switch should be good for 16-20 virtual machines. We should also state that in numerous implementations VERY few VMs have ever surpassed the 100Mb mark without us forcing it to do so in performance and stress tests.

ESX Server Monitoring

One of the most common questions we receive is about how a VM should be monitored once it is on the ESX server. Often this question comes in one of two flavors. The first is in reference to a VM being initially created or P2V'd and determining which host that new VM should reside on. The second is in reference to how to monitor the VMs long term via monitoring and management tools. Let's take a look first at a process/tool we call "swing servers" then jump into the ways to monitor ESX server and VMs.

Swing Servers

One thing that we are totally convinced of is that each ESX environment that is larger than a handful of servers should have what we call

'Swing Servers'. The idea is that the swing server is used for newly migrated servers, new VM creation, or used for performance troubleshooting of a VM.

The swing server (or set of servers depending on volume) in your farm maintains a reduced load of VMs compared to the other servers. If you have a farm of quad servers hosting 20 VMs each, the swing server would only host 5 or so VMs. The concept here is that a newly created VM can be left to run on the swing servers for a length of time. This ensures that the VM runs in an environment with little if any contention for resources. After a set amount of time the performance of the VM can be reviewed and you can identify its most utilized resource(s). This will allow you to make a better determination as to which host the VM will eventually be moved to and help you to better manage your overall ESX Server performance.

Another benefit of having swing servers is that you can move a VM that seems to be having performance problems to them. This will allow you look at the VM on a different host that has more of its resources free. If the performance instantly improves when the VM is moved, you are already on the right track. If performance doesn't improve, you at least have the VM on a less busy host and can more easily troubleshoot and isolate the problems.

In a farm of 8 or 10 servers or more we recommend at least one swing server. As the farm grows you may need to add more. During p2v migrations you may have a number of swing servers that VMs are migrated to in order to ensure capacity. As the migration nears its end you can then turn some of the swing servers into standard production hosts.

Monitoring Using Native ESX Tools

One of the advantages of VMware ESX having such tight control over the core four resources (processor, memory, disk, and network) is that it continually checks and verifies what is occurring at the lowest levels of the hardware. Fortunately, VMware has provided several mechanisms that allow us to inspect the same information that it utilizes to keep track of these various resources.

It's extremely easy to create a new virtual machine and get it running within ESX, but if not properly laid out, a host could fall apart quickly from resource contention. Knowing how to utilize VMware's tools allows one to check for potential issues before things get out of hand. Analysis of the core four resources over a period of time assists with capacity planning, which will allow you to get the absolute most out of your hardware while maintaining a secure and stable environment.

VMware provides two tools with ESX 2.X that allow us to manage the hardware at its lowest level. Understanding and properly utilizing these tools will allow us to notice potential performance bottlenecks and cut them off before they negatively impact the environment. While the two tools provide similar information, they complement each other by combining to provide real-time and historical data in numeric and graphical formats. This data can be used for trend analysis, for capacity planning, or for troubleshooting purposes when things don't go as planned.

The first native tool we will discuss is 'esxtop'. The esxtop utility is the VMware version of the Linux command 'top'. For you Windows guys, "top" is kind of like a command line version of perfmon. It can show you CPU and memory statistics for the hardware along with running processes and information on each process. ESXtop on the other hand goes where the Linux 'top' command can't. Since the Console OS is really just a high priority VM and only sees the first processor and its assigned memory, it cannot see the processes for other running VMs and hardware dedicated to the VMkernel. This is where esxtop comes in.

Another tool available from VMware is called vmkusage. The vkmusage utilities (or webpages) are really nothing more than a GUI representation of performance data for the VMs and the overall system. This data is collected, by default, every minute and the charts and graphs are updated every five minutes. Vmkusage can also be changed to output data to a text file and to decrease the polling and data collection interval.

esxtop

The esxtop command provides real-time numeric monitoring of all system resources and their utilization levels on running virtual machines. There is a runtime option that may be specified that determines the frequency of the screen updates. Although this command may just as easily be run on the local console of the host operating system, unless there are technical reasons as to why it won't work, we generally recommend that it be viewed through an ssh session to the host.

To run this command simply access the service console via SSH and execute 'esxtop'.

Its default configuration will show you a display like the one below:

```
3:17pm up 61 days, 2:41,15 worlds, load average:
0.24, 0.02, 0.12, 0.38

PCPU: 28.73%, 5.98% : 17.36% used total

MEM: 1978368 managed(KB), 506880 free(KB) :   74.38%
used total

SWAP: 2227200 av(KB), 0 used(KB), 2204928 free(KB) :
0.00 MBr/s, 0.00 MBw/s

DISK vmhba0:0:0: 0.00 r/s, 16.85 w/s, 0.00 MBr/s,
0.11 MBw/s

NIC vmnic0: 4.60 pTx/s, 4.60 pRx/s, 0.00 MbTx/s, 0.01
MbRx/s

VCPUID WID   WTYPE   %USED   %READY  %EUSED    %MEM
128    128   idle    95.75   0.00    95.75     0.00
129    129   idle    76.60   0.00    76.60     0.00
127    127   console14.36    8.38    14.36     0.00
155    155   vmm     5.98    2.24    5.98      21.00
152    152   vmm     3.59    0.15    3.59      28.00
139    139   vmm     3.59    1.50    3.59      14.00
137    137   vmm     2.99    4.79    2.99      10.00
154    154   vmm     1.05    0.04    1.05      4.00
136    136   driver  0.00    0.00    0.00      0.00
```

```
135     135   helper 0.00    0.00    0.00    0.00
134     134   helper 0.00    0.00    0.00    0.00
133     133   helper 0.00    0.00    0.00    0.00
132     132   helper 0.00    0.00    0.00    0.00
131     131   helper 0.00    0.00    0.00    0.00
130     130   helper 0.00    0.00    0.00    0.00
```

The layout of the esxtop screen provides quite a bit of useful information. In order to make any sense of this data, you need to know what the various fields mean and how to decipher the information given. Notice the first 5 or 6 lines in the output. These are your basic metrics for the entire ESX Server. For most of the following information (and all the possible commands for esxtop) you can access its manual by typing 'man esxtop' in your shell session. But for our purposes let's review the standard output of ESX and go over what is important for performance monitoring:

Line 1: UPTIME and Load Average
This line shows you the current system time, the uptime for the server, the number of 'worlds' and the load averages for the server. The load average numbers are the really interesting numbers. These numbers indicate the average time that Worlds ran or were ready to run during the last refresh.

Before we get into how this average is worked out we should get a basic understanding of the World ID. Essentially a World is the process(s) wrapped around hosting an individual Virtual Machine. Basically a World ID is kind of like a Process ID (PID) for a process running on the server. Only in this case a single, VMware specific ID number is given to the VM as it is powered on. This ID is what is used when monitoring VMs and is used for troubleshooting.

In addition to the World ID there are also numbers given to each Virtual CPU instance for each Virtual CPU assigned to the VM. So if a VM has a single processor, it is pretty likely that it's VCPU ID and its World ID will be the same. But if the VM has multiple Virtual processors, it may have two VCPU IDs with a single World ID that both VCPUs are part of.

Now back to the Load Average line. The numbers shown in the load average line are shown as four comma delimited values. These values represent: Current Value, 1 Min Avg., 5 Min Avg. and 15 Min Avg. The interesting thing about this number is that it is shown as an average that can equate not only utilization but also potential utilization. Assuming that a value in this line of 1.00 equates to 100% of all your processors being utilized, the system has the ability to show you values higher than 1.00. The importance of this is that a value higher than 1.0 indicates that there is processor contention and waiting processes. Meaning if your average is 2.00, you would need exactly twice the amount of physical processors you have just to get to 100% utilized. This is a really cool counter since it can not only tell you if you are over utilizing the processor, but also tells you by how much.

Finally, one thing to be aware of is the reason for the 4 different averages on this line. As you move left to right in the report, you move from current average, 1 minute average, 5 minute average, and 15 minute average. The reason for this is simple: moving left to right increases the significance of the value reported. As an example, a value of .9 shown in the current average field is not that bad of a reading; it could mean a simple spike in utilization that will subside rather quickly. But if you see a value of .9 in the 15 minute average field, it means you have had sustained utilization for a pretty long duration and could indicate some serious contention on the CPUs.

Line 2: PCPU
This is a comma delimited field that has the current utilization of each processor followed by the average utilization of all processors. This easily allows us to see how hard individual processors are working. When considering taking advantage of CPU affinity settings, it is imperative to watch this field. Also you should note that this field only shows utilization of the processor and does not include time that processes were waiting to be scheduled.

Line X: LCPU
Another available line is the Logical CPU line. This line acts much like the PCPU return but is for Logical CPUs. This line is only shown if you have Hyper-Threading enabled on your system.

Line 3: MEM

This line shows the amount of physical memory managed by the system, the amount of physical memory that is in use, and the amount of physical memory that is free. If viewing this same information in the web interface for an ESX server (memory tab) the total memory managed would be the total amount of memory minus the memory assigned to the service console. The "Free" memory would match that value in the memory tab physical section, and the % of used total would be the % of all managed physical CPU used by the VMs and virtualization overhead.

Line 4: SWAP

This line shows the amount of ESX Server swap in use. This is the VMware swap files stored on VMFS and should not be confused with the Console's swap space. This line shows the amount of swap space that is configured for the host, the amount of swap that is in use, the amount that is remaining free, and rate of swap in and swap out in MegaBytes a second.

Line 5: DISK

Shows physical disk usage, including total reads/sec, writes/sec, MegaBytes read/sec, and MegaBytes written/sec. The most important numbers are the rate statistics (MB/sec values) for the disks. These numbers give us a raw value that shows the exact amount of throughput being handled by the HBA to access a particular LUN. Utilizing these numbers you can properly balance virtual machines across LUNs to optimize the disk throughput of ESX. The return in esxtop shows a unique line of output for each LUN per Target per HBA. This is extremely helpful when trying to isolate disk contention. For more information on disk pathing and configurations see Chapter 4.

Line 6: NIC

This line shows the statistics for NICs dedicated to the VMkernel. The line output shows total packets transmitted/sec, packets received/sec, MegaBits transmitted/sec, and MegaBits received/sec. For each vmnic in your system you will have a unique line in esxtop. The nice thing here is that you get a glimpse of the transfer rate in Megabits per second for each NIC, now you have a fairly useful number that you do not need to convert to get realistic statistics.

Once you have viewed this high-level information in esxtop you may need to get a little more granular in order to look at a specific VM. To do this you need to jump into the data for each unique world. A world is basically a process for a running VM. If you review the esxtop output again you will notice that the data (by default) is broken into the following columns:

VCPUID
Virtual CPU ID (will match World ID if VM has only one VCPU)

WID
World ID, much like a PID

WTYPE
Type of World (vmm for Virtual CPUs)

%USED
% of physical processor used by the VCPU

%READY
% of time the VCPU was ready to run but was NOT running (this value indicates CPU contention)

%EUSED
Effective % of Processor used by the VCPU

%MEM
% of memory used by the VCPU

With the basic output you can get a good idea of which VMs are using most of your resources. Looking at these columns you will notice that the first three basically identify the VM/Process running. Columns 4 and 5 are really the most interesting. %USED is the amount of physical processor used by that VCPU. If you have a VM that uses a lot of processor this number will be fairly high.

In addition you will notice the next column '%READY'. This shows the percentage of time the world was ready to run (it had instructions to execute) but wasn't able to because of processor contention. The idea is that the %READY number should be very low – generally 5% or less. The more time your VMs spend waiting to run, the more lag time there is in responsiveness within the VM.

%EUSED is the amount of processor the VM uses when compared to the maximum CPU it has been allocated. So assuming a maximum of 50% of a single CPU has been allocated as the maximum for this VM a %EUSED value of 100% means that the VM is using all of the 50% of a single proc you have allocated to it. Contrast that to a maximum value of 80% assigned to that VM, a 50% %EUSED value means that the VM is using 40% of a physical processor. This counter is useful when you need to determine how close a VM is to saturating the physical CPUs when using VSMP or other than 100% as a processor maximum threshold.

Finally, %MEM is the total amount of active memory in use by the VM. The % is based on the amount of active memory used by the VM when compared to the amount of memory assigned to it. If you had a number like 10% on a VM that had 512 MB assigned to it, you could review the memory tab in the web interface and will find that the active memory in use by the VM would be about 51 or 52MB.

Once you have identified the WID that is over utilizing one of your resources you can use that number to locate the VM that it is associated with. The ony way of locating the VM is to use the Web Interface status monitor and look at each VM's WID number right under its name.

Using esxtop
The nice thing about esxtop is that it is interactive. It updates itself every few seconds and you can change the output you are seeing within your session. While the basic output (shown above and below) gives you basic tools for identifying processor contention, it does not show you which VMs are eating up swap space or memory, etc.

Figure 8.1

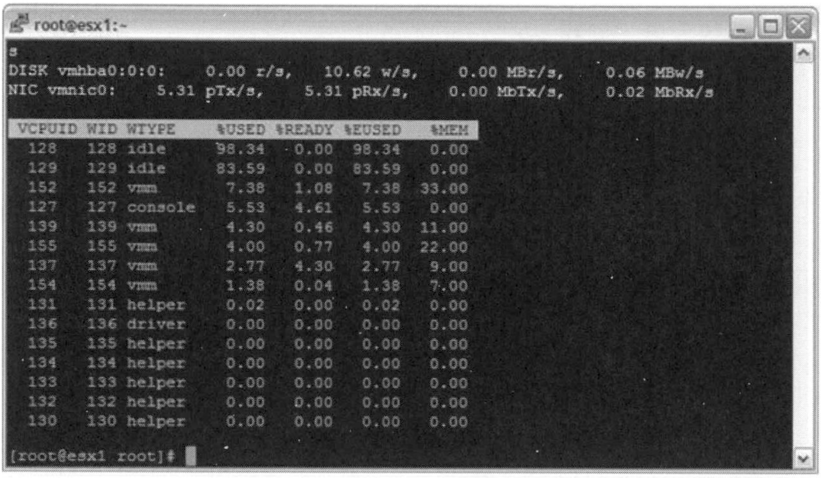

To add columns to esxtop simply start the tool using the esxtop command, then hit the 'f' key (lowercase 'f'). This will present you with a menu for adding additional metrics to monitor (seen below:).

```
Current Field Order: ABCDEfghijklmnOPqRSTuvwx
Toggle fields with a-x, any other key to return:
```

```
* A: VCPUID     = VCPU Id
* B: WID        = World Id
* C: WTYPE      = WORLD Type
* D: %USED      = CPU Usage
* E: %READY     = CPU Ready
  F: %SYS       = CPU System
  G: %WAIT      = CPU Wait
  H: CPU        = CPU Last Used
  I: AFFINITY   = CPU Affinity
  J: HTSHARING  = HT Sharing
  K: MIN        = CPU Shares Min
  L: MAX        = CPU Shares Max
  M: SHARES     = CPU Shares Allocated
  N: EMIN       = CPU Shared Effective Min
* O: %EUSED     = CPU Effective Usage
* P: %MEM       = MEM Usage
  Q: UNTCHD     = MEM Untouched (MB)
* R: SWPD       = MEM Swapped (MB)
* S: SWAPIN     = MEM SwapIn (MB/s)
```

```
* T: SWAPOUT    = MEM SwapOut (MB/s)
  U: MCTL       = MEM Ctl (MB)
  V: SHRD       = MEM Shared (MB)
  W: PRVT       = MEM Private (MB)
  X: OVRHD      = MEM Overhead (MB)
```

Fields with an '*' next to them are the fields that will be shown. In this case I have added fields R, S and T to view swap information about the VMs. This changes my esxtop output to include this new data.

Figure 8.2

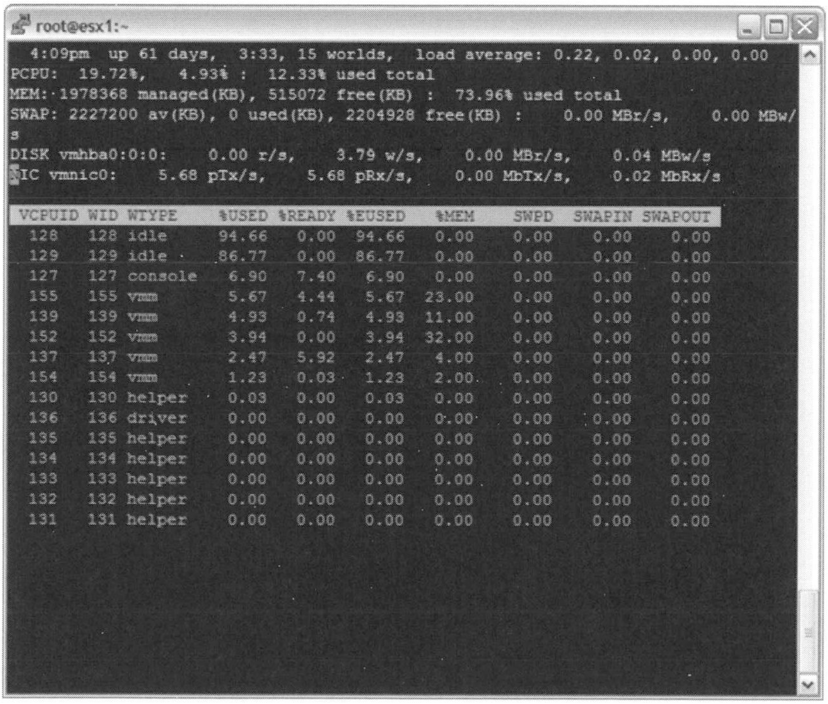
root@esx1:~

```
  4:09pm  up 61 days,  3:33, 15 worlds,  load average: 0.22, 0.02, 0.00, 0.00
PCPU:  19.72%,   4.93% :  12.33% used total
MEM: 1978368 managed(KB), 515072 free(KB) :  73.96% used total
SWAP: 2227200 av(KB), 0 used(KB), 2204928 free(KB) :    0.00 MBr/s,    0.00 MBw/
s
DISK vmhba0:0:0:    0.00 r/s,    3.79 w/s,    0.00 MBr/s,    0.04 MBw/s
NIC vmnic0:    5.68 pTx/s,    5.68 pRx/s,    0.00 MbTx/s,    0.02 MbRx/s

 VCPUID WID WTYPE     %USED %READY %EUSED   %MEM    SWPD  SWAPIN SWAPOUT
  128   128 idle      94.66   0.00  94.66   0.00    0.00    0.00    0.00
  129   129 idle      86.77   0.00  86.77   0.00    0.00    0.00    0.00
  127   127 console    6.90   7.40   6.90   0.00    0.00    0.00    0.00
  155   155 vmm        5.67   4.44   5.67  23.00    0.00    0.00    0.00
  139   139 vmm        4.93   0.74   4.93  11.00    0.00    0.00    0.00
  152   152 vmm        3.94   0.00   3.94  32.00    0.00    0.00    0.00
  137   137 vmm        2.47   5.92   2.47   4.00    0.00    0.00    0.00
  154   154 vmm        1.23   0.03   1.23   2.00    0.00    0.00    0.00
  130   130 helper     0.03   0.00   0.03   0.00    0.00    0.00    0.00
  136   136 driver     0.00   0.00   0.00   0.00    0.00    0.00    0.00
  135   135 helper     0.00   0.00   0.00   0.00    0.00    0.00    0.00
  134   134 helper     0.00   0.00   0.00   0.00    0.00    0.00    0.00
  133   133 helper     0.00   0.00   0.00   0.00    0.00    0.00    0.00
  132   132 helper     0.00   0.00   0.00   0.00    0.00    0.00    0.00
  131   131 helper     0.00   0.00   0.00   0.00    0.00    0.00    0.00
```

As you can see, esxtop now shows me memory that has been swapped and even breaks it down into the amount of memory swapped in and out in MB.

Command Options and batch mode

In addition to the interactive options of esxtop you also have 4 command line arguments available. Using these command line arguments you can set the screen refresh, set the utility to 'secure mode' stopping interactive commands, use 'batch mode' to output the data for logging, and finally, specify the number of refreshes you want to be done.

esxtop command line options

d	Sets the screen refresh interval (Default 5 seconds)
s	Secured Mode. No interactive commands accepted
b	Batch Mode. Used to output to STDOUT
n	Number of times to refresh stats. Often used with b option

Special attention should be drawn to the batch mode option. With a little bit of scripting, the output generated in this mode can be utilized to determine hard numbers as to how the hardware is being utilized over a period of time. This data can then be complimented by the graphical output provided by the vmkusage utility described later in this chapter.

Using esxtop in batch mode, a continuous log file can be generated that contains real-time utilization statistics collected at a set interval. Since this batch collection must run as a process and will consume system resources, it is strongly recommended that it be utilized only to collect statistics during an application test or for troubleshooting purposes.

To generate a statistics log file, issue the following command:

```
# esxtop -b -d X -n Y > outputfile.log
```

The value for X is the delay between screen refreshes. This value will vary based on the amount of time you wish to run the test for. Intervals of 5 seconds will consume a lot of disk space if a test is run for 12 hours. The value for Y represents the number of collections you wish to run. As a simple example, to collect data for 1 hour with collections every 10 seconds you would use a value of 10 for X (sample every 10 seconds) and a Y value of 360 (6 collections per minute for 60 minutes).

```
# esxtop -b -d 10 -n 360 > outputfile.log
```

The data in the output format of batch mode is extremely difficult to work with. To counter this we like to use a vbscript called parse_esxtop.vbs that digs through this data and sorts the data into a useful CSV file (of course you can write your own, but why start from scratch). Once the data is collected you can sort it yourself or use a script like our parse_esxtop to convert it into a CSV. The script and it can be found at www.vmguru.com under "downloads."

More information (actually way more than you need to ever use) about esxtop can be found in the man pages for the command. Simply run "man esxtop" in your shell session.

VMkusage

In addition to esxtop, VMware provides the vmkusage tool to analyze data similar to that obtained by using the esxtop utility and displaying it with a series of graphs. This type of display can give you a great visual representation of utilization trends.

Data can be provided in recent, daily, weekly, or monthly charts, so they can provide trend analyses of both the console operating system and the virtual machines running on the host. The various data analyses are displayed in the vmkusage output for each time interval.

	Console OS	Virtual Machine
CPU	CPU utilization of all CPUs	Utilization of assigned Virtual CPUs
Memory	Active, Ballooned, Shared and VMware Swapped	Active, Ballooned, Shared, Locally Swapped
Network	I/O of all physical NICs	I/O of virtual NIC assigned
Disk	I/O of Each HBA	I/O generated by guest of each HBA utilized

Installing vmkusage

The vmkusage packages are installed during the ESX install process, but they are not enabled by default. In order to properly configure vmkusage to start gathering information and generating graphs, the following commands must be entered:

`vmkusagectl install` – This will set up the proper cron job to run the vmkusage data collection process every minute to collect the data. It is important to wait for virtual machine data to generate, which could take up to 5 minutes, before proceeding to the next step.

Modify `/etc/cron.d/vmkusage-cron.sh` – This is a one-line script that must be modified to collect statistical data for a monthly interval. The original file contains the following line:

*/1 * * * * root /usr/bin/vmkusage > /dev/null 2>&1

It must be modified with the monthly switch as follows:

*/1 * * * * root /usr/bin/vmkusage -monthly > /dev/null 2>&1

`vmkusage -regroove` – This will clear the databases and begin to collect the monthly data specified by the previous step.

We should note a couple of things at this point:

1. The regroove command empties your current databases. So if you are already collecting vmkusage data and want to change it to a monthly interval, be aware of this little caveat.

2. You don't have to enable vmkusage if you don't want to, if you have another reporting tool (like VMware's Virtual Center) and are using that for VM monitoring, you may not need to enable vmkusage at all.

Finally to view the data reported to vmkusage simply use your browser and navigate to: http://myesxserver.company.com/vmkusage.

Using a Guest's Native Tools

In this section we are talking about the native tools available within a VM's guest OS. For Windows OS's this would be things like Task Manager or Performance Monitor. For Linux guests this would include tools like vmstat, free, and iostat. The problem with using tools within a VM is that they suffer from the problem of 'time drift'.

Since the ESX Server only allows the VM to access the processor as needed, the system clock 'drifts' from second to second. This means that a second in your VM may at one point in time be a second, and in another be longer than a second. In the case of performance counters, specifically ones that count items on a per second interval, these items can be extremely skewed and the results misleading.

The best bet is to use metrics that have hard numbers, queue lengths, amount of memory used VS free, etc. These numbers will be fairly accurate and will be more consistent than counters that rely on the system clock (such as pages per second, CPU utilization, etc).

Monitoring Using Third Party Tools

Third party tools generally come in a variety of flavors. The first is the management or monitoring tool that uses the Console OS but is not aware of VMware, the next is the agent or tool that uses the console OS and is aware of VMware, and finally there are agents that install within the guest and can be of the same varieties (aware of VMware or not).

ESX Host Monitoring

Monitoring tools that install on or use the Console OS but are not aware of VMware will do you little good. These software packages will only see what the Console OS sees, the first processor, and the amount of memory assigned to it. They do not have the ability to use the VMware APIs or data from the VMkernel.

Monitoring tools that are aware of the VMkernel are the ones you really need. These tools allow you to look at overall host performance (like using esxtop) and can isolate individual VMs for performance related data. Recently BMC announced its Performance Assurance product for Virtual Infrastructures. This product works like any other third party product will in a VMware enabled environment. The basic idea is that a data collector of some type will collect the standard Linux statistics from the service console and will use the VMware APIs to collect the VMware metrics from the VMkernel. The result of this configuration is a management utility that can look into all of your ESX servers and VMs and track all the data in a single point.

This same design is used by VMware in its VirtualCenter software (discussed later in this chapter).

Using the tools that become available with an ESX Server install limits your ability to view the ESX farm utilization as a whole. Sure these tools are fine for a single server, but that is what they were designed for, to show you data from only that single server. These were not designed to allow you to view data from all the servers in your farm as a whole.

What you need in this instance is a single interface that allows you to view the performance data for all the servers in your farm. In addition to the ability to view this farm performance data you may also be required to create reports about all the hosts and have the ability to compare the host data side by side. The benefits of a software product like this are enormous. With a single management product you have the ability to view your entire farm's performance from a single package. This allows you to simply, and pretty easily, do trend analysis of your VMs and Hosts, and of course be proactive in your VM and farm performance maintenance. The drawback is that this software (like any) is not free, and generally comes with a price tag for both the Console, and each agent you wish to install.

VM Monitoring

Much like the monitoring tools that are used for the host, you may have the same compatibility issues with the guests. Often enterprise size environments will use packages like NetIQ, Tivoli, or HP OpenView to monitor their physical servers. As part of their standard build these tools are installed and the server is monitored for performance and OS and Hardware issues.

Much like using perfmon, these tools are based on the guest's APIs for monitoring performance metrics and are still susceptible to the 'time drift' issues inherent to VM technologies. A best bet when using these tools is to disable counters which are based on the system clock, and percentages of processor usage, and stick with hard numbers. Examples of counters that will be valid in a VM (for Windows):

- # of Processes

- Processor Queue Length

- Memory: Committed Bytes

- Memory: Available (MB, KB etc)

- Disk: Current Disk Queue Length

Obviously these are not all the valid counters but just a few samples. The really funny thing is that you might never know how many counters really use the system clock until you begin to look for valid counters for your VMs.

Another type of monitoring tool often used in VMs are application specific monitoring tools. This software generally looks for service failures, replication problems, disk space limitations etc. (something like a NetIQ for Exchange or Active Directory). These tools monitor the health of a given application based on the services running or errors generated in the event logs. These tools are known to work just fine within a VM as they don't use the system clock (generally) and should be fine in your environment.

VMware's VirtualCenter

Since it would be impossible to review the configurations for every possible management tool out there, and since this really is a book about VMware, we have decided to focus on the functionality of VMware's primary management tool: VirtualCenter.

VMware's VirtualCenter gives you the ability to have a single management interface for all of your ESX servers. Without a management tool like VirtualCenter, you would be required to manage each of your ESX servers independently. The creation of new VMs, the review of performance data, and the scheduling of tasks for VMs would be done on each ESX host without a consolidated view into the overall environment.

VirtualCenter, while not perfect, is currently the standard for managing your ESX hosts, and the VMs that run within the environment. It allows you to schedule tasks on your ESX hosts, set alarms and thresholds for performance, and review performance of both hosts and VMs. In this section we will review the components of VirtualCenter, go through the basics of setting up permissions for users and review the VirtualCenter functionality of scheduled tasks and performance monitoring.

VirtualCenter Components

VirtualCenter is really made up of 5 unique components. Each of the following components interact with each other to give you a usable interface for managing the ESX environment:

- VirtualCenter Client

- VirtualCenter Server

- VirtualCenter Database

- VirtualCenter Agent

- VirtualCenter Web Service

Let's review each of these separately to understand their place in the VC infrastructure:

VirtualCenter client

The VC Client is an application that provides the user interface to VirtualCenter. The client can be installed on a Windows workstation or server and interacts with the VirtualCenter server.

VirtualCenter server

The VC Server is really a service that is installed on a Windows server within your environment. This service accepts commands from the VC client, and interacts with the ESX hosts. It basically acts as a clearing house for all commands/tasks bound for the ESX hosts or VMs and gathers performance data from ESX hosts for storage in the VC database.

VirtualCenter database

The VC database is an ODBC compliant database that stores all VirtualCenter information. Data stored here will include information about the hosts, the VMs, VM configurations, VirtualCenter security, performance data, tasks, and VM permissions. The database is installed at the time of the VirtualCenter installation and is used by the VC Server. You can gather detailed information about the data map for this database in the VMware document: Using VirtualCenter Database Views.

Since the VC database is ODBC compliant you have 4 supported options for your database: Microsoft Access, Microsoft MSDE, Microsoft SQL (7 or 2000), or Oracle. Due to its inherent limitations, Access is not recommended for anything other than demo or proof of concept usage. If you wish to keep away from SQL or oracle and want to use a locally installed database, MSDE may be your best choice. In either case the database configurations and setup are well documented in the VC admin and installations guides available on VMware's web site. Please check their site for the most up to date installation steps.

VirtualCenter agent
The VC agent is installed on each ESX server that is to be managed. Once installed the agent coordinates the actions received from the VirtualCenter server. So if you issue a new task from the VirtualCenter client, it is accepted by the Server, then the server delivers the commands to the agent on the targeted hosts.

VMware VirtualCenter Web Service
The web service is an optional component of VirtualCenter that exposes VirtualCenter functions to third party applications. Most vendors that are developing tools for Vmware today are using the web service to allow their functionality.

VirtualCenter Licensing
Before configuring VirtualCenter you need to understand the licensing concepts associated with it. VirtualCenter requires a minimum of two licenses, but can take three. The first two licenses that are required are a license for the VirtualCenter server – one license per VirtualCenter server installed – and a license for each ESX host that is monitored. Additionally, a third type of license can be installed for each host. This third license is a VMotion license that enables you to VMotion (or move virtual Machines seamlessly) between hosts. The

VMotion functionality will be discussed later in this section, but for now it is important to understand that to do it, you need a license.

So at a bare minimum you will need the following:

1. VirtualCenter Server license for each VirtualCenter Server (generally 1 per data center).

2. A VirtualCenter Agent license for each host you wish to manage with VirtualCenter.

3. Optionally, a VMotion license for any host you wish to use VMotion functionality with.

VirtualCenter Configuration Options

There are numerous ways to configure VirtualCenter in your environment. Which one you select will depend on your organization's requirements for management, redundancy, and DR. VirtualCenter (in its current form version 1.2) is really a datacenter specific animal that requires pretty solid network access to each host being managed and to the VirtualCenter datastore. In some organizations a simple single server configuration will suffice, in other organizations a multiple server configuration with replicated databases is required. Let's take a look at each of the different options and give their benefits and drawbacks.

Single Physical Server Implementations

In this configuration the VirtualCenter database and Server services are all installed on a single server. You may use a small local database like MS Access or MSDE, or might even install SQL locally on the same server.

This configuration is generally good for smaller ESX environments with only a limited number of hosts or servers. It allows for the client to be installed on local workstations and you only have a single server to maintain/backup. Obviously this is one of the least expensive configurations but it does not allow for any server redundancy.

Advantages of a Single Physical Server Implementation

• Least expensive implementation

- Good fit for small, single datacenter environments

Disadvantages of a Single Physical Server Implementation

- Not redundant/Highly Available

- Limited Scalability when MS Access or MSDE is used

- Cannot be made redundant when using MS Access .

Multiple Server Implementations

In this configuration the Database is separated from the VirtualCenter Server. This configuration will generally use Oracle or MS SQL for the VirtualCenter database and is the most common configuration used in large environments. There are several different architectures for this implementation but they basically come back to the VC Server being separated from the Database. Let's review the possible configurations:

- Single VirtualCenter Server connected to a Clustered Database

- Single VirtualCenter Server connected to a hosted database that is replicated

- Two VirtualCenter Servers (one hot, one standby) with an external database

- Two VirtualCenter Servers (one hot, one standby) with a replicated database

Obviously there are a number of minor mutations of these four but by now you should get the idea. Notice how in the configurations with two virtual center servers they are not configured as active/active. The reason for this is the VirtualCenter agent. When the agent is installed, an ESX server can be managed by only one Virtual Center server. So having multiple VirtualCenter servers managing the same ESX servers is not possible, besides not really being needed.

When implementing VirtualCenter it is important to remember that the Server itself is really nothing more than a database application with an ODBC connection. All of the important data and security is stored in the database itself. This leads some organizations to adopt a configuration where the database is made redundant, through replication or clustering, and in the event of VirtualCenter Server failure, the server is simply rebuilt or the application is installed on another server and pointed to the same database.

Advantages of Multiple Server Implementations

* Highly scalable (VMware now says this model can handle upwards of 100 ESX servers)

* Better fit for database replication and redundancy

Disadvantages of a Multiple Physical Server Implementation

* More expensive to implement and configure

* More expensive to maintain

VirtualCenter Server as VM

One interesting configuration/mutation that can be implemented is creating the VirtualCenter server as a VM. The cool thing about this is that you can use it in any of the above configurations. In addition if you are using a multiple server config you can keep the VirtualCenter server on a different host than the database server to protect against a single host failure. And even in the event of a host failure, these VMs act like any other and can simply be started on another host if needed.

Often times large enterprises will create the VirtualCenter server as a VM then connect it to an external database server they have. This allows for a quick recovery of the Server in the event of a failure and guarantees consistency in the database through their normal corporate database procedures.

Structuring your VirtualCenter Containers

In Chapter 7 we looked at the 4 different roles available in VirtualCenter for security. These roles – read only, VM User, VM Admin, and VirtualCenter Admin – are used to assign rights to containers, VMs, and farms within VirtualCenter. Much like OU's within Active Directory, the containers that you can create for VMs within VirtualCenter allow you to assign different groups, with varying levels of permissions to, the VMs. How you organize this structure really depends on how you are going to manage the VMs and farms themselves.

Farm Groups, Farms, and Virtual Machine Groups

Within VirtualCenter you have the ability to create Farm groups, Farms, and Virtual Machine Groups. As their names describe, Farm Groups contain a number of farms. Farms are a set of managed ESX servers that are considered in the same farm, and Virtual Machine groups are Groups of VMs within a Farm.

Farms are generally made of like servers all sharing the same LUNs. If you are not using a SAN, then how you divide up your farms is up to you, and you can skip the next few paragraphs. But if you are using a SAN and you plan on using VMotion, then a farm is defined by the following two rules:

1. All Farm members must share access to the same LUNs.

2. All Farm members must be like hardware and software configuration.

Note on rule #2: software configuration here is in reference to the ESX configuration, number and names of virtual switches, and general configuration of the ESX Server that effects the VM configurations. Up till now most ESX updates allow you to run backward compatible VMs on newer hosts. As a rule of thumb, attempt to keep all the ESX servers in a farm at the same patch/build level. If you need to upgrade a farm over a period of time, try to limit VMotion usage to servers that are configured with the same build.

These two rules are really based around the requirements for VMotion. To understand these requirements we really need to understand how VMotion works. If you do not plan on using VMotion, even between a number of like servers, then you can can simply break them apart any way you want. But if VMotion functionality is going to be used this is how you will structure your farm's groups of servers that VMs can be VMotioned between.

Let's take a look at Figure 8.3 and walk through the basic VMotion process:

Figure 8.3 VMotion process overview

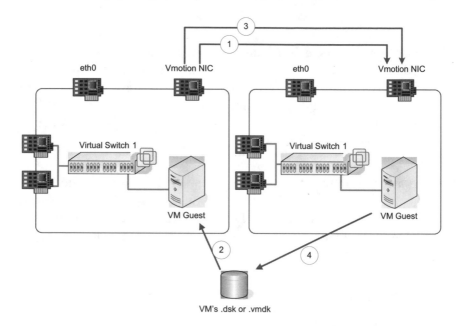

1. The VMotion process is started, a check is made on the target to ensure there are enough available resources to start the VM, and if so, a copy of the VM state – including memory, nvram, configuration, etc. – is started from the source ESX server to the target.

2. Once the copy is complete and the delta of the VM memory between the target and source machines is small, the VM is suspended on the source ESX server and the lock on the VMDK file is released.

3. A final delta copy of the VM's running memory and nvram is made between the source and target servers.

4. The VM is resumed on the its new ESX host and the disk file for the VM is locked by the new ESX Host.

As you can see, the VM itself is not really copied. Instead a new VM is created on the target server, the memory is copied to the server, and then the Guest is essentially stopped on one machine and then almost instantly restarted on another. The trick here is that the guest requires access to all the same devices it had when it was 'stopped' on the source server. The other thing is that the hardware and software configurations between the servers should be identical. If the VM was connected to a virtual switch labeled Switch2 and the Virtual switch was configured with specific port groups, that same configuration must be in place on the target server. Also you should be aware that in the current versions (ESX 2.5 and VirtualCenter 1.2) the resource check done during the first step does not check to see if there are enough available 'ports' on the virtual switch that the VM will be connecting to. This means that if the target host's virtual switch has all 32 ports filled, the VMotion will proceed, but the final step 4 (the resumption of the VM) will fail because it can not connect the VM to a network port. .

Another thing to note is that the processor model on the ESX servers is very important. The idea that processes are pretty much going to be paused and restarted is a big deal. The VM being moved has been running on a specific type of processor and is sending instructions to the processor assuming a certain model. If the model has changed (like switching between a 3.0 GHz MP to a DP) the VM will most likely fault.

A final note on this process is that VMs with large amounts of dynamic memory may not be able to be VMotioned. The basic idea is that the algorithm used in step 2 to determine the point at which the memory deltas are small enough for the suspend on the source server to occur, never sees a small enough number of differences to send the suspend commands. This can happen with a VM that is using lots of memory that is constantly updating (think 2GB + and highly active). The best bet with these types of VMs is to schedule them to be VMotioned during off peak hours. This will ensure the lowest amount of changes to the memory and help to guarantee a successful move.

The most interesting thing that VM newbies note about the VMotion process is that the VM disk file is NOT copied between hosts. This would be a huge constraint to the process – trying to copy gigs of disk between hosts. Instead the VM is simply suspended and restarted on another host. This means that the hosts MUST share the LUNs and see them as the same paths to the VM's files. This is one reason to always use the VMFS volume name when locating VMDK files in VM configurations instead of the VMHBA path.

Now that you know how you will create your farm if you use VMotion, we need to look at Virtual Machine Groups. These are containers for Virtual Machines within the ESX server farm. It doesn't matter what ESX host the VM is currently on, the Virtual Machine group is simply a logical container for you to assign permissions to. How you create these groups is up to how you will manage the VMs.

If you manage the VMs by OS type (i.e., you have a UNIX team that handles the Linux VMs, a Windows team for Windows, and an Exchange team for Exchange) you can simply create groups for each of the specific types of VMs you have and dole out permissions at that level. On the other hand if VMs are going to be managed by their specific business unit and a business unit may have Exchange, Windows File, and Print etc., all in one farm, then your containers may have a structure matching that of the business.

Much like Active Directory OU design, some thought should go into how you structure the containers and groups within VirtualCenter. While it is possible to assign permissions to specific VMs, it can become cumbersome to manage as your environment grows. Try to keep the design simple, determine how you will give access to the VMs and who will need access, and then create the strategy for the containers. If you don't get the structure right the first time, that's OK. Much like an OU structure, it's not the end of the world to change the structure in VirtualCenter. If you find you need to change the design later, it's a pretty simple process to move VMs and VM groups around and change the structure of the tree.

Connecting to an ESX Server

Once you install VirtualCenter you will need to begin to connect to the hosts you wish to manage. To do this you will simply add a new host within the VC client and supply its name or IP address and the root credentials to that server. This will 'install' an agent on the ESX server and create a local service account for use in executing commands you issue from within the VirtualCenter client.

One of things that 'bothers' some people is that VirtualCenter requires the root account password when adding an ESX server to be managed. When the root password is used in VirtualCenter, it is used to install the VirtualCenter agent then create a service account that will handle commands being issued from the VirtualCenter server. Instead of using the root account, VirtualCetner uses this service account to handle all of the VC interaction. In fact, the VirtualCenter server does not store the root password anywhere and 'forgets it' as soon as the agent is installed and the service account is configured.

You will also be asked if you wish to enable VMotion on this host. If so it will require you to select a VMNIC that will be used for VMotion traffic and will require you to assign an IP address and gateway to the NIC. In Chapter 4 we discussed the benefits of dedicating a NIC to this process. As you saw in the VMotion example, it is possible that a gig or more of data may be copied from one host to another. We strongly recommend you dedicate to this feature an NIC that is not normally used by the VMs to help make the process faster and reduce or eliminate the potential impact on running VMs.

Once the host is added, VirtualCenter will discover any existing VMs on the new host. These new VMs will be dropped into a 'discovered VMs' Virtual Machine group. You can leave these here as you wish or you can create your new security and management structure and move the VMs into the groups you have created.

Reviewing ESX Server Performance Data
Once the server has been added you can look at its performance data (at least from an overview level). With VirtuaCenter just installed, little to any data will be available right away. The performance overviews can be seen by simply selecting the Performance Tab of the host you wish to review. You can then select the time frame you wish to view (Past Day, Week, Month or Year) and review the data.

Once the data does begin to collect, you will also be able to run reports for the Core Four resources from the VC management interface. These reports are output as Excel spreadsheets and can show performance statistics from the last day, week, month, or year of activity. Depending on the duration of time you are looking at, the sampling interval for the report changes. For reports from the previous day, you will get the last 24 hours at 5 minute intervals. If you look at the last week, it will be samples at 1 hour intervals, the past month will be at 6 hour intervals, and the past year will be comprised of one day samples.

Changing the Sampling Intervals

The default reports and data collected by VirtualCenter are, at the most frequent, done once every 5 minutes. At times this may not be granular enough to get into the detail of a VM or hosts performance. One way around this is to add your own sampling interval. When in VirtualCenter you can edit the VirtualCenter properties from the File pull down menu. In the VC properties you can add or remove performance intervals as you like.

While this does give you the ability to see more granular data, it also causes an increase in your database size and can cause an increased load on your console operating system. I tend to set up a single additional sample as a standard that I call 'Last Hour'. This sample will collect data once a minute with a duration of 60 samples. This will let me look at the data more closely if needed without drastically increasing the size of my database.

Reviewing VM Performance

Much like the host, the same reports and overview charts can be seen for each individual VM. By selecting the specific VM you are interested in, and selecting its performance tab, you can see the same types of performance information that you see for the host. This information is the same information you can see by viewing the output from esxtop. The one lacking point here is that there is no way to view information about the overhead the VM is seeing or the amount of time it is waiting, like what is shown with the %READY field in esxtop. Still there are very few tools out that will even accurately record and show a VM's resource usage so this is better than nothing.

It should be noted that while the data you see in these reports and charts is based on the same basic metrics esxtop uses, it is possible that the data may not exactly match between the two different tools.

This is generally due to the different sampling intervals used by the two tools and likely occurrence of different start times and the duration of the monitoring. So while there may be some variances between the two tools, they should show the same basic trends.

Host and VM Alarms

One of the features that VirtualCenter offers is the ability to create custom alarms for host and VM performance. These alarms can be triggered by a number of things including host resource usage, host state, VM resource usage, VM heartbeat, and VM states. Once a defined threshold is exceeded, the alarm is triggered and an automatic action can be taken. This action can be as benign as sending an e-mail or SNMP trap, or as drastic as shutting down or suspending a VM.

Alarms can also be created at the group or container level and not just at the individual host or VM level. The nice thing about this is that it allows you to create a single alarm and have it monitor a large number of hosts or VMs without having to reconfigure the same alarm over and over again. So if you have a general alarm for Host state or Host resource usage, and you want it applied to all hosts, you can simply apply it at the Farm or Farm Group level. But if you need to get granular and look at a specific host or VM, you can do that, as well.

A good example of a situation where you might want to fire an alarm is a VM that runs batch jobs. These batch jobs may run flawlessly 95% of the time. But once every few weeks the job hangs and it spikes the processor on that VM and creates a situation where other VMs are starved for processor time until that VM or Process is reset. In this case, you could create an alarm for that individual VM. The trigger would be VM CPU Usage, and the action could be to suspend or shutdown the VM. If you wanted to be nice, you could also send off a simple e-mail to the application owner to let him know that, once again, he has caused you another sleepless night.

To create a new alarm for a host or VM, simply right click on the object you wish to create the alarm on (whether it is a specific host, VM or group) and select New Alarm. From that point configure the

Alarm's name, your desired triggers, and the action you wish taken when that alarm occurs. It should be noted that if you are basing your alarms on performance data, they will only respond as quickly as your shortest sampling interval. This means that if you are triggering an alarm on a CPU spike to 90%, that generally lasts 4 minutes, the default samples of 5 minutes may not catch the spike. Of course this is a little extreme as short duration spikes are generally not an issue, but you should be aware of the limitations.

Script Actions on Alarms

One of the interesting features we hear about a lot is the ability to run scripts on custom configured alarms. The idea here is that if you run into a situation where the 'canned' actions aren't enough, you could write a script. Then instead of just sending an e-mail you could also send an e-mail and have VirtualCenter run the custom script for you.

The script that you specify here should be located on the VirtualCenter server. When the script executes it will execute on the VC server using the account information used to run the VC services. So if you want to run scripts that interact with the Virtual Machines, change power states, or run processes on ESX hosts, you have to design the script to run from the VirtualCenter server.

Configuring VirtualCenter for SNMP

VirtualCenter 1.2 allows you to configure up to four receivers for your SNMP traps. So what's an SNMP receiver? Well, an SNMP Receiver is a software program made to interact and receive SNMP traps/messages. An SNMP trap is like a system log message, however it is sent over the network via a standard protocol. So if you use an SNMP management software you need to configure VC for the receivers on your network. If you only need a single receiver, ensure that it is number one. Then if additional receivers are required put them in numerical order from 1 to 4. Each SNMP trap requires a corresponding host name, port, and community. These can be configured by editing the VirtualCenter properties from the File pull down menu, then selecting the advanced tab.

Here you will be presented with receiver configuration fields, for example:

- snmp.reciever.1.name: The DNS name, or IP address of the SNMP receiver.

- snmp.reciever.1.port: The port number of the receiver. (Default 162)

- snmp.reciever.1.community: The community name or community string.

A community name/identifier is a plain-text password mechanism that is used to weakly authenticate queries to agents of managed devices or software platforms. The idea is that devices on a network are grouped into a managed 'community'. This allows you (albeit weakly) to somewhat restrict the who/what has access to the SNMP messages on the network.

Configuring VirtualCenter for SMTP

If you want to send e-mail notifications from VirtualCenter, you will need to tell the VC server which SMTP server you want it to use, configure a "from:" address, and tell it which port you wish it to use. Virtual Center does not contain the ability to authenticate to your mail server (if your server requires it) so you may need to allow for any SMTP traffic from this server to be relayed via your mail server.

To setup mail notifications from within VirtualCenter, edit the properties again and go to the Advanced tab, scroll past the SNMP configurations, and you will get to the three SMTP settings:

- mail.sender: This is the address that will show up in the "From" field in the e-mail

- mail.smtp.server: This is the DNS Name or IP address of the SMTP server that will relay the messages

- mail.smtp.port: This is the port that VC will use to connect (default 25)

If you run Exchange server within your organization, the easiest way to allow this relay is to simply set the SMTP Virtual Server to allow

Relaying from the IP address of the VirtualCenter Server. Access the System Manager in Exchange, browse to the server you wish to use as a relay, browse to protocols, then SMTP and Right click on the SMTP Virtual Server and select properties. From within the properties, select the Access tab, and under Relay, add the IP address of the VirtualCenter Server.

Using VM Templates with VirtualCenter

One of the more valued features of VMware and VirtualCenter is its ability to store and maintain Template VMs. Template VMs are a lot like a "Gold Image". The basic idea is that a VM's disk file is copied to a deployment point (generally a VMFS volume, but templates can also be stored on the VirtualCenter Server) and used for the deployment of new VM's.

Before staring the creation of your first templates you should ensure you have a location to store them. In most large environments you would have a 'deployment LUN' zoned to all the ESX servers. Sometimes this is not possible, either for political or technical reasons, or it does not fit with your design – like if you don't use SAN storage. In that case you can use a Windows share as a deployment point. It won't be as fast as a SAN connection, but it will allow you to have a central repository for VirtualCenter templates without a SAN.

Before we get too deep into this topic, it is probably a good idea to review the difference between a template and a clone. Within VirtualCenter, you have the ability to right click on a Virtual Machine and create either a template or a clone.

Templates are typically stored in a central repository that you will use to deploy new VMs and their guest operating systems. You have the ability to keep a large number of templates so that you can support multiple guest OS builds. For Windows guests, templates are typically images that have had "sysprep" run against them so they are ready to deploy as new systems that will receive new SIDs, etc.

A clone of a virtual machine is just that: a clone. It is an identical copy of an existing virtual machine. While you can (in some cases) use this clone as a new VM and guest OS, cloning is generally used to create a copy of an existing virtual machine for troubleshooting or testing purposes.

With that out of the way, we can now get into creating our templates and configuring our central storage. Storage strategies were reviewed in Chapter 4 and what should go into a VM template or 'Golden Master' was reviewed in Chapter 5. Here we will simply look at what you need on the VirtualCenter side to make this happen.

Creating the Template

The creation of a new template can be done from the Inventory screen or Template screen within VirtualCenter. We assume here that you have already created the VM, installed its operating system, configured any support tools such as anti-virus and backup agents you need in your basic build, and installed any applications required within the template. Also, if this is a Windows guest you will probably want to sysprep the Windows operating system. Well, don't do that just yet. While some admins do sysprep their VMs and use a copy function for deploy the VM, VirtualCenter (when using its Template Functions) integrates with Microsoft's sysprep tool. (See 'Templates and sysprep files' later in this section.)

When creating a new template, you will need to determine if the VM you are using as a template is a managed VM or not. A managed VM is a VM that shows up in the VirtualCenter console. A non-managed VM is a VM that is not registered on the ESX host you are connected to in VC. If the VM is managed by VirtualCenter, the process is pretty simple. You can simply right click the VM and select the 'New Template from this Virtual Machine' option. This will kick off the template creation process.

If the VM is not managed by VirtualCenter—meaning it is really just a set of files—then the files (both the configuration and VMDK file) must be located on the VirtualCenter server (the system running the VirtualCenter service). If you select the option for a non-managed VM, you need to enter the path to the .vmx. This path should be the path that the VirtualCenter server would see and not the VirtualCenter client. I know, it sounds a little complicated, right?

Well this is really used more for imported VMs than for creating new templates. In any case, once you point the wizard to the configuration file or select the source VM from within virtual center, the process from there is pretty much the same. You will be required to give the VM template a name/description, and then you will need to select a storage location for the template files.

Template File Storage

As mentioned earlier, Template files can be stored on a SAN volume or on the VirtualCenter server itself. The trick with the SAN volume is that it needs to be available to all of your ESX servers. The upload directory on the VirtualCenter server, on the other hand, can deploy templates over the network to any host you can manage, regardless of SAN connectivity. The draw back with using the VirtualCenter server as a repository is speed and network bandwidth. The deployment of VMs from templates stored on the VC server is much slower than SAN based templates. In addition you may be talking about 10 or 20 GB worth of file that needs to be transferred over the network. This can have an impact on overall network performance depending on your network design, seeing how templates deployed over the network are transferred to the ESX server via the console NIC.

If you choose to put the templates on a SAN, a good practice is to create a centralized deployment LUN. This LUN can be zoned to all of your ESX servers regardless of the Farm they are configured in. Even though this may seem to break the rule of no more than 10-16 ESX servers per VMFS volume, these VMs are never powered and therefore you will see little if any activity on the LUN, so those rules don't apply to this particular scenario.

If you choose to place the templates on the VirtualCenter server, then you need to configure the VirtualCenter upload directory. From the File pull-down menu select VirtualCenter settings and browse to the Templates tab. Here you should specify a location on or available to your VirtualCenter server with enough space to host your expected templates.

Templates and Sysprep Files

One of the interesting things that VirtualCenter does is to integrate its template deployment functionality with Microsoft's sysprep utility. The concept here is that you can sysprep a Windows guest, then shut it down and begin the template creation process. When the template is deployed, VirtualCenter has the ability to run what it calls a Guest Customization Wizard. The concept here is that even without VMware the sysprep utility allows you to leave a configuration file on the prepared machine. This file is kind of like a mini unattended setup file that answers the normal questions you would see from the mini-setup program that runs at first boot after a sysprep.

VirtualCenter uses the sysprep files in this guest customization wizard and allows you to answer all or some the questions beforehand. This allows you to create a completely automated build process for the VM with unique information for the guest OS. This feature really comes in handy when you schedule the deployment of the VM to happen in the middle of the night.

Anyway, in order for VirtualCenter to accomplish this customization it needs access to the sysprep files that were used to sysprep the guest operating system. VirtualCenter stores these files in a preconfigured structure in the "\Program Files" directory on the VirtualCenter server computer. In a default installation, Virtual Center installs the following directory structure:

```
c:\Program Files\VMware\VMware VirtualCenter\resources\
```

Under that directory you will find the following structure

```
...  \windows\sysprep\1.1\
...  \windows\sysprep\2k\
...  \windows\sysprep\xp\
...  \windows\sysprep\svr2003\
```

Notice that there is a directory for each sysprep version, 1.1, and the versions from the support folders for Windows 2000, Windows XP, and Windows 2003 Server. As a best practice I like to extract the files for each of these versions into their respective directory, as this keeps me from having problems when someone uses a 'non-standard' version of the program. But if you know you only use a specific sysprep version, you can simply extract those files into the correct directory.

If you have version 1.1 of sysprep, your directory structure under 1.1\ will contain the following directories:

```
...  \sysprep\1.1\docs\
...  \sysprep\1.1\samples\
...  \sysprep\1.1\tools\
...  \sysprep\1.1\contents.txt
```

If you are using a sysprep version from the support folder on the Windows CDs, the content of your OS's subdirectory will contain the following:

```
...sysprep\<guest>\deptool.chm
...sysprep\<guest>\readme.txt
...sysprep\<guest>\setupcl.exe
...sysprep\<guest>\setupmgr.exe
...sysprep\<guest>\setupmgx.dll
...sysprep\<guest>\sysprep.exe
...sysprep\<guest>\unattend.doc
```

Once syprep files are in place on your VirtualCenter Server, you are ready to create your Windows templates. It should be noted that in addition to the Windows customization using sysprep, a similar functionality can also be used with VirtualCenter for Linux guests. An executable can be downloaded from VMware's website that installs the open source components for customizing Linux guest operating systems. Simply running this executable on the VirtualCenter server adds the proper functionality for Linux customization.

Configuring ESX Server to Allow Concurrent Template Deploys

If your templates are created by ESX Servers version 2.5 or later you are (by default) limited to deploying one Virtual Machine at a time, per template. With 2.5 you need to enable a feature called "allocated template disks" to allow you to simultaneously deploy multiple VMs from the same template. To create templates as allocated disks you need to make a configuration change on your ESX server. Templates created prior to making this change will only allow a single VM deployment at a time. To make this change you need to edit the /etc/vmware/config file. Using a text editor like nano or vi, edit the config file and add (or modify if the line already exists) the following line:

```
template.useFlatDisks="TRUE"
```

Once you have saved the file, you need to restart the VirtualCenter agent on the host. You can do this by selecting the Host's properties in VirtualCenter, going to the advanced tab, and clicking the restart agent button.

This change will ensure that all template disks created on your ESX Server are allocated and will allow multiple concurrent VM deployments.

Deploying the Templates

Deploying the VM template is really the easy part of using templates. Within VirtualCenter, you can deploy a new VM from a template by simply right clicking on a target ESX host and selecting the Deploy Virtual Machine from Template option. Alternately you can also do this from the Scheduled Tasks screen if you wish to deploy the template at a later time. In either case the process is pretty much the same.

When you start the wizard you will follow the steps listed below:

1. Select the template you want to use for the new VM.

2. Give the VM a name (this is not the OS name, it's a VM name as seen in VirtualCenter).

3. Select the Virtual Machine group the VM will be deployed into.

4. Select a VMFS volume to hold the newly created dsk or vmdk files.

5. Determine whether you want the VM to power on automatically once created.

6. Select the Virtual Switch that the VM will be linked to.

7. Set the RAM settings and Resource Priorities for the VM.

8. Start the guest customization wizard or import the settings from a XML file.

9. Deploy the template. Allow the VM to boot and give the VM a few minutes to allow the post configuration scripts to run and complete the server deployment process.

When reading it, it seems like a lot of steps, but really it's just a few clicks through about 4 or 5 screens. The longest part of the process is probably the guest customization wizard, and even that can be shortened up some. Most of these steps are pretty straightforward and don't require an explanation, but the options for the guest customization wizard and XML files are pretty interesting, so lets explore them a bit.

The Guest Customization Wizard
As stated earlier, the customization wizard ties into Microsoft's sysprep utility, but that is not all it does. Besides being able to add in items like admin username and password, Microsoft product ID's, Machine name and IP settings, you can also save all of this information into an XML file for later use. That way, when you create the next VM, you don't have to re-enter all of the information for the new server, you can just edit the settings that are different.

The XML files are nice since they can contain all the settings for autologins and even applications to run after the machine is done setting up and the autologin has occurred. In addition, the settings for adding a machine to the domain will be saved to the XML file and will contain the domain account and the password for the domain user and local admin account. Since this account information is saved in the XML file it is obviously secured with encryption, and this allows you to have users or admins deploy VMs without the need to have special domain access or permissions to add a VM to a domain.

Below we have an example of a Customization Wizard XML file. We have truncated the encrypted passwords for readability, but everything is fairly intact:

```xml
<?xml version="1.0" ?>
<autoprep xmlns="urn:sysimage-vmware-com:autoprep1"
xsi:type="Autoprep"
xmlns:xsi="http://www.w3.org/2001/XMLSchema-instance">
<options>
 <changeSID>true</changeSID>
</options>
<sysprep>
 <GuiUnattended>
  <AdminPassword plainText="false">XcnjpRR3=
  </AdminPassword>
  <TimeZone>020</TimeZone>
  <AutoLogon>false</AutoLogon>
  <AutoLogonCount>0</AutoLogonCount>
 </GuiUnattended>
 <UserData>
  <FullName>Ronoglesby</FullName>
  <OrgName> Ronoglesby </OrgName>
  <ComputerName>RAMOM</ComputerName>
  <ProductID>XXXXX-YYYYY-ZZZZ-AAAAA-BBBBB</ProductID>
 </UserData>
 <Identification>
 <JoinDomain>Rapidapp.net</JoinDomain>
 <DomainAdmin>roglesby</DomainAdmin>
 <DomainAdminPassword plainText="false">eqEkoWPs0=
 </DomainAdminPassword>
 </Identification>
 <LicenseFilePrintData>
  <AutoMode>PerSeat</AutoMode>
 </LicenseFilePrintData>
</sysprep>
<adapters>
 <adapter>
  <MACAddress>MAC00</MACAddress>
  <UseDHCP>false</UseDHCP>
  <IPAddress>192.168.165.202</IPAddress>
  <SubnetMask>255.255.255.0</SubnetMask>
  <Gateways>
   <Gateway CostMetric="1">192.168.165.1</Gateway>
  </Gateways>
```

```
<DNSFromDHCP>false</DNSFromDHCP>
<DNSServers>
  <DNSServer>192.168.165.235</DNSServer>
  <DNSServer>192.168.165.236</DNSServer>
</DNSServers>
<DNSSuffixes />
<NetBIOS>EnableNetbiosViaDhcp</NetBIOS>
 </adapter>
</adapters>
</autoprep>
```

Obviously the more options you select in the wizard the larger this file can become. But for the purposes of not having to type in the same information a couple of hundred times, these files are life savers.

Scheduling Tasks

The final VirtualCenter feature we want to take a look at is the ability to schedule tasks. The task scheduler within VirtualCenter works a lot like the Windows task scheduler. It is basically a wizard driven system that allows you to schedule a number of different tasks at some point in the future or to schedule recurring tasks.

There are basically six different tasks that you can schedule using VirtualCenter:

1. Deploy a Virtual Machine from a Template.

2. Clone an Existing Virtual Machine.

3. Change the power state of a Virtual machine.

4. Migrate a Virtual Machine.

5. Migrate a Virtual Machine using VMotion.

6. Change the resource settings of a Virtual Machine.

This allows you to schedule VM migrations or changes to occur during off hours where there is potentially less impact to the environment. Also, if you are creative, you may find ways to use these scheduling options to save horsepower on your VMs. One client we had is toying with the idea of using these scheduled tasks to power off or suspend VMs that are not in use. Most of the VMs the client is considering are VMs that run batch jobs at night or once a week.

The theory here is that the VM could be suspended or powered off most of the day, then a half hour or so prior to the batch job is scheduled to run, the VM can be powered on or resumed from its suspended state. Obviously a configuration like this requires that the jobs being run by these servers be of a consistent duration. However if they are, and you have the possibility of having a large number of these types of VMs, it may be a way to save a bunch of horsepower.

While not as interesting as the previous use, a more typical use of the scheduling features is to migrate VMs from host to host. While migrating a VM with Vmotion is fairly seamless, migrating a host from one server to another without VMotion requires downtime. Using the scheduling tools you can schedule this to happen during off hours and not have to sit around all night eating your precious beauty sleep time.

## Chapter 9

Automated Installations and Provisioning

While VMware's boot CD provides a simple way to install and con-figure ESX, it is not necessarily efficient if you need to configure sev-eral identical machines. A typical installation contains three major steps: ESX Installation, The ESX Configuration Wizard, and Third Party Software installation. The ESX installation and configuration wizard steps can be easily automated using VMware's scripted instal-lation process. We cannot safely tell you that all third party software installations may be automated, but a vast majority of them have options built into installation scripts that allow for a hands-off instal-lation.

Once we tackle the ESX installation and configuration through auto-mated means, we will take a look at guest deployments and the vari-ous ways we can automate their deployment. There are a wide vari-ety of ways to do this and many are currently in use in datacenters for deployment of physical machines. In addition, many hardware vendors are jumping on the virtualization bandwagon and placing VMware host and guest deployment functionality in their enterprise deployment and management products.

ESX Installations

Although it may not be apparent at first, VMware utilizes an extreme-ly flexible installation process for ESX. The installation of ESX uti-lizes the same application that all versions of RedHat Linux (at least as far back as we can remember) have utilized. The Anaconda installer is a flexible installer that utilizes a kickstart configuration file that has a list of installation options. We will see the flexibility and usefulness inherent in Anaconda when we get into creating our own configuration file later in this chapter.

VMware's Scripted Installation

VMware provides a mechanism integrated into ESX that assists in creating a configuration file for an automated build. By utilizing a web-based wizard, you are stepped through the various options for creating either a kickstart configuration file or an installation boot floppy. As ESX has evolved as a product, so has its scripted installation wizard. With ESX 2.5, it is possible to completely configure ESX without ever utilizing the MUI of the target server.

Preparation

One of the most common problems typically associated with attempting to set up ESX scripted installations is improper sizing of the /var partition. To successfully run the script as stated in the next section, you must have a /var partition that is large enough to fit the contents of the installation media (450–500MB depending on ESX version). You should also keep in mind that this directory needs to store the system's log files, so that fact should also play a role in sizing your partition.

Assuming the proper amount of space is available in your /var, we may now kick off the scripted installation setup script. The first thing that must be done is mounting the ESX installation CD-ROM in the COS of the host server. You should know the proper command for this by now (See Chapter 5 if you need a reminder). Once the CD is mounted we can execute the following script as root:

```
# /usr/bin/scriptedinstall-setup.pl
```

Since this script copies the entire contents of the CD-ROM to the /var directory, it will take a few minutes to run. You will be notified of its completion and will be ready to begin creating an automated installation. While you can easily create an automated boot disk at this point, there are some things that we need to point out that will assist in creating a truly automated installation of an ESX host.

We feel it is important to note that running this script will slightly reconfigure your server and the Web Interface to also listen on port 8555. This allows remote hosts to connect over standard http and retrieve the proper files for an http-based network installation. If firewall rules or router ACLs are utilized, you will need to open additional connectivity to this port. The traffic over this port for the remote installation is not encrypted.

Before you Begin

One item that is often overlooked is knowing the hardware configuration and layout of your host system. As you will see throughout this chapter, the more knowledge you have of your hardware's configuration, the easier and more complete the automation process becomes. This especially becomes true when the option for allocating hardware devices based on their bus numbering presents itself. If possible, the following information should be documented before attempting to complete the scripted installation configuration wizard.

Hard Drive Configuration

You should know the size and configuration of your hard drive array. This will prevent you from allocating too much space to partitions and generating critical errors during the installation process.

Memory Configuration

It is typically a good idea to know the amount of memory in your system, the amount of memory you wish to assign to the service console, and the amount of memory you wish to assign to virtual machines. This will also assist in properly sizing the VMkernel's swap file.

License Information

Make sure you have your license information available. You will be prompted for this information if it is not entered during the installation process. By entering the license numbers at this point, you prevent a future reboot.

Network Configuration

You should have a good idea as to how you want your ESX network configuration to look. If you are unsure of how you want your virtual switches configured, we recommend you review Chapter 4 and jump back to this section. You should also know your TCP Settings and Hostname at this point.

System Bus/Device Numbering

Unfortunately, this is one of those configurations that is different on every model of computer. There are no set standards, even with similar hardware from the same vendor. To make things even more difficult, hardware vendors do not always make these values the easiest things to determine. This information is rarely displayed on the system's case in a diagram and is occasionally (at best) shown in the system BIOS configuration. This numbering is often referred to as the "Bus, Slot, Function" format. One of the easiest ways we have found to determine this on a per-model basis is to begin an ESX GUI installation. When it comes time to allocate devices to the COS, Virtual Machines, or Shared, each device will be listed. One of the values listed next to each device will be its "Bus, Slot, Function" number. This is typically a two or three part number separated by colons (9:8:1 or 15:8:0). The first number will always be the system bus number the device is connected to. The second number represents the PCI slot number where the device is located. The third number represents the function, which is often used when working with HBAs or NICs that have multiple ports. If you plan to perform a fully automated installation, this information should be well documented.

Configuration Wizard

Armed with the above information, we can finally kick off the scripted installation wizard. By pointing our web browser to the MUI of the ESX server that the scriptedinstall-setup.pl script was run on, we may kick off the scripted installation from the options menu. If the Perl script mentioned was successfully run on the host, you will see the first screen of the Wizard, which should contain "Kickstart Options".

While the ESX 2.5 Installation Guide does a good job of describing the various options, we feel more focus should be placed on several of them. If a specific option is not mentioned, there is nothing special to take note of when walking through the wizard. We will also try and avoid boring you with the obvious.

Kickstart Options

The title of this configuration section is actually quite deceptive as technically, every option we specify using the wizard is a kickstart option.

Installation Method

There are four options available to us in the MUI wizard: CD-ROM, Network, Remote, and NFS. These values represent the location of the installation files. Choosing CD-ROM will require that the ESX installation media be in the CD drive of the target system. You may need to modify the system boot order so the system properly boots off the floppy drive to kick off the automated installation.

The Network and Remote options are nearly identical. The sole difference is the "Network" option automatically configures the current server as the source HTTP server (and disables the "Remote Server URL" field). When choosing "Remote," you must specify a "Remote Server URL" which may be a remote (to the target system) HTTP or FTP server. You are not limited to the http protocol. We will further discuss the various options in the "Customizing your Boot Floppy" section.

If you choose NFS as the Installation Method, you should be aware that the scriptedinstall-setup.pl script does NOT setup your ESX host as an NFS server. You will either need to modify your ESX security settings and manually configure an NFS share or point to a remote system that has been properly configured. We have found that it is best (and most secure) if you do not use your ESX servers as installation distribution servers. We strongly recommend using either a standalone server, or, at the very least, a virtual machine with an HTTP/FTP server or with NFS configured. Running unnecessary services should be avoided on your console operating system whenever possible.

Network Method
You are only given two simple options for the "Network Method" configuration: DHCP and Static IP. If Static is chosen as an option, you will perform the proper configuration in the next screen. If DHCP is chosen, you will skip the IP configuration page and move forward to the EULA page. It is VERY important to note that if DHCP is chosen for this section, you will not be able to configure a hostname, which will cause major problems with the SSL certificate when you attempt to configure a permanent hostname. It is strongly recommended that you always have your IP information available ahead of time. At the very least, fake information should be entered for the IP address so the hostname may be properly configured. It is safe, and quite easy, to change the IP information after the host has been built.

Boot Device
If you are planning to take advantage of the "Boot from SAN" capabilities of ESX 2.5, make sure you choose "SAN" for the "Boot Device" option.

Networking Options
There are no out of the ordinary options when configuring the networking section. As mentioned before, it is always recommended that the hostname information be entered to prevent issues with the SSL certificate.

Virtual Switch Options
Starting with ESX 2.5, VMware has provided functionality to automatically configure virtual switches during the installation process. On this screen you have the capability to configure multiple virtual switches and define the amount of physical NICs that are assigned to Virtual Machines by the VMkernel. When naming your virtual switches, you want to avoid using a number as the first character of the name. Typically, you want to name your virtual switch something meaningful. If using VLAN tagging at the network switch, you could name the virtual switch based on its VLAN, such as "VLAN120". If using VLAN tagging at the virtual switch, you can use something along the lines of "ProdVLANs" or "DevVLANs". It is not possible at this point to create port groups in the automated installation process. This can be performed as a post-configuration script. More details on the advanced configuration of networking options within ESX can be found in Chapter 4. You should also keep VMotion under consideration, as it requires its own virtual switch. Typically, a name such as "VMotion" will suffice for this virtual switch.

When configuring the "Number of Network Cards", it is important to remember that this value is the amount of cards assigned to Virtual Machines and not the total amount of adapters installed in the host. At this point, we have not configured which adapters are assigned to the service console and which are assigned to virtual machines. We will actually assign the network adapters that each switch will use on the next screen.

NIC Configuration

On the next screen, after assigning your virtual switch names and number of virtual machine NICs, you will get an entry for each physical NIC. For each NIC, you can properly assign it to one of the virtual switches, created on the previous screen, from the dropdown box. When determining which physical NIC is associated with the NIC on the configuration screen, you should remember that virtual machine NICs are assigned in the order the system scans them on the system bus. There are no guarantees that the bus numbering follows the PCI slot order on the back of the system. After building your first system, you will want to thoroughly check the network configuration and ensure you have achieved the desired results. Once you have the proper configuration, you will know how to configure additional systems.

Console Configuration

Although VMware temporarily stops labeling configuration pages at this point in time, we can clearly see that the next screen configures values for the console operating system. The serial number information is straightforward. Remember, each server requires its own unique serial numbers.

Reserved Memory

When configuring the memory reserved for the console OS, the MUI provides the proper default values in the dropdown box. They also define the mappings of amount of virtual machines to the amount of memory to configure. We have found that while VMware's recommendations are solid values, it never hurts to assign a little more memory to the service console. Please review Chapter 3 for more information on assigning console memory.

PCI Configuration Method

There are two options available for PCI Configuration: Automatic or Manual. VMware has done a very good job with their Automatic PCI configuration. For most default configurations, this option will work extremely well. Choosing "Automatic" configures your devices in the following manner: The first detected NIC gets assigned to the service console. The first detected SCSI device gets assigned to Virtual Machines and shared with the Service Console. All remaining devices get assigned to Virtual Machines. If you choose Automatic, you will jump forward to the disk partitioning section. If you choose Manual, the next screen you will be presented with will allow you to completely configure your PCI devices.

PCI Device Allocation

This screen is the reason you had to research and document your device numbering when attempting to create an automated installation. When you have a configuration that is beyond the default "Automatic" configuration mentioned previously, you can utilize this screen to allocate your devices as needed. Unfortunately, there is a limitation of being able to configure only 8 devices using the MUI. If you have a system crammed full of NICs, you will either have to configure the initial deployment as "Automatic", and reconfigure after the final reboot, or read further on manually configuring a ks.cfg file. When entering information, it is important to remember that all values entered here should be in hexadecimal format. For values of 10 and higher, this should be considered.

Partition Configuration

The partition configuration section is extremely similar to what you would see during the standard installation process. The one item you want to watch closely is that you choose the proper controller configuration. The Installation Wizard can configure several different device controllers for partition configuration. It is important that the proper configuration is chosen because if the wrong option is chosen, your partitions will not be configured during the build process.

- IDE Disks (hdx)

- Standard SCSI Disks (sdx)

- HP SCSI Controller (cciss/cxdx)

- Compaq Smart Controller (ida/cxdx)

- Mylex DAC960 Controller (rd/cxdx)

IDE Devices are typically utilized on blade chassis. You may not configure a VMFS partition on an IDE Disk. This will generate an error during the verification before proceeding to the next configuration screen. Unless you are using an HP or Compaq system, there is a good chance that the standard SCSI disk will work. If you are unsure of what choice to make, you can verify against a configured system by running the "df" command as the root user. This will provide you with a list of partitions and their device mappings.

Create and Name Swapfiles

This configuration option is new to ESX 2.5 and allows us to configure the swap file as part of the installation process. Combined with the other options new to ESX 2.5, you can actually configure a system during its installation process or with a configuration script to boot the first time with ESX in a fully configured state.

Select Partitioned Volume

This section provides a dropdown list of VMFS partitions that were created in the previous step based on the Volume Label that was assigned. There is also the option to configure the swap file on an already existing VMFS partition (in the event of a system rebuild while leaving the VMFS volumes in tact).

FileName

VMware provides the option to leave this field blank if you are utilizing a static IP address to configure your system. We have to recommend against using this option as it will name the VMware Swap File with the IP Address that you have configured your system for. Although it has no functional difference over any other name, it just doesn't look right. The default value assigned if using the VMware MUI in a standard installation is "SwapFile.vswp". Since this is just a name, and function is not modified if it is named differently, there is no reason to change it. Troubleshooting issues with ESX is easier if the file is named using the standard, as it is obvious what the file is and what it is used for.

Size

When sizing your VMware swap file, make sure that it is not configured larger than the VMFS partition that was created. This will cause errors during the boot process and will prevent the swap file from properly starting. The size is specified in Megabytes, so make sure the proper math is performed if you are sizing your values in Gigabytes.

When all options are properly set for the Swap File, it is important that you actually click on the "Create Swap File" button. The options specified will be placed in the list on the bottom half of the configuration page. Once you have at least one swap file, you can move to the final screen of the Scripted Installation Wizard.

Floppy Image or Kickstart File?

After completing the wizard you are given two options: "Download Floppy Image" or "Download Kickstart File". The floppy image is an image file that can be written to a floppy disk and booted from. The proper ks.cfg file is located in the image file. Based on the installation method and decisions made previously, the boot disk will read the installation from the proper source and install ESX based on the ks.cfg file. There are several ways to create the bootable floppy disk depending on your operating system.

From a Linux system

Linux has the proper tools to natively write an image file to a disk. As shown in Chapter 5, we can utilize the dd command to create an ISO image file from a CD-ROM. We can utilize the same utility to write an image file to a disk. With the IMG file on the local computer (whether it was copied or the CD-ROM drive was mounted), and a blank diskette in the floppy drive, run the following command:

```
# dd if=/mnt/cdrom/images/bootnet.img of=/dev/fd0
```

From a Windows system

Windows does not have native support for writing floppy images. Fortunately, VMware has provided a dos utility called rawrite that can be found on your installation media under X:\dosutils (where X is your CD-ROM drive). It is easiest if both rawrite and your image file reside in the same directory on your computer. After inserting a formatted diskette into your floppy drive, you can utilize the following command to create your boot floppy (The command assumes your files are in "C:\directory" and your floppy drive is lettered "A"):

```
C:\directory> rawrite -f bootnet.img -d A
```

If you choose to download the ks.cfg file directly, the easiest way to utilize this would be to place it on a blank floppy disk. You can then boot off of the ESX installation CD and enter the following at the lilo boot prompt:

```
esx ks=floppy
```

What this actually does is tells the system to perform a standard esx boot as specified by the syslinux.cfg file. It also passes a boot parameter (ks=floppy) that is used by the Anaconda installer to override the ks.cfg file in the local initrd.img file and use the one located on the floppy drive. We will discuss some advanced ks.cfg file options when we talk about building a custom ks.cfg file later in this chapter.

PXE Deployment Tools

PXE deployment tools for ESX server are still in their infancy stage. Although the ESX installation is based on the installer for Red Hat 7.2, there is a lot of custom functionality written by VMware to simplify the configuration of ESX during the installation process. While we have not tried every product available, we have found those that we have tried are limited in their capabilities to completely configure an ESX host. Often times utilizing a deployment tool is equivalent to installing off the CD-ROM media and the same amount of post-configuration needs to go into finalizing the host build.

Most of the major hardware vendors have integrated functionality into their deployment tools that allow automated installations of ESX. Some are better than others, and each has its limitations that are already well documented. Although the primary use advertised by the vendors is for deployment onto blade servers, the deployment software configurations can often times be modified to support most hardware.

Customizing your Boot Floppy

We feel it is important to briefly describe the Anaconda installation process. Since the preferred way to execute a custom installation is from a boot floppy, we will focus our attention to those components. It should be noted that booting off the installation media CD contains the same components, but is structured slightly different.

ldlinux.sys
The ldlinux.sys file is the first file read during the boot process. The boot sector of the floppy disk tells the system to utilize this file to begin the boot process. This file reads its settings from the syslinux.cfg file.

syslinux.cfg
Syslinux.cfg is the configuration file that is used by ldlinux.sys to prompt the user for the various boot options available. A typical syslinux.cfg file for an ESX automated installation will look like the following:

```
default esx


prompt 1
timeout 100
display boot.msg
F1 boot.msg
label esx
      kernel vmlinuz
      append apic ramdisk_size=10240 vga=788
initrd=initrd.img ks=floppy
label noapic
      kernel vmlinuz
      append ramdisk_size=10240 vga=788 initrd=ini-
trd.img
label driverdisk
      kernel vmlinuz
      append apic driverdisk ramdisk_size=10240 ini-
trd=initrd.img
label text
      kernel vmlinuz
```

```
    append apic text driverdisk ramdisk_size=10240
initrd=initrd.img
```

There are several components of this file that are important to make note of for the purpose of a customized installation disk. The very first line that states "default esx" tells the system to load the specific settings listed under the "label esx" section of the file. The timeout value is the amount of time given before the default prompt times out and the default settings load. It is measured in 1/10th of a second, making our listed value 10 seconds. The "display boot.msg" line will display a custom friendly message as described next in this section.

The last portion of this file contains the various boot options. By letting the timeout value expire, the configuration under "label esx" is automatically loaded. This can be intercepted by pressing any key at the boot prompt before "esx" begins to load. If a different boot option is required, you may type a valid entry at the prompt that matches a specified label. It is extremely rare that anything but "esx" will ever be needed. The "kernel vmlinuz" tells the system which kernel executable to load during the system boot process. Further details on the kernel executable can be found later in this section. The "append" section passes boot parameters that tell the kernel to load in a certain way. The most important options are "intrd=initrd.img" and "ks=floppy". Both of these options are explained later, as they pertain to different files on the floppy disk. The boot parameters basically tell the kernel the exact files on the boot device that it should use while loading.

boot.msg

The boot.msg file is an ASCII based file that contains information about the boot disk and displays friendly instructions to the end user. It is this file that displays the colored "Welcome to the VMware ESX Server Install" message during the initial boot sequence. There is a Windows utility called "IsoLinux Mate" that can be downloaded that can add colorization and flashing text to a customized boot.msg file. It is not required that this file be in a Unix format, so creating and copying it to the boot floppy are the only steps necessary to customize your message. This is actually useful in situations where you are using different hardware models. The splash screen could state that this diskette should only be utilized for a particular model. The

"IsoLinux Mate" utility can be downloaded from the author's home-page at http://members.chello.at/bobby100/.

vmlinuz
The vmlinuz file is a compressed executable image file that contains the Linux kernel files. The Linux kernel contains the "core code" behind the Linux operating system. Without this kernel file, we do not have a Linux operating system. The kernel on the floppy disk is a small optimized kernel with the specific purpose of booting from a floppy and loading only the components that are needed for a functional system.

initrd.img
The initrd.img file is the "INITial Ram Drive" image file. This compressed file contains the root (/) file system of the boot floppy and the init file, which tells the system what services to load and applications to start during the boot process. It contains the driver files necessary to configure the hardware of the system. It also contains basic applications that allow us to perform specific Linux commands at a console. The initrd.img file is uncompressed into a ramdisk created as specified by the "ramdisk_size=10240" kernel parameter of the syslinux.cfg file.

ks.cfg
The final file of the boot disk is the ks.cfg file. If a "ks" option is listed as a kernel parameter, the init file that was decompressed from our initrd.img file knows to pass this configuration file on to the Anaconda application. If this value is not present, a full Linux installation will be performed without any automated options. By specifying "ks=floppy" as a kernel parameter, the Anaconda application knows to load the file named "ks.cfg" off of the floppy disk. Nearly all customization of a host is configured utilizing this file, so we will take a good look at its contents and structure. There are several main sections of the ks.cfg file that we will look at closely: General ks.cfg Options, ESX Specific Options, %packages, %pre, and %post.

General ks.cfg Options
As mentioned earlier, VMware utilizes the Anaconda installer to perform its installation. Anaconda is an amazingly flexible installer that

allows us to configure nearly every operating system configuration automatically using a kickstart configuration file. A complete list of every option can be found at the following URL:

```
http://www.redhat.com/docs/manuals/linux/RHL-7.2-
Manual/custom-guide/s1-kickstart2-options.html
```

This is quite an extensive list of options. There are far too many options available to us to review every single one. We do feel it is quite important that we discuss the options that should be included in an ESX ks.cfg file. We will not discuss every value for the required options, as the URL above does a great job at accomplishing that. The easiest way to create a base ks.cfg file is to run through the Scripted Installation Wizard. This will create a ks.cfg file with the listed configuration options and assign the proper values. This section is meant for those who need advanced customization capabilities for their systems and those who do not want to run through the wizard for every new host.

Installation Method
```
nfs
cdrom
url
```

An installation method must be chosen. This refers to the location of the source files for the installation. This may be contained on an NFS share, on the ESX installation CD, or on an HTTP or FTP server. We have found that network based installations are often times better choices than a CD-ROM based installation. Once you copy the proper files to the network server, you do not need to hunt down a disk to perform an installation. Before we go too far into the various connection methods we have to strongly recommend against using an ESX host to host network based files. Doing so requires you to open additional ports on your host, potentially putting your system at risk.

To point your ks.cfg file to an NFS share you need to use the following two options:

--server and --dir. The completed line in your ks.cfg will look like the following: (A valid hostname may be substituted for the IP address assuming you properly assign a DNS server in the network configuration section described shortly.)

```
nfs --server 10.0.0.100 --dir esx
```

CD-ROM based installations require the installation CD to properly function. There are no special options to configure. The value that should be listed in the ks.cfg should simply be:

```
cdrom
```

If you put the source installation files on an HTTP of FTP server you can configure kickstart to read from a remote URL. For Windows administrators it is often times very simple to set up an IIS HTTP or FTP instance on an existing server. Anaconda can handle multiple forms of a URL including adding port information to an http request or adding authentication to an FTP request. In fact, creating a custom ks.cfg file is the only way to enable authentication for an FTP connection request, as the Scripted Installation Wizard will generate an error checking the FTP URL value. The following are some examples of ks.cfg lines that may be utilized to connect to a remote URL:

```
url --url http://10.0.0.100/esx_source
url --url http://10.0.0.100:8000/esx_source
url --url ftp://10.0.0.100/esx_source
url --url ftp://user:pwd@10.0.0.100/esx_source
```

Root Password
```
rootpw
--isencrypted
```

You can configure a root password in your ks.cfg file in one of two ways: Clear Text or Encrypted. If you use Clear Text it is strongly recommended that the password be temporary and that it be changed either manually or as part of a script after the installation is complete. To use an Encrypted password it is recommended that you generate a ks.cfg file using the Scripted Installation Wizard and copy the rootpw line in whole.

```
rootpw password
rootpw --isencrypted $1$NNyrc3hGW$PxalIY4dZAQR0M2WFEc
```

Authentication Options
```
auth
--useshadow
--enablemd5
```

If you took the time to review the URL that lists the configuration options, you will notice that a lot of values have been left out. There are many different authentication methods available to automatically configure including SMB, Kerberos, and NIS. We feel that while it is possible to configure these items in the ks.cfg file, that it should be performed as a post-build step. Please refer to Chapter 7 in regards to configuring external authentication.

The --useshadow option is very important. It configures a shadow file as a user password database. When a shadow file exists, the user passwords are encrypted in /etc/passwd and cannot be viewed by a person with read rights to any file. The --enablemd5 option turns on md5 for Linux authentication, which is the default authentication method utilized for local accounts.

```
auth --useshadow --enablemd5
```

Boot Loader
```
bootloader
--location
--uselilo
```

We have yet to see an ESX installation that does not utilize LILO as its boot loader. It is the only boot loader that is supported by ESX. The only option that may vary is the location value. Depending on the system you are installing ESX on, you may choose either "mbr" or "partition" for the location value. It determines where the boot record for the system is written. Choosing mbr will work on nearly all systems, especially if the server is a recent model. There are rare circumstances which may require LILO to install the boot record to the first sector of the partition containing the kernel boot files.

```
bootloader --location=mbr --uselilo
```

Timezone
```
timezone
```

This is a required option in the ks.cfg file. The only reason it is mentioned in this section is that you will generate an installation error if you attempt to configure your system without this value specified.

```
timezone America/Chicago
```

Network Configuration
```
network
--bootproto
--ip
--netmask
--gateway
--nameserver
--hostname
```

This option actually serves two purposes: It sets the configuration of the system during the installation process and it specifies the final network configuration for the server. Things get tricky if you are building the server over a network connection on a staging VLAN before moving it to production. In that case, which is quite common, the system will need to be configured using DHCP, but a hostname should be specified to prevent errors with the SSL certificate. This type of configuration is not possible using the Scripted Installation Wizard so it must be performed with a custom ks.cfg file.

The --bootproto value can be either "static" or "dhcp". If dhcp is selected, the only other value that may be utilized is --hostname. Again, we recommend dhcp never be selected without statically setting your hostname. If static is chosen as the installation method, every value must be specified for the system to properly configure itself for the network. When reading the ks.cfg lines below, please keep in mind that each line should be read as an entire line without line breaks. Also, when specifying static IP information, you should remember that only one DNS server may be specified automatically.

The addition of a second DNS server may be scripted in the %post section of the ks.cfg file.

```
network --bootproto dhcp --hostname
esxhost.domain.com
network --bootproto static --ip 10.0.0.100 --netmask
255.255.255.0 --gateway 10.0.0.1 --nameserver
10.0.0.10 --hostname esxhost.domain.com
```

Language Settings
```
lang
langsupport
--default
keyboard
```

The three options for languages settings must be set in the ks.cfg file. The "lang" value sets the language that is used during the installation process. The complete list of language codes can be found at the URL specified at the beginning of this section.

```
lang en_US
```

The "langsupport" value is slightly different in that it specifies the language that is installed on the system for use in the operating system. You may specify a default language that is utilized by the operating system and install additional language support. For example, with the following line you can configure the default language of your system to be English, but also provide German language support:

```
language --default en_US de_DE
```

If you intend to use only one language, utilize the following line, substituting the proper language code:

```
language --default en_US en_US
```

The final regional value that requires configuration is the keyboard layout. Like languages, there is a list of keyboard layout codes available at the previously mentioned URL. The ks.cfg line should look similar to the following:

```
keyboard us
```

Partitioning
```
clearpart
--linux
--all
--initlabel
part <mountpoint>
--size
--ondisk
--fstype
--asprimary
--grow
```

The partitioning section of the ks.cfg file is one of the most comprehensive and important configurations. It has been our experience that automated partitioning alone has justified the creation of an automated build process. Typically we have seen Windows administrators have a hard time understanding the way Linux configures its partitions. If someone mistypes some information or clicks an incorrect box, it could potentially cause issues on the ESX host in the future.

The first option, "clearpart" is used to erase existing partitions of an existing disk. If you wish to completely rebuild a system and delete all partitions on the system, the --all value should be specified. In the event that you have a local VMFS partition for virtual machines, you may wish to specify the --linux option, which will only delete ext and swap partitions. VMFS partitions will remain intact. At this point, we would like to remind you that ANY time you are modifying the partition table of a system you should ensure you have a solid up-to-date backup of all files on the system. The --initlabel option will prepare newly configured hard drives for use. It is the equivalent of writing a signature on a new hard drive in Windows. If the disk has already been initialized, the --initilabel value will be ignored. The following is an example entry for preparing your hard disk for partitioning:

```
clearpart --all --initlabel
```

The second option allows us to lay out our partition scheme for the hard disk. The "part" option may be specified multiple times—once for each partition we wish to create. The --size value is specified in Megabytes, so be sure you properly calculate the value if you are measuring in terms of Gigabytes.

The --ondisk value specifies the physical disk that the partition will be created on. Depending on the SCSI controller you have installed in your system this can be one of several values. This was mentioned under partition configuration of the Scripted Installation Wizard section of this chapter. If you plan on using local storage for your virtual machines it will not be uncommon to see partitions created on multiple physical disks.

The --fstype value specifies the file system that should be utilized for the partition. There are only four values that should ever be utilized in ESX for this specific option: ext3, swap, vmkcore, and vmfs2. As we will see with an example shortly, a base installation utilizes at least one of each partition type.

The --asprimary value is utilized to specify which three partitions are configured as primary. The remaining partitions are configured under an extended partition of the system. Linux best practices dictate that the /boot, / (root), and swap partitions should always be listed as primary.

To fully utilize the entire space of a hard drive, we may specify the --grow option for a particular partition. Often times this is associated with either the VMFS partition or the /vmimages partition, as these are the two that typically require the most space. After all static partitions have been defined, a partition with the --grow option takes up the remaining space on the disk and maximizes the capacity utilization for the host.

When we put all of these values together we get an entire section of our ks.cfg built. A typical configuration will look like the following:

```
part /boot --size 50 --ondisk sda --fstype ext3 --asprimary
part / --size 2500 --ondisk sda --fstype ext3 --asprimary
part swap --size 1500 --ondisk sda --fstype swap --asprimary
part vmfs --size 10240 --grow --ondisk sda --fstype vmfs2
part vmkcore --size 100 --ondisk sda --fstype vmkcore
part /var --size 1024 --ondisk sda --fstype ext3
part /vmimages --size 10240 --grow --ondisk sdb --fstype
ext3
```

In the above configuration block we notice that we utilize the --grow
option twice. This is because we actually have two physical disks: sda
and sdb. The /vmimages partition is configured to take up the entire
second disk configured on the SCSI interface.

Reboot After Installation

There is one final optional component that determines the behavior
of your system upon completion of the installation process. If you
want your system to automatically reboot, simply add the following
line to the ks.cfg file:

```
reboot
```

If this line is not present you will be presented with a screen prompting you to hit "Enter" to perform a system reboot. Many times this
option is left out so system administrators know when the build has
actually completed.

Miscellaneous Options

There are several options which must be included in the ks.cfg file in
order for the installation to proceed. There are no options available
and they cannot be left out. Those options are listed here:

```
skipx
text
mouse none
firewall --disabled
```

ESX-Specific Options

Anaconda affords us several useful options for installing and configuring the Linux portion of ESX. By default, Anaconda cannot assist
us with the post configuration of ESX. Luckily, VMware was nice

enough to program several options into anaconda that can read custom kickstart commands to complete the majority of the ESX configuration tasks. As always, following the configuration wizard will place
the proper options and values in your ks.cfg file. If, like us, you do
not wish to run through the wizard every time you build a new
machine, you can modify a standard ks.cfg file and utilize the following options. We should note ahead of time that the option and its values all reside on a single line of the ks.cfg file. It is possible for more
than one value for a specific option to be specified. For example, the
following entry would be utilized to specify your serial number information:

```
vmserialnum --esx=12345-12345-12345-12345
--esxsmp=12345-12345-12345-12345 (This is all one line)
```

vmaccepteula
There are no values associated with this option.

This will automatically check the box that states you have read and
understand the terms of VMware's End User License Agreement.

vmservconmem
```
--reserved=xxx
```

The vmservconmem option specifies the amount of memory you
wish to utilize for the console operating system in megabytes. For
more information on properly sizing your COS memory, please
review Chapter 3.

vmpcidivy
```
--auto
```

`--host=x/y/z` – Configures the specified device for the COS

`--vms=x/y/z` – Configures the specified device for Virtual
Machines

`--shared=x/y/z` – Configures the specified device for both the
COS and Virtual Machines

No, this option is not a typo. VMware coded the vmpcidivy option to allow us to automatically allocate our devices during installation. As mentioned several times in this chapter already, in order to automate the allocation of your devices you must already know their configuration. VMware provides the "--auto" value that will allow ESX to attempt to automatically configure the devices in the host. We have had extremely good luck with this option, but must still recommend that if the configuration of the devices is known that it be hard-coded in the configuration. When utilizing the "--auto" value no other values should be specified.

If hard-coding the configuration of your devices, a combination of "--host", "--vms", and "--shared" should be utilized to configure every device in the system. It is not uncommon to have the "--vms" value utilized several times in the ks.cfg file. An example of a vmpcidivy option is as follows. Remember, all numbers are in hexadecimal, so numbers greater than 9 will need to properly reflect their hex notation.

```
vmpcidivy --host=3/1/0 --shared=3/8/0 --vms=3/1/1 --
vms=6/8/0 --vms=c/8/0
```

vmserialnum
```
--esx=xxxxx-xxxxx-xxxxx-xxxxx
--esxsmp=xxxxx-xxxxx-xxxxx-xxxxx
```
(This is all one line)

This option is very straightforward. It provides a mechanism to automatically apply the serial number information during the build process. This option works well when combined with "vmaccepteula" as the installation will not stop and prompt you for acceptance of the EULA or serial information.

vmnetswitch
```
--name="NetworkX"
--vmnic=vmnicX
```

This option is new to ESX 2.5 and it allows us to build virtual switches as part of the scripted installation process. On previous versions of ESX, this step needs to be performed manually. Don't worry, we will show you how to script this configuration shortly. There can be several "virtualswitch" options in a configuration file to configure more than one virtual switch. The "name" value defines the name as ESX sees it. This name should never start with a number! Something meaningful should be utilized for this such as "VLAN120" or "VMotion". The "vmnic" value defines which physical adapters will be assigned to each virtual switch. You will need one "vmnic" value per physical NIC you wish to assign to the virtual switch. For example, the following two lines will create 2 virtual switches and utilize 4 physical NICs. Please carefully note where quotation marks are and are not utilized:

```
vmnetswitch --name="Network1" --vmnic=vmnic0 --
vmnic=vmnic1 --vmnic=vmnic2
vmnetswitch --name="VMotion" --vmnic=vmnic3
```

vmswap
```
--volume="vmfsname"
--size="XXXX"
--name="filename.vswp"
```

Like the vmnetswitch option, this option is new to ESX 2.5. It allows us to configure the swap file that the VMkernel utilizes for memory reclamation. The "volume" value ties back to the label assigned to the VMFS2 partition in the partitioning section of ks.cfg file. This is the partition that will house the VMware swap file. As we have stated multiple times in this book, but cannot stress enough, it is strongly recommended that the VMware swap file reside on a local VMFS partition rather than on the SAN. The "size" value is specified in megabytes. Make sure you do the proper conversions if you plan on measuring your swap file size in gigabytes. Finally, the "name" option specifies the name of the swap file. If you were to use the ESX MUI to configure this file it would automatically be named "SwapFile.vswp". We can see no reason to change naming standards for this file, so recommend that you stick with the ESX defaults on this one. Your vmswap line should look like the following when properly constructed:

```
vmswap --volume="vmfs" --size="5120" --
name="SwapFile.vswp"
```

%packages
The %packages section provides a package group name as defined in the /VMware/base/comps file on the ESX installation media. The package group in the comps file defines the individual packages that will be installed for the specified group.

%pre
After the options section there is an optional %pre section. This is used to run shell commands before any files are copied to the local hard drives. This is often times not utilized as much as the %post section of the ks.cfg file.

%post
In addition to a %pre section, kickstart also offers a %post section. This is used when running commands after the installation completes but before its final reboot. This is utilized in automated installations to set up the automated configuration of advanced ESX configurations, which are not fully integrated into Anaconda and kickstart. Like the %pre section, this is simply shell script that can be utilized to perform a variety of functions.

We have covered A LOT of information in regards to creating a custom ks.cfg file. On the following page let's take a look at what a complete ks.cfg file should look like. We have added the appropriate comments to help identify what each line is doing.

```
# Kickstart file manually created by Scott Herold and
Ron Oglesby

# Installation Method
url --url ftp://anonymous:esxbuild@10.0.0.50

# Temporary root password
rootpw temproot

# Autconfig
authconfig --enableshadow --enablemd5
```

```
# Bootloader
bootloader --useLilo --location=mbr

# Timezone
timezone America/Chicago

# X Windows System
skipx

# Text Mode
text

# Network configuration
network --bootproto static --ip 10.10.10.10 --netmask
255.255.255.0 --gateway 10.10.10.1 --nameserver
10.10.10.100 --hostname esxhost.company.com

# Language
lang en_US

# Language Support
langsupport --default en_US en_US

# Keyboard
keyboard us

# Mouse
mouse none

# Reboot after install
#reboot

# Firewall Settings
firewall --disabled

# Partition Information

clearpart --all --initlabel
part /boot --size 50 --fstype ext3 --ondisk sda --
asprimary
part / --size 2560 --fstype ext3 --ondisk sda --
asprimary
part swap --size 1024 --ondisk sda --asprimary
part /var --size 1024 --fstype ext3 --ondisk sda
```

```
part /vm --size 9216 --fstype ext3 --ondisk sda
part vmkcore --size 100 --fstype vmkcore --ondisk sda
part vmfs --size 10240 --fstype vmfs2 --ondisk sda

# VMware Specific Kickstart Options

# Accept the license
vmaccepteula

# Console Operating System Memory
vmservconmem --reserved=272

# PCI Device Allocation
vmpcidivy --host=1/2/0 --shared=1/1/0 --vms=1/2/1 --
vms=2/1/0 --vms=2/2/0 --vms=2/3/0 --vms=2/3/1

# VMware License Information
vmserialnum --esx=XXXXX-XXXXX-XXXXX-XXXXX --
esxsmp=XXXXX-XXXXX-XXXXX-XXXXX

%packages
@ ESX Server

%post

# Configure Speed and Duplex of console NIC
echo "options bcm5700 line_speed=1000 full_duplex=1"
>> /etc/modules.conf

# Add additional DNS server to /etc/resolv.conf
echo "nameserver 10.10.10.101" >> /etc/resolv.conf

# Copy Tools Folder from CD to /vmimages
cd /vmimages
/usr/bin/ncftpget ftp://10.0.0.50/tools.tar.gz

/bin/tar zxf tools.tar.gz
/bin/rm -f tools.tar.gz

# Prepare the system for the automated script execu-
tion
/bin/mv /etc/rc3.d/S99local /etc/rc3.d/S98local
/bin/cp
/vmimages/tools/scripts/S99_3rd_party_setup.sh
/etc/rc3.d/S99_3rd_party_setup.sh
```

```
/bin/chmod 770 /etc/rc3.d/S99_3rd_party_setup.sh
```

Third Party Software Installations

Many third party applications such as backup and monitoring agents come with a scripted installation process. This is typically done by utilizing command line options or an installation configuration file. It allows for simple single command installation of your support applications. Every application is set up a different way so some research will have to be performed to determine how a specific installation can be scripted, if at all.

You will notice that at the end of our %post section of the example ks.cfg file we have 3 lines defined that modify one of our startup scripts (S99local). What happens in the small section of script is the file that is currently S99local is moved to S98local. By itself, this doesn't change the way the system functions. By copying the S99_3rd_party_setup.sh file into the specified directory the system will automatically kick it off after all other services and scripts on the server have started. A simple example of what can be placed in the S99_3rd_party_setup.sh file is as follows:

```
#!/bin/bash
# Install Director Agent (RSA II on x365 ONLY)
rpm -Uhv /vmimages/tools/director/ibmusbasm-1.09-
2.i386.rpm
cd /vmimages/tools/director/diragent
sh IBMDirectorAgent4.20.sh -r dirinstall.alt
/opt/IBM/director/bin/twgstart

# Configure vmkusage
vmkusagectl install
cp -f /vmimages/tools/system_files/vmkusage-cron.sh
/etc/cron.d/vmkusage-cron.sh

# Reset system to normal boot mode
rm -f /etc/rc3.d/S99_3rd_party_setup.sh
mv /etc/rc3.d/S98local /etc/rc3.d/S99local
reboot
```

While this script is simplified, and is actually a small chunk of another script, it gives an example of what can be performed in a post-build script. Here, we automatically install and start the IBM USB ASM driver and install the Director 4.2 agent based on a custom configuration file. After Director is configured a custom vmkusage-cron.sh file is moved into the proper directory. In our case, our custom vmkusage-cron.sh file is preconfigured with the -monthly switch to allow for more data to be stored and graphed. Finally, we delete our S99_3rd_party_setup.sh file and move the original S99local file back to its original name. After a final reboot our system is fully configured. Using shell (or even Perl) scripting it is entirely possible to configure your system without doing anything more than sticking in a floppy disk and pressing the power button!

Guest Installations

Everything that we have configured up to this point gets us to where we need to be to deploy guest operating systems. Since we have automated everything to this point, why stop? There are several methods to automatically deploy virtual machines. Here we will talk about the two most popular methods: Using VirtualCenter and using a PXE based installation tool.

VirtualCenter Installation

VirtualCenter provides simplified management to the virtual infrastructure as a whole. One of the more useful features is the capability to automatically deploy new virtual machines by either cloning existing guests or deploying templates. VirtualCenter has the capability to utilize Microsoft's Sysprep to customize the unique information of your new Windows guest. In addition, VMware provides an "Open Source Components" package to assist with customizing supported Linux Distributions.

Configure the Sysprep Tools and Open Source Components

VMware has good documentation on the processes that must be performed to configure the guest customization components. Regardless of this documentation there seems to be some confusion as to where these components need to be installed. These components should be installed and configured on the VirtualCenter Management Console server. There have been several posts in VMware's Community Forums about the guest customization components not functioning. This is typically because people attempt to configure these on their master image or system that they wish to clone. The ONLY way these components will work is if they are installed on the VirtualCenter Management Console.

Clone a VM

The first method that can be utilized to configure a Virtual Machine is cloning an existing machine. This is extremely useful in a case where you have several servers with applications that need to be configured in an identical fashion. Instead of going through a 2 hour application installation 6 times you can simply perform the installation once and clone the server 5 times to achieve the required result. One thing to be careful of is ensuring the application configuration isn't dependent on a server name. Some applications are NOT friendly when a server needs to be renamed. While going through the "Clone VM" wizard make sure you choose to start the "Guest Customization Wizard" to properly configure the settings of the cloned virtual machine.

Deploy from a Template

Deploying images from a template is similar to cloning a guest. The exception is the "Master Server" is imported and stored in a repository. As soon as the template image is created there is no dependency on the source VM. Templates often include up to date service packs and a base set of applications. Using templates we can create different server profiles. We could have different templates for different operating system versions or applications that are installed. We could have a Windows 2003 server with IIS installed that has a security policy for a DMZ server as one template while having a Windows 2000 server optimized for a SQL installation as another. There is no limit on the number of templates that are configured beyond storage space for the image repository.

DHCP Requirement

One of the "features" of VirtualCenter that has reared its head in the past is its dependency on DHCP while deploying a new template. This requirement is not documented very well in the VirtualCenter administration guide. A majority of data centers do not allow any DHCP on production server subnets. This causes complications if you are attempting to deploy a new production virtual machine and having it join a domain as part of its deployment process. When VirtualCenter deploys a new virtual machine it takes the settings that were entered into the Guest Customization Wizard and integrates a limited amount of that data into Sysprep. Basically, the only items Sysprep attempts to configure are the hostname, domain information and SID resets. For all other functions, VirtualCenter runs a post-deployment script after the operating system boots. This script includes configuring the network devices with static IP addresses. Since this information does not get configured until the system completely boots after deployment, the Sysprep configuration that runs when the guest is first powered configures itself with DHCP. If DHCP is not available, you will get an error when attempting to join a domain. You must manually click past the error and wait for the system to reboot and configure itself using the post-deployment script, which can take up to 5 minutes! Once the IP information is applied, the system can be properly joined to a domain.

PXE Installations

VMware integrated PXE boot capabilities into virtual machines starting with ESX 2.1. This functionality makes it easy to integrate the deployment of a virtual machine into the every day practices of the data center. VMware guests do not support "Magic Packets" so cannot be automatically powered on from a PXE server. This should be considered when planning your deployment process. There are two different ways to boot from PXE. The first method is to change your boot order in the system BIOS to set the Network Adapter as the first boot device. You may need to reset this value after the server has been deployed to properly boot form the HDD. The second option is to press the "F12" key during the boot process. This will automatically force the system into a network PXE boot. This is the easiest option and does not change any configurations of your system to perform.

ESX guests support PXE on both vmxnet or vlance network adapters. You will have to ensure that the proper drivers are loaded in your operating system image or scripted installation if you choose to use the vmxnet driver to build your guest.

There are many 3rd party options available from various software vendors. These tools are generally specialized applications with a wide range of compatibility with many systems. These are typically the best tools to use. In addition to third party deployment tools many hardware vendors have proprietary deployment solutions such as IBM's RDM and HP's RDP. These are typically programmed around a specific set of hardware and tend to be less friendly when attempting to deploy virtual machines.

There are plenty of third party tools available. Fortunately, VMware has a certified list of applications that can deploy guest operating systems to virtual machines. As VMware matures you can expect to see a larger list of compatibility from 3rd party software vendors. For now, these are the supported applications for automated guest deployments:

- Microsoft Automated Deployment Services (ADS)
- Microsoft Remote Installation Services (RIS)
- Red Hat Enterprise Linux 3.0 AS PXE Boot Server
- Symantec Ghost RIS Boot Package
- Altiris Server
- IBM RDM
- HP RDP

Chapter **10**

High Availability, Backups, and Disaster Recovery

In this chapter we will review the different backup and recovery, and High Availability strategies for your ESX environment. First we will start with the basics: single server backup and recovery, and the backup and recovery of VMs on a day to day basis. Once that is done, we will jump into the different ways to handle high availability and DR in a larger ESX environment, and some of the common issues you will run into in a disaster recovery scenario.

"DR" versus "Backup and Recovery"

People often confuse the terms "disaster recovery" (DR) and "backup and recovery." In reality they are two different types of processes/problems and they are *not* interchangeable. For that reason, let's define them here so that you understand where we are coming from.

Backup and Recovery (as far as this book is concerned) are the daily procedures you will use to backup and restore your systems, on site, during a failure of some type. This failure may be a hardware problem, a loss of data due to corruption or malicious destruction, or a simple "oops, I didn't mean to delete that" moment.

Disaster Recovery in this chapter is described as a recovery from a massive failure or loss of data. In this scenario, you have either lost your entire server farm at a location or a large portion of the infrastructure supporting it. This loss may be due to a natural event or man made destruction. In either case, you have to recover almost all your VMs and or hosts to new or different hardware.

Some environments utilize their same recovery/restoration procedures during a disaster recovery scenario. Obviously, this is very efficient and makes the process much simpler since the IT staff uses it every day. If that is your environment, then you are lucky. However here we have split the two procedures into different sections since most organizations don't have the ability to utilize just one.

Backup and Recovery Strategies

The first topic that needs to be discussed is the difference between backing up the ESX host/Service Console and backing up the VMs. For backup strategies and disaster recovery purposes, you need to think of these two items as two separate and distinct systems that need to be backed up and planned for. As a matter of fact, it is perfectly fine to use two different strategies for each of these components.

So why do these two strategies need to be separated? Simply stated, they are different systems with different needs and requirements. The ESX server is the platform or infrastructure, while the VMs are like your traditional servers using that infrastructure. Since the ESX host serves up network connectivity and physical server resources to the guests, it can be most easily associated with other network infrastructures like routers, switches, or even racks and power.

If the ESX Server is the infrastructure, then the Virtual Machine guests are your servers and applications that utilize it. Virtual machines by their very nature provide you with a number of different ways to do backups and therefore, recover. VMs themselves can be viewed as either a set of individual files or viewed as (and treated as) normal servers. If they are viewed as files, then the VMDK and vmx files are backed-up or replicated. If they are viewed as servers, then the data on the VMs is backed-up in a more traditional manner, just like traditional physical servers.

ESX Server Backups

Much like a router or switch, an ESX server is really the sum of its hardware, its base OS, and its configuration. Let's assume a Cisco switch didn't come with the IOS already installed on it. If you had a switch fail, you would simply reinstall the IOS on a like piece of hardware, restore the config, and you would be up and running. In this case the IOS would be a simple implementation, and the really important piece of the restore is the configuration. With that in place, the switch would become fully functional, and your connected systems would be back online.

In an ESX environment, the important piece of the recovery puzzle – from an ESX Server perspective – is the configuration. Assuming you are recovering on like hardware, you can simply do a default install of ESX Server and restore or copy all the VMware configuration files to the server and reboot.

At this point it should be stated that we are assuming you are backing up the server for recovery to like hardware. Later in this chapter we will discuss disaster recovery and business continuity, but in this section we are only looking at a single server recovery scenario on the original server or like hardware.

Backup and recovery of an ESX server is a fairly simple process. All you really need to backup is the configuration files for your server and any files you have changed besides VMware configurations (such as NTP settings, user accounts etc). Since this isn't a database host or a file server, the backup job should be relatively small and easy to maintain.

Following this line of thought, you need to determine if you are going to backup your ESX servers at all. If you have a completely scripted install of ESX, that covers all of your configurations, additional packages for monitoring, security changes, etc. And if you have decided to recover your VMs by storing their VMDKs on a SAN and creating new VMs on another server in the event of a failure, then you may have no need to backup your ESX Servers at all. Of course recreating VMs is often a tougher proposition than you may think, but let's cover that in the VM section.

Assuming you have a requirement to be able to recover a single server failure with the VMs that were running on that server, then the easiest way to do this is by restoring the configuration after a base OS install.

It should be noted we are talking about the ESX Server OS itself here and not the data within the VMs. VM recovery options will be covered later in this chapter. Below is a list of the types of failures you need to plan to recover from:

- Data Corruption: Files or data required for use become unreadable by the system.

- Data Loss: Files or data required are accidentally deleted or removed.

- Disk Failure: Failed hard drives on the host. Because of RAID configurations this could become a non-issue unless you loose a controller or multiple drives at once.

- Host Failure: Complete failure of the ESX host server or one of its primary hardware components.

When creating a backup plan for the console operating system, we want to temporarily forget about the configured virtual machines, as they will possibly be recovered differently. VM backup and recovery has its own special set of considerations that we will look at in a minute. In this section we want to focus on what it takes to sufficiently backup the ESX host operating system for maximum recoverability.

Assuming we can rebuild an ESX to its original specification (partition sizes, etc) either via a scripted build or simple 'how to' build document then we just need to look at the following configurations:

Critical components of the console operating system
- *Console OS Configurations.* Although VMware provides a fairly standard installation procedure, there are still files that are modified to meet security requirements or optimize performance. It can be tedious, and could potentially impact return to service, if each file had to be modified by hand if a host needs to be rebuilt. To make this recovery simpler and faster, we recommend ensuring that each of the following files in the console operating system are backed up.
    - /etc/profile
    - /etc/ssh/sshd_config

- /etc/pam.d/system_auth
- /etc/ntp and /etc/ntp.conf (optional depending on NTP configuration)

Depending on your security configuration and replication model for accounts, you should back up the account and password database files. If you have a "master" server from which these files are replicated, you can just back these up from the master server and use those during a recovery to synchronize your newly rebuilt host to the rest of the farm.

- /etc/passwd
- /etc/group
- /etc/sudoers
- /etc/shadow
- *VMware ESX Configurations.* All configurations of ESX and the VMkernel are stored in the /etc/vmware directory. Files stored in this directory tell ESX how to allocate hardware devices during startup, where the VMware Swap File is located, and advanced configurations made to customize ESX to your environment.

  Like the console operating system configuration files, it can be extremely time consuming to reconfigure ESX to its exact pre-failure state. By backing up the entire contents of the /etc/vmware directory, you can easily return ESX to its original state after a base installation using the installation media.

- *Virtual Machine Configurations.* The directory containing all of your VM's vmx files. Generally within this directory there are sub-directories for each of your VMs. Within these sub-directories are the VM's vmx file, the NVRAM file for the VM, and the virtual machine's log files.

  The NVRAM file contains the BIOS information and configuration of the virtual guest. Without these configurations it is still possible to rebuild your guest operating system, but you need to keep a solid inventory on all virtual guest settings such as memory, processor, and VMDK file usage. It's a best practice to make a backup of the entire directory to make a single server recovery very simple

At this point the plan is to backup and restore only configuration files. That means during the recovery of a server, you will perform a base install of ESX using the original name and IP information, then restore that server's configuration to its previous state. With that in mind, the next step is to install the backup agent onto the console and configure it for your backups.

Which backup software should you use?

Since the COS is really a RedHat Linux based system, you will need a backup agent that works for a Linux OS. Most major backup software available today has Linux agents, and these can be installed within the console OS for use. If your software does NOT have a Linux agent, then it might be possible to use a script to copy the required files and directories to another server or share then backup the files from there.

Right now there are about a half dozen "certified" backup technologies for use with ESX. The list of backup vendors can be found at: http://www.vmware.com/pdf/esx_backup_guide.pdf. In this list you will see products like Netbackup, Backupexec, Tivoli Storage Manager, etc. Mostly these are the major backup utilities in use in larger environments. Now is this list the definitive list of backups that will work? No, it's not. But if you want support from VMware, these are the vendors they have tested. However in most cases, if you have a Linux agent, it will run within the console and do the backups required for recovery of the Service Console.

Backup Schedule

Once all configurations are made and everything is properly running, changes are rarely made to the files mentioned above. Since the console operating system uses text configuration files for all settings, the amount of data being backed up is extremely small. For this reason, we recommend a nightly backup schedule on the files and directories listed above that have changed. While nightly may not be necessary, the required capacity and amount of time should have no impact on the performance of other backup jobs.

Options for Backing Up the Service Console

Now that you know what to backup on the Service Console, and have a general strategy for Console backups, it is time to decide how you are going to do it. If you run an enterprise-type backup software, this may be a simple decision. If you are running ESX server in a smaller environment, you may have more flexibility in determining how ESX will be backed up. In either case it really comes down to three options:

- Backup the Service Console Over the Network

- Backup the Service Console from a Local Tape Device

- Backup the Service Console via Local Device used by a VM

Let's examine each of these individually and see which of them fit your environment

Backup the Service Console over the Network

Almost all larger environments will already have a backup system like this in place. In this configuration, a backup server (or servers) manages a tape device or tape library and will use remote backup agents on servers to backup and restore data over the network. This is the method of backups commonly utilized in all but the smallest environments.

If you already use network backups, implementation of this system is fairly simple; all you need to do is install the backup agent on the Service Console and then schedule and run the backups.

Advantages of backing up over the network

- Easy and inexpensive to implement if you already use this type of system

- Fits with many datacenter standards

- Best design for multiple server environments

- Does not increase load on the Service Console

Disadvantages of backing up over the network

- Does not work well for remotely located ESX servers

This is generally the standard in environments running ESX Server. Since it is the most often used, there are very few problems with this configuration and it allows you the most flexibility in larger environments.

Backup the Service Console to a Local Tape Device

In this configuration you will install a local tape device on the ESX server, install the device's driver, and install backup software on the Service Console. Finally, you will configure the software to backup your machine configurations on a regular schedule. It is strongly recommended that when attaching an external tape drive to a system, that it be connected to an additional controller whenever possible. This will prevent SCSI locking errors that can only be cleared by an ESX host reboot. If a secondary controller is not possible, a secondary interface of the primary controller should be utilized. We do not recommend sharing SCSI tape devices with the same interface as your SCSI storage.

Advantages of backing up to a local tape device

- Simple to use and implement

- May work well for a remote location ESX without access to a Network Backup server

Disadvantages of backing up to a local tape device

- In multiple server environments, this becomes tough to manage

- Local console software may not be able to backup VMs

- Will increase load on the Service Console which may or may not be an issue depending on when you need backups and restores

Local Tape Drive Assigned to a VM

While this method is not used very often, I have seen it designed into some remote office configurations and in VMware documents, so it is worth mentioning. In this configuration, the local tape drive is assigned to a VM rather than the Service Console. Here, the VM runs the backup server software and backs up the Service Console via backup agent (much like the first method we described).

The issue with this configuration is that you must have the VM up and running to restore the ESX Server files. So if the problem you are having is that you have lost all of the ESX configurations, how are you going to get the VM up?

In this case you would have to import the VM to another host, and then restore the ESX server from the VM on a separate host.

Advantages of backing up to a local tape assigned to a VM

•   Removes load from the Service Console

Disadvantages of backing up to a local tape device

•   Cannot restore a host without first recovering a VM

To implement this configuration you will need to do the following:

1.   Install the tape drive on the ESX server.

2.   Using the vmkpcidivy or the Web Interface, assign the device to the Virtual Machines. Then, using the Web Interface, assign the device to your specific backup VM.

3.   Install the device drivers within the VM and install any back-up software required.

4.   Verify that the VM has network connectivity since the back-up will work like a backup over the network. (Traffic will flow from the VM's VMNIC to eth0 over the network.)

5.   Ensure a backup agent is installed on the Console and sched-ule your backups.

The same rules apply for attaching an external SCSI tape device in this scenario, as well.

Virtual Machine Backup and Recovery

In this section we are discussing the normal backup and recovery strategies for a guest VM. The idea here is that the strategies are for "normal" backup and restorations and not strategies for business continuity or DR. We should note that you may wind up using the same recovery procedures for DR that you use on a daily basis, but we are not focusing on that in this section.

As mentioned at the beginning of this chapter, there are two basic ways to do virtual machine backups. First, you can treat the VMs as a set of files – large files, but files, none the less. Or you can treat the VMs just like physical servers. You may choose to do either option individually, or you may eventually combine both in your backup and recovery plans, but for now, let's take a look at each

Treating a VM like a Physical Server

In this scenario, the VM is treated just like any other server on your network. Generally, a backup agent is installed within the guest OS, backup jobs are then created and run on a regular basis, and recovery is handled just like it would be with any physical server.

Figure 10.1

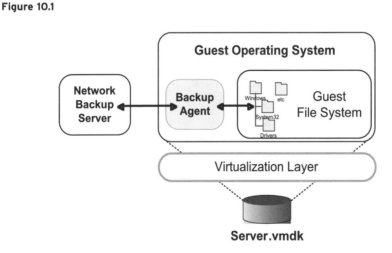

The advantage of this design is that it can simply integrate into your existing backup system, and provide for full, partial, or file level restores to the VM. The primary disadvantage is that is does not tap into the abilities of a VM to be completely restored in its entirety. Instead, to do a complete restore, you would have to load an OS, install the agent, and then do a complete restore from the backup software, just like a physical server.

Advantages of treating a VM like a physical server

- Allows for partial or file level restores

- Easily fits into most existing backup schemes

- Requires no advanced scripting or VMware knowledge

- Day-to-day procedures for backing up a server do not change

Disadvantages of treating a VM like a physical server

- Does not allow for a VM to be recovered in whole (like from a snap shot)

As you can see, this is obviously the simplest way to backup your VMs, but might not meet all of your needs. If you have a requirement to restore a VM in whole, then you may need to backup VMs as files. Of course if you also have the requirement to be able to restore individual files within a VM without restoring the entire VM to its previous snap shot state, you will most likely have to implement a file level backup with a Backup agent.

Treating a VM like a set of files

In this scenario, the VM is treated like a set of files on a machine. Here, the VMDK files, the logs, and possibly even the .vmx configuration file are backed-up. This allows for the files to be stored off site or on some type of backup media, then restored, as needed.

The obvious benefit of this configuration is that with the restoration of a few files, you have successfully restored your VM to its previous backed up state. The draw backs of this configuration though can be cumbersome for some smaller environments. The first thing that comes to mind is that these files (the VMDK files) are generally very large. The backup of these files could take a LONG time and can require a substantial increase in the amount of backup storage you will need in your environment. While there are some ways to decrease the space required, it may not decrease it enough to justify this type of backup.

Let's looks at the obvious advantages and disadvantages further.

Advantages of treating a VM like a set of files

• Allows for a complete restore of a VM to a previous state

Disadvantages of treating a VM like a physical server

• Does not easily allow for file level restores within the VM

• Large amounts of data could require an increase in your environment's backup storage

• Backup times may be extremely long

• Some backup software has problems with files larger than 2 GB

• VMs must be stopped to ensure a 'perfect' recovery

• VMs that aren't stopped during a backup are backed up in a 'crash consistent state'

Wow, what a list. Some might ask why people do this at all with a list like that. The simple reason is 'recovery'. This option gives you the ability to recover an entire server with the restore of a few files. While this may not fit your backup needs for day to day operations, it may fit better into your DR scheme. This is why some organizations do both.

Of course there are many disadvantages here so let's look at them. First, this mechanism does not allow you to recover individual files. Some may argue that you could restore the VMDK file to another partition, mount the VMDK with another VM or use the VMware Diskmount utility, and then copy the files needed. My answer to this solution is that I don't want to restore a 10GB VMDK file to copy two Excel spread sheets that some accountant deleted by accident. You're better off running a backup agent if you need to have file-level recovery capabilities.

The next disadvantage is the pure amount of data being backed up. Unlike GSX or Workstation that allows the disk files to grow as space is needed, ESX server VMDKfiles are created to their entire size specified for the VM. So if you have a 10GB VMDK for a server,

422   VMware ESX Server

with only 3 GB in use, you will be backing up 10GB, unlike the three you would backup using an agent installed within the guest. Of course to help overcome this you could use the vmkfstools –e command to export the VMDK file into a series of smaller "COW" format files. This will chunk the VM into a series of files and help save space by stripping away a lot of the 0 byte 'padding' within the VMDK file.

The other issue with this method is that there are no differential or incremental backups. Even if you use the vmkfstools and get the size down, it would still be the equivalent (size wise) of a full backup, and will take just as much time as a full backup. So if you have a large environment that cannot run a full backup each night due to the amount of time it takes, this could be an issue.

Finally, not all backup agents can deal with files larger than 2GB, and sometimes they can't even see the VMFS volumes. Again, this would require that you use vmkfstools to first export the files, and then back them up from an ext3 partition.

Backing up using the VMware API

The next item we should address is the state in which the VM will be when it is backed up. This question is critical since the state of VM at the time of backup will determine the state the VM will be in if, and when, it is recovered. If a Virtual Machine is turned off, then the backup is very simple and straightforward. The files for the VM are simply backed up as is, or are exported and backed up. The trick really comes when you wish to backup a running VM, as a set of files, without interrupting service. This requires using VMware's snap shot abilities.

This snap shot is just what it sounds like: it "freezes" the VM at a point in time and the state that the VM is "frozen" in is what is backed up. The idea here is that the VM is saved in a running state. If you need to recover it, you will have a bootable disk and mostly solid data. However since the memory wasn't all committed and possible transactions were pending or in the middle of being committed, you may wind up with some missing application data. The benefit of this backup is that the server is never unavailable, but you still have a recent image of it to restore without taking it out of service.

Before we delve into more details, let's look at the process of backing up a running VM as a set of files. This process uses the VMware API that allows you to snap shot a VM and add a redo log file to the VMDK. Let's go through the process following the chart below:

Figure 10.2

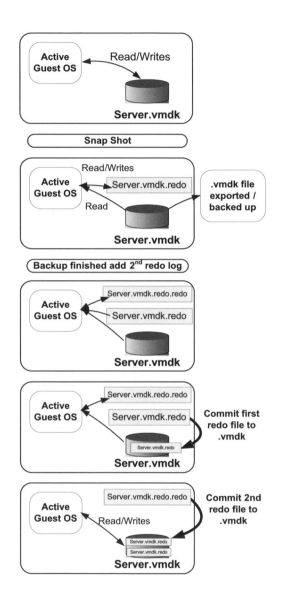

As the process starts, the snap shot essentially "freezes" the VMDK. For any changes to the VMDK, a .redo log file is created. This file is named with the VMDK's name and a .redo extension. With the VMDK frozen it can then be backed up, exported, or simply copied (though most organizations use the export command in vmkfstools). Once the file is backed up or exported to an image, a second redo log is created and the first one is applied to the original VMDK. This

second file is named the same as the first with another .redo extension at the end of it. So if your VMDK was named server.vmdk, the
second redo log will be server.vmdk.redo.redo.

Once the first redo log is committed, the final step in the process is
to commit the second log's changes and begin accessing the VMDK
file as normal. At the end of this process the VM guest is back to
reading and writing changes directly to the VMDK, at least until the
next hot backup.

While this may sound a little complex and seem to be too much if
you are not familiar with using scripted backups, never fear, others
have already figured it all out. If you wish to use a script to do hot
backups as shown above, I would highly recommend you look at
Massimiliano Daneri's site and research his VMBK (VMware backup)
perl script that allows for a hot backup of ESX guests. He has recently added features to support FTP and even backup of the vmx and
CMOS files for the VMs. His page can be found at:
http://www.vmts.net/vmbk.htm

If you don't like to write scripts and don't have a lot of
Linux/UNIX/perl scripting background, then you may need to find
another solution. A company in Illinois called VizionCore has a small
software package to fit the bill. Their program is called 'esxRanger
CLI' and is a basic Windows exe that simplifies the process of backing up your VMs as files. Based on the VMware COM interface, it
allows you to perform the types of backups described above without
any scripting. The basic idea is that you can run this exe from your
desk or from a Windows sever, specify the source location to be
backed up, and the destination, and you are off and running.

In addition, since it is a Windows executable, it can be scheduled to
run using the standard Task Scheduler. The cool thing about their
tool is that it comes with a compression ability built in that removes
the compression execution from the console OS. Doing compression
this way makes it much faster and removes the burden form the ESX
Server's Console OS, freeing up the CPU for use by your virtual
machines.

Like any other snapshot type of backups, esxRanger should be used in conjunction with your regular backup procedures depending on the type of data that may be stored inside the VM guest. Using this software, you also have the option to stop VM guest services like SQL or Exchange, and then start the esxRanger backup while the services are stopped. After the backup begins you can resume the services immediately without waiting for the backup to complete. This ensures that esxRanger captures the files in a closed state prior to the backup. Nice huh?

I don't want to sound like a salesman for this company, but this really is a great way to do backups for your VMs. If you are looking at using the snap shot technology from VMware, I would highly recommend that you to take a look at this tool before you spend time and money on developing scripts. Don't get me wrong – it is possible to create large perl scripts with lots of error checking, etc. – this will do a lot of what you would get from esxRanger. However for a fairly minimal cost, you can get a simple application (that has a support group behind it) to do everything for you.

The one drawback to esxRanger is that a cost is associated with it. But in this case, comparing the cost of the software to what you get from it, and to the time it takes to develop your own system, is fairly inexpensive. (They have both "per processor" and enterprise licensing.) There is nothing here that is going to break the bank, but you sure do get a lot of features with it. I would highly recommend you check out this product at www.vizioncore.com.

High Availability within the Datacenter

In this section we will discuss the designs organizations are using to provide high availability VMs within their infrastructure. Here we will focus on high availability (HA) within the datacenter and not for DR. While some of these configurations may be used for DR, we will discuss their specific DR configurations later in the chapter.

VMware supports a number of clustering technologies for its VMs. These include products like Microsoft Cluster Services (MSCS), Veritas Clustering, NSI's Double-take, etc. Using these technologies for your VMs is fairly simple. And while clustering itself can be (and is) a topic requiring its own book, here we will focus on the VMware specific configurations for getting this to work.

Virtual to Virtual Clusters

It was probably about week after the first VMs started to go into production that the first official production admin was asked about clustering. More than likely, it was even before then. With today's business requirements for available systems, almost all mission critical apps have some type of high availability configuration built into their design. With the move to a virtual infrastructure, you as an engineer or architect need to understand how these work and when they should be implemented.

Using a Virtual to Virtual cluster is just as it sounds: two VMs participating as cluster nodes to server-up a common resource. These VMs can be located on the same ESX Server or spread across ESX Servers to protect against a host or hardware failure.

The basic concepts of the clustering technology you use will not change. If using MSCS, you will still need some type of shared storage, will still require a front-end and heart beat network, and will still be dependent on the common data remaining intact. Remember a cluster only protects against hardware failure (in this case virtual hardware) or possibly a service failure. It will not keep data from becoming corrupt.

Figure 10.3

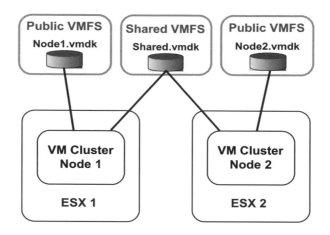

In a Virtual to Virtual cluster, the most common configuration is to store each cluster node on a separate ESX Server. This protects against hardware or host failure. Next, the VMDK files for the cluster node's OS's should (hopefully) be located on different LUNs (Did I mention you still need a SAN to cluster across ESX Servers?). Keeping the VMDK files for the cluster node OS's on different LUNs will ensure that a problem with a single LUN will not bring the entire cluster down. And finally, you will still need some shared type of storage. This storage can be a "raw disk" or a VMDK file stored on a VMFS partition configured in 'Shared Mode'.

With the introduction of ESX 2.5, VMware now recommends that you use raw disks (or at least a raw disk with a Device mapping, which will be explained in a second) for both Physical to Virtual, and Virtual to Virtual clusters. Prior to ESX 2.5, the recommendation for Virtual to Virtual clusters was to maintain the shared storage as a regular VMDK file and not as a raw disk.

With 2.5, VMware introduced Raw Device Mapping. The basic idea is that you will create a special mapping file (a type of VMDK) that will reside on one of the VMFS partitions in your environment. This file will allow you to manage and redirect all access to the physical disk like it was a standard VMDK file. In other words, the VM thinks it has a VMDK file but really VMware is "spoofing" it and redirecting all access through the file to the raw disk.

Figure 10.4

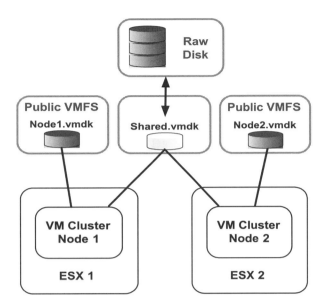

So why do this? One advantage is that it gives you the ability to add redo logs to the raw disk and treat them more like VMs. It also allows you to easily VMotion a VM that is accessing a raw device; to the VM, all they see is another file on an LUN. In addition, there are two different modes of the device mapping, Physical and Virtual. Virtual allows you to manage and use the mapping file just like a VMDK, which includes the use of redo logs. The Physical mode allows for more direct access to the device for applications requiring lower level control of the storage.

Which shared storage should I use?

If you are on 2.5, the answer should be simple. Use raw device, since VMware recommends it. But if you are on 2.5 and need to run 50 Virtual to Virtual clusters, you may begin to have an issue since the number of LUNs you may need to create to support each cluster, in addition to all the storage for the regular VMs themselves, may drive your local storage guy to drink.

If you are going to have a small number of clusters, it's not a bad idea to follow the recommendation and use a raw device mapping. But if you plan to have a number of different Virtual to Virtual clusters, and you see your storage configuration getting more and more complex, it may be a good idea just to use a shared mode VMFS partition and store shared data on it in the form of VMDK files.

Advantages of using Raw Device Mapping and Raw Disk

- Allows raw disk to be treated like a VMDK file

- Allows for simpler configuration and use of raw devices

- Recommended by VMware for Virtual to Virtual and Physical to Virtual clusters

- Some applications may require low level access to the disk

Disadvantages of use Raw Device Mapping

- Does not ease storage configurations for large numbers of clusters

Once you have the storage issues decided on, you then need to ensure you have adequate network connectivity. Using a product like MSCS, you are often required to have two network connections for each node; one for the production network, and another for a heartbeat network.

In this configuration you should put the heartbeat network on its own virtual switch. If using clustering within an ESX environment that uses VMotion, this will allow you to configure your hosts with a "heart beat" virtual switch that is possibly uplinked to a specific VLAN. On a physical network, these machines are generally connected via a cross over cable or isolated on their own segment. In the VMware world, we must design our hosts to accommodate the extra NICs.

Figure 10.5

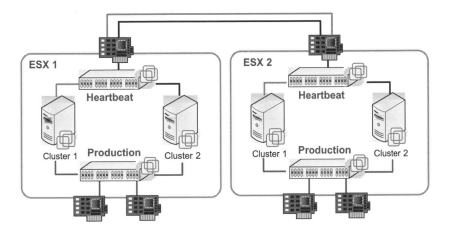

As you can see by the image, the additional heartbeat network reduces your number of available (for production at least) VMNICS by at least 1. You can make that redundant by associating two VMNICs with the heartbeat network, but the cost of that is a reduction of two available NICs in your server.

If you think back to Chapter 4, another possibility is to utilize 802.1Q VLAN tagging on your physical NICs. This will allow you to create several VLANs on the same virtual switch, eliminating the need to add additional physical NICs to your ESX hosts.

For more information on setting up a Microsoft Cluster within your VMs, please visit the following VMware article:

```
http://www.vmware.com/support/esx25/doc/esx25admin_clu
ster_setup_esx.html
```

Physical to Virtual Clusters

Another way VMs are being used is to consolidate the number of passive cluster nodes on the network. Let's assume you have plans to implement 10 active-passive clusters in your environment. Assuming that you went with a simple configuration like a pair of HP DL 380's for each cluster, you would wind up with 20 processors, which basically sit around all the time waiting for a failure that rarely occurs.

Some companies have decided that using VM's as the passive cluster nodes in this scenario makes perfect sense. Assuming you have 10 passive nodes, that will use very little processor and memory unless there is a failure, it is possible to consolidate these nodes onto your ESX servers and use the Raw Device mapping feature in ESX to connect the VMs to the shared storage that the physical machines will be using.

Figure 10.6

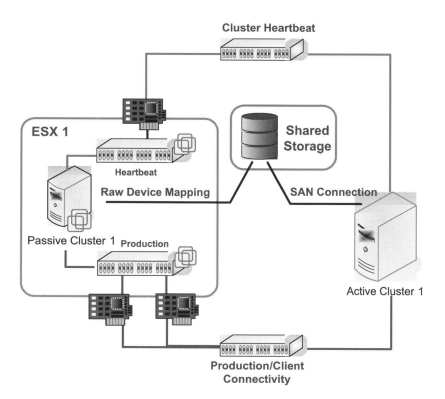

Using this configuration, the VM Passive Nodes have the ability to access the production network, the shared data and quorum, and maintain a heartbeat with the active node. In this situation it is possible to consolidate as many as 8 to 10 passive nodes onto a single dual or quad processor piece of hardware. In the event of a failure of a single node or the need to induce a failure for maintenance on the active node, the ESX Guest will pick up the load and maintain its active status until failed back.

The drawback here is that you do not retain 100% failover capacity. In other words, if you happen to have a situation where multiple active nodes fail and your ESX host is underpowered, your users may experience a decline in performance.

Clustering Without Shared Storage

Another common technology used in both the VM world and in physical environments is the use of clustering or software mirroring technologies that do not require shared storage. This clustering is often called software clustering or SMB clustering. The basic premise is that the backup node in the cluster maintains a duplicate of the primary node's data. This data is often replicated via SMB.

The nice thing about this technology is that it requires no shared storage between the VMs. This allows for simple configuration and often the ability to replicate your data to servers that are not in the same site (can anyone say DR?). Many companies have turned to this technology instead of some of the more expensive SAN replication technologies. There are a few vendors on the market that offer quality software clustering like NSI's DoubleTake, and Legato's Co-StandbyServer. In either case, you have the ability to create a software cluster without the need for shared storage. This is nice for smaller environments that are struggling with DR or have the need for high availability but don't have the funding or expertise for a SAN.

Since these technologies use replication to create their passive nodes, I highly recommend dedicating a heartbeat/replication NIC in your ESX server. Some version of NSI's software will require this. In either case, it's a good practice to separate the replication and heartbeat traffic from your production network, and may only cost the price of an extra NIC or two.

How About Clustering the ESX Server?

While not one of my favorite topics, I think we should discuss clustering none-the-less. There are some cluster services coming to market (i.e., Veritas Cluster Server for Linux) that allow for the clustering of the ESX host itself. The idea is that the VMs running on a host are nothing more than a process running on a Linux server. So if that process were to stop, or if the server were to become unavailable, why not start the VM on another server?

This is not a bad idea in theory, but it doesn't cover all the bases. Let's assume we cluster the ESX host, with a complete standby host waiting for a failure (classic cluster configuration). On this host we have 5 VMs; 2 running IIS with some static content and some session based ASP pages, and 3 running Microsoft SQL Server. In the event that the server losses power, has a mother board failure, etc., those processes are moved to the standby server and your VMs are still running. Of course this software may not solve the problem when a service running within a VM stops. In this case, there is no passive node for the VM and the application becomes unavailable, anyway.

Another problem here is that you have created an environment with N+N redundancy. For each 'active' ESX host with running VMs you have a standby server. Of course you could drop that redundancy down and only place the clustering software on specific hosts, and then keep the most mission critical VMs on those hosts, but then you are creating two farms, and different levels of service for different VMs.

At the time we wrote this book, the Veritas Cluster Server just introduced its support for ESX servers and very little is know about it presently. The way it works is that it replicates the configuration of guests between servers, then if a failure occurs, it will start the VMs from the failed host onto a known, good host. This leaves your VMs in a state as if they were shutdown hard, and just brought back up on another server. Of course you could also do this manually, or via scripts within the ESX hosts, or via event driven scripts within VirtualCenter. VCS offers a way to do this much faster than a manual process and without all the scripting required to build your own automated process.

Advantages of clustering the host

* Provides for automatic restart of VMs

Disadvantages of clustering the host

* Does not provide for service failure within a VM

* Does not move the VMs over seamlessly (its like a power on after an improper shutdown for the VM)

* Additional Cost

* Additional level of complexity

Disaster Recovery Considerations and Options

There are only a few things that are for sure about DR. First, it takes a lot of planning and preparation to do right, and second, it's never cheap when done correctly. DR with ESX server is no different. We have all heard the sales pitch as to how easy DR is with VMware, but is it really easy or cheaper? Maybe it's easier, however I am not sure about cheaper. To recover a VMware environment, we need to analyze the same two items that we looked at when we were reviewing what to backup in the environment. The first is the ESX Servers themselves. Without them, we won't get a single VM up and running. The second is the VMs. We will look at a few different ways to handle each of these and let you see which fits best into your environment.

VMware Disaster Recovery "Dream" Environment

By now we have all heard the dreams of having our VM's instantly available in a disaster recovery (DR) site in the event of a massive failure in the primary location. The dream sold to everyone was that you could simply drive over to your local DR site or contracted DR location, power up your ESX servers, and turn on your VMs. The reality, unfortunately, is a little more difficult than that.

This section will not tell you that it can't be done—it will tell you that it won't be cheap. Before we jump into this, let's look at what you would want to accomplish in your dream environment. The following are steps to take after the failure of an entire primary datacenter:

1. Drive to secondary facility

2. Power on or verify configuration of ESX hosts

3. Verify you can "see" the VMs on the SAN

4. Power up VMs in order of DR plan priority

5. Get coffee while watching VMs power up

6. Get raise for getting all servers back up in under an hour

That sounds pretty good, huh? Let's look at what this might require to make it a reality. The cool parts of this recovery scenario hinge on having the VMs at the DR facility. Notice that I didn't put the step 'restore VMDK files from tape' in this dream process.

1. Must have SAN replication to DR site for VMs

2. Replication must meet business data consistency needs (done frequently enough to ensure the data is up to date)

3. Need to have enough hardware to run your ESX hosts at the DR location

4. Possibly need to have ESX installed and ready to go live

5. Hopefully you will have all the VM configurations saved or backed up

6. IP subnet that VMs reside on must be located in both datacenters

7. A VirtualCenter implementation that manages the hosts in both sites would be nice for moving the VMs

In this dream scenario we are able to start the VMs and get them going on a bunch of pre-configured ESX hosts. However, as you learned throughout this book, the VM is configured to connect to specifically-named virtual switches. Also, these virtual switches were linked to specific subnets back to your primary datacenter, so if the subnet is not the same in the DR site, all the IP information will have to change. Note that IP changes are the least expensive of your problems.

The most significant expense will be the standby hardware and the storage. The first key to this scenario was having the VM's replicated offsite. This requires a SAN infrastructure capable of block level replication (something like EMC's SRDF). In addition, replication of all this data is going to take a significant amount of bandwidth between the two sites. Dark fiber would be ideal in this scenario and would allow you to sleep at night. Finally, you will need a lot of servers, and hopefully these servers are preconfigured with ESX and ready to go. If they aren't, then you will most likely have to install ESX, get the network and SAN configurations right (zoning can be a pain when the storage guy is trying to get his systems recovered), then find the VMs, and bring them up. If you don't have their configurations, then you will most likely have to create new VM's and associate them with the proper VMDK files (this is where that VM inventory comes into play).

Anyway, in an ideal VM DR environment, you would have a single IP subnet that would span between both datacenters. This would hopefully be a multi-gig connection that is redundant. You would also have enough storage capacity at your DR site to handle all of your VM storage requirements, and you would have some sort of SAN replication to ensure that the data in the VMs is current enough to recover from.

With these pieces in place, the final piece would be to have a series of DR servers configured identically to you primary site servers. These servers would have access to the replicated SAN LUNs, or the LUNS could be masked until the DR plan was invoked. In either case, the most work that would have to be done to get the VMs up would be to unmask the LUNs, rescan within ESX for new mass storage devices, and use VirtualCenter to create and/or start your VMs.

Well, even writing this has been a bit of a bummer. Most companies don't have the ability to put in this type of infrastructure for DR, and those who do, sometimes won't invest in the cost. So let's take a few pages here and review ways to work through each of these items, from servers through to storage.

ESX Server Recovery/Deployment

It would be nice during a DR scenario to have a bunch of preconfigured DR hardware setup and ready to go. If this is the case in your company, then ESX DR is easy. Have the server built, and ready for the situation, and you are ready to go. However in most business this is not the case. Basically, if you don't have a bunch of standby hardware, you are dealing with one of two solutions:

- A contract facility that will provide you with "like" hardware

- The repurposing of existing company owned hardware

The first option is used by a majority of companies out there. The basic idea is that they contract with someone like SunGard, so that in the event of a disaster, SunGard guarantees them X amount of rack space and bandwidth and Y amount of different types of hardware.

The issue here is that you will most likely not get the SAME EXACT hardware. Or you may get the same model, but will it have the same HBAs in the same slots, the same types of NICs plugged into the same speed network ports, etc? If not, your unattended install for ESX that does all the cool NIC and HBA configurations just went out the Window. So when planning for the redeployment of ESX, or when trying to ensure that you get the correct contract level that will ensure you get hardware as close as possible to your existing configuration, you will need to adjust your DR builds for ESX to be extremely flexible and allow for manual configuration of the server.

The second option of repurposing existing hardware is much more interesting. In repurposing, you are taking existing hardware that you own and rebuilding it as ESX servers. This gives you a little more flexibility as you will have a better idea of the hardware that will be used during DR. Some organizations will attempt to repurpose other "less critical" production servers for the critical production boxes. This is a poor plan, as you are really robbing Peter to pay Paul. You will eventually have to bring back those production servers that were "less critical".

One thought for this scenario that a client of mine had was to split his VMs into two groups of hosts. The first group of hosts would only host production VMs. The second group would only host Test and Development VMs.

Figure 10.7

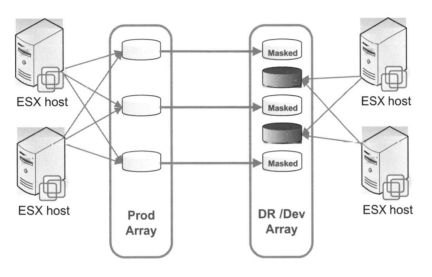

Their idea was to maintain the Test and Development VMs at a second datacenter. In the event of an emergency, the test and development VMs would be shut down and the hardware (which already had ESX on it and running) would instantly be repurposed to host the production VMs. This configuration, combined with SAN replication and masked LUNs, would basically give them the ability to bring up their production VMs in another site in a very short period of time.

Recovering the VMs

The entire purpose of DR is to get the VMs back up and running. In the dream DR scenario, you would simply use a tool like VMotion to move the VMs between your production site and the DR site, ensuring a smooth failover. SAN replication would ensure your VMDK files are already in place, and configuration of the VMs would be handled during the migration of the VM. Of course some of us will never see that type of setup, so we need to deal with what we have.

Recovering Using Restored VMDK Files

First of let's determine what is really needed for DR purposes. If you have been backing up the VMDK files, then you will at a minimum need those VMDKs. If your VM backups have included the vmx configuration files and NVRAM file, then you are almost set.

The whole idea of backing up these files in the first place is to facilitate recovery. If you have the files, you can simply restore them and register and start the VM on the target ESX server. This registration can be done by using the vmware-cmd tool with the following syntax:

```
vmware-cmd -s register /path/file.vmx
```

Using the register option will allow the VM to been "seen" by the ESX Server. The VM will now be available in the Web Interface and will be able to be seen/discovered in VirtualCenter.

If you have not been backing up the configuration files, and only have the VMDK files, you will be required to make a new VM for each VMDK you wish to recover. The vmx files tell the ESX server how the Virtual Machine is configured, so a relatively accurate vmx file when recovering would be nice to ensure that the VMDK files are booted into a like virtual hardware configuration.

Without the configuration files, you will be required to keep a pretty good inventory of your virtual machines and their settings, so, during a DR scenario, you can recreate them all.

Recovering Using "Normal" Backups

While this type of recovery doesn't really take advantage of the concept of the VM, it is still a possibility. If you are using agent-based backups within the VMs, then you do have the ability to create new VMs on your DR severs and restore the data from the backup.

The idea here is that the VMs are treated just like physical machines. During DR, a new VM can be built (maybe even from a template) and a backup agent can be installed to do a complete restore of the server. While this process only saves you time in the initial install of the VM to restore to, it can be a good alternative to VMDK files backups or SAN replication if cost simply puts them out of the realm of possibility.

Recovery Using a Combination of Methods

One issue that you should consider in your DR plan is creating a tiered level of service for recovery. The concept here is that you create a top-level tier that requires near instant recovery, a mid-level tier that will need to be recovered after the first level, and a final, third-level tier that will be the last servers to be recovered.

Along with this tiered model comes different SLAs for recovery at each tier. Let's look at the following table as an example:

Tier	SLA for Recovery	Types of Applications	Types of Backups for DR	Examples
1	24 hours	Business critical	SAN replication or VMDK files to off-site facility	Email, line-of-business apps, point-of-sale apps
2	72 hours	Non-critical, but required	VMDK files backed up and shipped off-site, or "normal" backups of the VMs	accounting systems, IT mgmt servers, file servers with non-critical data
3	1 week	Infrequently used servers	Normal agent-based backups within the VMs	small file servers, dev and test servers, HR data

With this type of model you can employ multiple backup and recovery processes depending on the criticality of the servers being recovered. This system not only creates a priority and order for VMs to be recovered in, it also defines the methods in which the VMs will be backed up for DR purposes.

Assuming you have a limited amount of offsite storage and bandwidth to the remote site, you may only be able to replicate so many GBs of VMDK's per night. Alternatively, you may only be able to copy off so many of the backed up VMDK files to the remote site depending on your available bandwidth. However you could take second or third-tier VMs and keep their VMDK's or normal backup data on tape media that is shipped off-site.

During a recovery scenario, the tier one servers would be the first VMs to be brought up. Depending on the type of configuration, the VMs are started or registered then started in a very short amount of time. The tier two servers can be recovered from backup tapes of the VMDK's or even have new VMs created and have the data restored as if it was a physical server. Since these are 'less critical' servers, you would have more time allocated to complete the restore. Finally the tier three servers are brought back on-line. These servers are used infrequently, not used by many people in the organization, and don't drive or hurt the business if they are done for a week or so. These VMs can be restored as if they were normal servers. A new VM can be built, the backup agent installed, and the recovery performed.

Obviously this is a simplified model for the book, but the concept is sound. You and your company will have to determine which of your servers fit in which of these tiers, what your SLAs are for recovery of these types of servers, and what you can afford as far as DR planning and provisioning.

Appendix & Index

Appendix: Linux Commands for Windows Folks

Command's Purpose	Command Name	Linux Example
Copies files	cp	cp thisfile.txt /home/
Change file permissions	chmod	chmod [options] filename
Type a file to the screen	cat	cat Filename.txt
compare two files	cmp	cmp FILE1 FILE2
Change Directory	cd	cd /home/test
Check current path	pwd	pwd
Moves files	mv	mv thisfile.txt /home/
Lists files	ls	ls (option) /dirname
		ls -l /dirname
Clears screen	clear	clear
Closes prompt window	exit	exit
Displays or sets	date	date date
Deletes files	rm	rm thisfile.txt
Delete a directory	rm -rf	see above
"Echoes" output	echo	echo this message
Edits files	pico[a]	pico thisfile.txt
Compares the contents	diff	diff file1 file2
Finds a string of text	grep	grep this word or phrase thisfile.txt
Creates a directory	mkdir	mkdir directory
Screens through a file	less[d]	less thisfile.txt
Renames a file	mv	mv orgfile newfile
Create an empty file	touch	touch filename
remove empty directories	rmdir	rmdir /dirname
Mount a file system	mount	mount /mnt/floppy (see more examples below)
Shows amount of RAM	free	procinfo
Check Disk space	df	df
dump file to the screen	cat	cat /dir/filename.txt
Check network interfaces	ifconfig	ifconfig
Show loaded drivers	lsmod	lsmod
Show PCI buses and devices attached to them	lspci	lspci
Show running processes	ps	ps
Current users logged on	who	who
Show performance info.	top	top
Log out current user	logout	logout
Reboot a machine	reboot or shutdown	reboot or shutdown-r
Poweroff a machine	/sbin/halt or shutdown -h	after issuing the halt command and the system halts you can power off the box
Add a user to local system	adduser or useradd	useradd [userid] -p [pass word]
Add group	groupadd	groupadd
List users on the system	users	users
change current password	passwd	after entering passwd you will be prompted for a new passwordln

Index